PRAISE FOR

Disgracefully EASY

"It is all too easy to forget that in World War II, however much they wanted to be in the action, uncounted thousands of men and women in uniform 'did their bit' without leaving our shores. Bill Hanchett was one of them, a pilot so skilled he was kept 'stateside' to train others. In *Disgracefully Easy*, his thoughtful and perceptive letters to his parents open a window onto the feelings, frustrations, and experiences of 'those who also served,' as well as a running commentary on how young men of his time felt about politics, duty, the war, and the postwar future to come."

—WILLIAM C. DAVIS, CIVIL WAR HISTORIAN AND AUTHOR

"The combination of Tom Hanchett's research and his father's collected letters make this an interesting story, beautifully told . . ."

—DR. PAUL HOFFMAN, DIRECTOR, AIR UNIVERSITY PRESS, USAF AIR EDUCATION AND TRAINING COMMAND

"As time progresses there continues to be an avalanche of books about World War II. But there are very few about the citizens who fought it, their sacrifices, lives and deaths, and the heart they gave up into it. Now along comes *Disgracefully Easy*, a true-to-life book that uneasily tells it like it was. Here's your chance to see the war from the bottom up versus the top down."

—PETER STEKEL, AUTHOR OF *FINAL FLIGHT, THE MYSTERY OF A WWII PLANE CRASH AND THE FROZEN AIRMAN IN THE HIGH SIERRA*, AND *BENEATH HAUNTED WATERS, THE TRAGIC TALE OF TWO B-24S LOST IN THE SIERRA NEVADA MOUNTAINS DURING WORLD WAR II*

"*Disgracefully Easy* is an important contribution to our understanding of World War II. While it does not contain any new information on campaigns or battles, it does contribute to our understanding of the Homefront and the military personnel stationed there. William 'Bill' Hanchett had a front row seat to life at air bases throughout the United States. From Miami Beach to Randolph Field, Texas, Hanchett spent the war training for combat missions that he never flew. Millions of men and women participated in World War II and hundreds of thousands of them gave the last full measure of devotion. Equally worth remembering are those who raised their hand and volunteered for service only to find their particular path never left the United States. This book tells the story of one of those greatest generation individuals, who felt the call to service, but who served only at air bases around the United States, the war ending before his B-24 unit flew west. Passed over by technology (the B-29) and campaigns far from his location, Bill returned to civilian life and rose to be one of the nation's leading scholars on Abraham Lincoln. His letters home provide insight into the war years and will be useful to scholars and history buffs alike."

—**DR. BRIAN D. LASLIE**, COMMAND HISTORIAN AT THE UNITED STATES AIR FORCE ACADEMY, AND AUTHOR OF *FIGHTING FROM ABOVE: A COMBAT HISTORY OF THE U.S. AIR FORCE*

"This is a superb compilation of wartime letters."

—**KARL ZINGHEIM**, HISTORIAN, USS MIDWAY MUSEUM, AND LECTURER, SAN DIEGO STATE UNIVERSITY

Disgracefully EASY

A B-24 Pilot's Letters Home

WILLIAM HANCHETT
with
THOMAS F. HANCHETT

*Helping talented writers
publish exceptional books.*

www.AcornPublishingLLC.com

For information, address:
Acorn Publishing, LLC
3943 Irvine Blvd. Ste. 218
Irvine, CA 92602

Interior design and formatting by Debra Cranfield Kennedy

Printed in the United States of America

ISBN-13: 979-8-88528-118-8 (hardcover)
ISBN-13: 979-8-88528-117-1 (paperback)

ALSO BY
William Hanchett

The Transformation of America:
Readings in United States History
Since the Civil War
Edited with Richard T. Ruetten

Irish: Charles G. Halpine in Civil War America

The Lincoln Murder Conspiracies

Out of the Wilderness: The Life of Abraham Lincoln

To Ian, youngest grandchild

and

Ralphy and Alice Jean, great-grandchildren

of Bill Hanchett

Expanded Table of Contents

Chapter 3
College Training Detachment 46—Tennessee Polytechnic Institute

Participates in an experimental Army Air Forces College Training Detachment, Cookeville, Tennessee
College courses while waiting to enter flight training
First flights
Bill and three other aviation students chase down a runaway horse-drawn wagon.

Chapter 4
Preflight and Primary Flying School

Maxwell Field, Montgomery, Alabama
Bill describes the strict regimen and hazing of "rats" during preflight training
Burma Road
Struggles with Morse Code
Fear of being "washed out" becomes a recurring concern
Leisure time with BMC graduate Harriet Engelhardt
First impression of Primary Flying School in Douglas, Georgia
Bill's naivete, thinking that aviation cadets received relaxation time because learning to fly is difficult
Link Trainer introduction
Learns to fly a PT-17 biplane with a tough civilian instructor
Concern about Nazi sympathizer working with his father
Italy surrenders
Jean Forster graduates from Swarthmore College
Miss Mabel Dodd.

Chapter 5
Basic Flying School—Bainbridge Army Air Field

Bainbridge Field, Georgia and commanding officer Colonel Mills S. Savage
Learns to fly a BT-13 Valiant training plane
Differences between a civilian and a military instructor
Spends spare time reading classic literature
Parachute mishap
Class 44B statistics
Bill uncertain on type of plane he wants to fly, medium bombers or fighters
Bill "dogfights" with three P-47 Thunderbolt fighters and decides he prefers a single-engine plane.

Chapter 6
Advanced Flying School and Wings

Marianna Army Air Field, Florida
Bill hopes to fly "hot ships," the best fighters in the Army Air Forces
Sensitive controls of an AT-6 Texan trainer
War room studies
Flying the beam
Gives instructor a good laugh and earns the nickname "Flaps"
Flying preferences
Turning point after high-altitude chamber test results
Bill proudly receives his hard-earned officer's commission and pilot's wings from commanding officer Colonel John W. Persons.

Chapter 7
Instructor-Pilot School—Randolph Army Air Field and Return to Bainbridge

Family experience on D-Day
Graduation from one of the toughest programs in the Army Air Forces, the Central Instructors School at Randolph Field, San Antonio
Bill returns to his old Basic Flying School in Georgia as an instructor-pilot
First group of aviation cadets
Hours flying in the backseat of BT-13, Vultee "Vibrator"
Instructor-pilot camaraderie
Learns to play a Tonette
Merry rat races
Instrument flying training
Infantry training bivouac
Visits Jean in Philadelphia
German prisoners of war working on a peanut farm
Basic Flying School closure.

Chapter 8

Learns to fly the B-24 in Montgomery and Courtland, Alabama

First impressions of a B-29 Superfortress

General William O. Butler's welcome to Maxwell Army Air Field

Flight Engineer experience

Hitler's "Big Lie" theory

The Fala affair

The B-24, one of the most difficult airplanes to fly

Amidst the 1944 presidential election, Bill engages in lively ongoing correspondence with his father

Bill supports President Franklin D. Roosevelt, breaking politically with his father, who supports Thomas E. Dewey

Pearl Harbor attack investigation report

Bill describes the experience of holding a 36,000 pound, four-engine bomber in his left hand

Link Trainer flying versus real flying

Memories of Eleanor Roosevelt and Addie Daniels' toe

Christmas 1944 with relatives.

Chapter 9

At Lemoore Army Air Field, Bill loves California's fertile central valley

Tonopah Army Air Field, Nevada

Colonel John A. Feagin improves flight safety and morale

In the high desert, Bill trains his bomber crew for what seemed to be an inevitable combat assignment in the Pacific

Bill wishes he could study U.S. History as hard as he studies the B-24 Liberator

Applauds Okinawa invasion

Bill practice "bombs" his future hometown of San Diego, California

Physical strain of flying

Engine fire emergency handled by a disciplined crew

Victory Europe (VE) Day

Possible transition to the new B-32 Dominator very heavy bomber

Describes preflight briefing

Flying with P-63 Kingcobra fighters

Feeling the absence of President Roosevelt

Postwar plan, raising chickens

Bill's training flights include an unscheduled overnight trip to see relatives in Tucson, Arizona

Introduction

We salute and thank those who fought for freedom against fascism on distant battlefields around the globe during World War II. We should also acknowledge the service of those who trained diligently and prepared with apprehension for what they thought would be the inevitable overseas combat assignment—an assignment that never came.

Before William (Bill) Hanchett became a professor of American History and an authority on the assassination of President Abraham Lincoln, my father served as a B-24 four-engine heavy bomber pilot in the U.S. Army Air Forces (AAF) during World War II. This book is a selection of his correspondence written during the war era. The total correspondence consisted of 206 letters and 98 postal cards written from the late 1930s to December 1945. The correspondence has been edited with an introduction to each group of letters.

The letters are divided by each phase of flight training, or flying school, as it was called during the war, to assignment as an instructor-pilot in BT-13 basic trainers, to transition to B-24 heavy bomber pilot training, and subsequent assignment to a B-24 training squadron at Tonopah Field, Nevada. The letters provide first-hand descriptions of flying different airplanes, from the PT-17 primary trainer bi-plane to the B-24 Liberator. All the chapters, except the first, which covers several years before Bill's enlistment in the AAF, include his letters.

The title *Disgracefully Easy* comes from a postal card my father wrote on August 19, 1945, ten days after the second atomic bomb was dropped on Nagasaki, Japan. Bill Hanchett indicated that his military service had been "disgracefully easy" when compared to other servicemen who had served in combat. This assessment reflects my father's feeling at the end of the war and his awareness of the sacrifices of so many. Through his correspondence, Bill Hanchett tells another side of the history of World War II.

My father kept B-24 flight manuals and booklets published by the U.S. Army Air Forces, describing all phases of flight training and the air fields where he trained. Through the years, dad told me about flying and about his experiences during the war. The discovery of the correspondence, combined with his stories, the flight manuals and air field booklets, provided a trove of primary source material.

In the fall of 1944, as he learned to fly the B-24, the correspondence also describes the critical election when President Franklin D. Roosevelt ran for a fourth term against Republican Governor Thomas E. Dewey. Bill's father supported Dewey, but Bill supported and admired Roosevelt, "our greatest President," he wrote. That year, Bill found his own political voice—separate from his father. The letters reflect a continuity in American politics and society, with politicians and writers stoking division and promoting controversial conspiracy theories and voter suppression, themes which resonate today.

The correspondence reflects a time when families communicated with each other through handwritten and typed correspondence, which was delivered via "snail mail"—long before email, text messaging or social media were even imagined. The letters are naturally written in language commonly used in the 1940s. The letters are a snapshot in time, of course specific to the Hanchetts, but they also reveal family experiences and situations during the war years that many will recognize and identify with on a personal level.

My father received frequent correspondence from his immediate and his extended family, but as service members do, Bill sometimes complained about the lack of mail from home. He especially enjoyed receiving cookies and other treats. The correspondence sent to my father from his family is unavailable, so we do not know exactly what he heard from home, but from his correspondence we can infer the other side of the "conversation."

Throughout the correspondence, various family activities and family members and friends are mentioned, and through Bill's comments and expressed opinions, the reader learns something about them and about him. In some of his letters, my father "lectures" his parents about various things, from politics and finances to even winding a new watch. Bill had a lot to say and at times every blank space on a page—front, back, top, bottom or side—were filled with questions or comments.

Bill joined the U.S. Army Air Forces in October 1942. His correspondence tells the story of basic training in Miami Beach, drilling on a golf course, and his experience in a unique Army Air Forces College Training Detachment (CTD) program where aviation cadets attended college courses while waiting to enter flying school. This experience reinforced his interest in history.

The story also includes some of the instructors and AAF officers who directed the training. Bill discusses them, not always by name, but by rank. End notes are included on several who were influential in his development as a pilot. They are unsung heroes of the AAF, not typically mentioned in books on the air war.

In the letters, at times he is the actor in the events described, at other times, the observer, critic, and self-critic. In addition to telling his story of military service, the correspondence reveals Bill's developing interest in history and evaluation of daily and world events, showing a political and social awareness in a tumultuous era. His willingness to admit mistakes and laugh at himself comes through in his letters. For example, when he made a mistake in advanced flying school, for which he received the nickname "Flaps," he wrote a six-page letter about it.

Bill mentions the friends he made and activities he participated in with them while in the service. As with the people many of us encounter in life, they make their appearances and then sometimes disappear. Other than a very few, several who were friends in high school, and one or two others, no evidence or documentation was found that he kept up with any of the people he served with during the war.

Bill's correspondence reflects an evolution in how he felt and thought about his world. Before he enlisted in the Army Air Forces, Bill's enthusiasm for learning grew at Black Mountain College. When he had the opportunity, he read a great deal. His study of literature and history broadened his perspective and contributed to his development as an historian. He always said that period literature is a way to better understand history. Some of the books he mentioned reading were, and still are, well-known classics. Other books are not so well known, so bibliographic information about these books is included in the chapter endnotes.

In order to better understand the correspondence, some background on the Hanchett family and the various people Bill mentions will be helpful. The Hanchett family of English origin has been in America since the early 1630s. One direct ancestor fought the British and was captured during the siege of Quebec early in the American Revolution.

Bill's father, William, known in the family as Will, was born in 1880 in Westfield, Massachusetts and worked as a page during the 1893 World's Columbian Exposition in Chicago. Will attended Evanston Township High School until the death of his father at an early age compelled him to go to work to help support his mother and four siblings, so he never graduated from high school. By 1905, Will worked as a bank teller, and in November of that year, became a salesman for Trowbridge and Niver Company, a Chicago municipal bond company.

Will married his boss's daughter, Lucie Alice Trowbridge, in March 1910. Alice, the daughter of Lucius Atwater and Caroline (Cobb) Trowbridge, was born in Rockford, Illinois in 1888. She was the eldest of three sisters, and attended Wellesley College from 1908-1909. After a honeymoon trip to the Bahamas, Will and Alice resided near her parents in Evanston, a Chicago suburb on Lake Michigan.[1]

In October 1910, the Hanchett Bond Company was formed and originally composed of Will, his two brothers, John and Harold, who also worked at Trowbridge and Niver, and the president and his father-in-law, Lucius Trowbridge. Will served as Vice President and General Manager until 1922, when Mr. Trowbridge retired, at which point Will became president of the company.[2]

Along with his parents, Bill's Aunt Leila, his father's older sister, was a frequent correspondent. Leila trained as a nurse at Chicago's St. Luke's Hospital. During the First World War, before going overseas, she served at Camp Sherman, Ohio as a Red Cross nurse treating soldiers during the 1918 flu pandemic. In the summer of 1918, Leila embarked for France with the American National Red Cross Nursing Bureau, serving there through August, 1919. Leila worked at a U.S. Army hospital during the decisive Meuse-Argonne Offensive, which led to the end of the war in November, 1918. President Woodrow Wilson signed Leila's American Red Cross Foreign Service Certificate.[3]

Bill was born on May 25, 1922. Bill and his five sisters, Jane (Calamity), Josephine (Jo or Sally), Frances (Fran), Alice Ann (AA) and Louise (Wese or Louie) came of age in Evanston. Despite their age differences, the eldest Jane, born in 1911 and the youngest Wese, born in 1923, the siblings were close and carried on congenial life-long relationships.

The Hanchett children lived a comparatively privileged life until the Depression, but they were not immune to the world around them. During

Christmas, 1918, the four older sisters became ill during the flu pandemic but recovered.

In 1925, Will bought a vacation home called "Ye Olde Maple" on White Lake in Michigan. The family spent the summer months on the golf course, swimming, motor boating and sailing. Will would commute there every weekend from Evanston. Home movies from the 1920s depict an active family life. Friends of his older sisters taught Bill to sail. It was there that he developed a lifelong love of water and sailing.[4]

Wese was just one year younger than Bill, and they spent a lot of time together. They walked or rode bicycles around Evanston and spent time with cousins who also lived in the city. On weekends they would pass the ornate Orrington Hotel on their way to a nearby movie theater with their German Shepherd, Mac, who would wait patiently for them outside. Bill especially liked action-adventure movies like Errol Flynn and Olivia de Havilland's *Captain Blood*. At home he read books like *The Story of Roland*, about a knight in the Middle Ages. From an early age Bill's imagination was sparked by historical adventure stories and historical events. For example, playing in the snow, he pretended to be one of General George Washington's soldiers at Valley Forge. Bill's interest in history was further developed through books like *Minute Biographies* and *Great Moments in History*.

The Hanchett Bond Company made Will quite wealthy. Yet, during the Great Depression, which began in October of 1929, the local municipalities in whose securities the Hanchett Bond Company dealt with were unable to make payment on their bonds. The company was forced into voluntary bankruptcy during the winter of 1931-1932. Like describing a sinking ship, Bill's mother, Alice, wrote that the company "went under." Alice's analogy was good, the Hanchett Bond Company *had* been the "ship" the family sailed in and relied upon. Now it was gone, and the family moved into an unfamiliar, less privileged lifestyle. For Christmas 1931, in what must have been one bright spot in an otherwise dreary time, the Hanchett children gave their parents a small book called "We Are Six," in which the older children had been writing since 1924. Each child contributed written stories describing themselves, or various family experiences.[5]

Both the business and the family homes were lost in the Depression. During the war years, Bill's parents were apart because his father, in his mid-sixties, spent a great deal of time on the road as a business consultant, traveling around the country and in Canada. Much of Bill's correspondence to his father was addressed to him at hotels or YMCAs. Between 1937 and 1945, Alice recorded living with her youngest daughter, Louise, in at least ten different addresses in Evanston. When his parents were apart, Bill sometimes wrote long letters to each parent on the same day. Which topics were emphasized in the letter differed depending on the recipient. At times, he addressed his father as "Fat." Years before I knew of the existence of this correspondence, my father told me that he and his dad referred to each other as "Fat" just for fun. Proof positive is found in this collection.[6]

As a young boy, Bill's mother took him to the Chicago Historical Society to see the Charles Gunther collection of Abraham Lincoln memorabilia. Andrew Ferguson describes this exhibition and its origins in his book, *Land of Lincoln: Adventures in Abe's America.* One of the displays included a reproduction of the bedroom of the Petersen House, where Lincoln was carried after being shot at Ford's Theater on April 14, 1865. The exhibit included the actual bed with a bloodstained sheet where Lincoln died. My father told me that after seeing this display and the bloodstained sheet, he hated John Wilkes Booth, Lincoln's assassin. This exhibition no doubt contributed to my father's academic interest in American history and his lifelong interest in Abraham Lincoln.[7]

While in high school, Bill worked in a local food store, National Tea Company, bagging groceries. He would frequently see Jean Haire-Forster, an ETHS classmate and her mother, Christina. Jean was a year younger than Bill, but in the same grade level. They later became romantically involved and, as described in the correspondence, married at the end of the war.

Jean's father, my maternal grandfather, Dr. Arthur Haire-Forster, was an Anglican/Episcopal Minister and an Irish immigrant who came to Evanston via Toronto, Canada. He was a Professor of Hellenistic Greek at Seabury-Western Theological Seminary. In 1916, while in Toronto, Canada, Arthur met and married Christina Kammerer, the daughter of an American businessman working in Canada. Christina's grandfather emigrated to the United States from Hesse-Darmstadt, Germany in 1851 and settled in New York.[8]

Unknown to my father, his parents saved all of his correspondence. After they passed away in the late 1950s, the letters went to his sister, Jo, who later gave them to him. They were tucked away in the closet of his study, forgotten.

My father never revealed the existence of this correspondence. My nephew Colin discovered it in late July 2016 around the time my father passed away. The correspondence was bundled in a plain brown wrapper tied with string. On the wrapper was a note my father wrote dated 12 July, 1961, stating that he did not know his parents had saved the correspondence. Bill wrote, "I am saving them now on the chance that they may be of interest to me or someone else when they have acquired enough years to qualify as historical documents." Through moves to different residences over many years, the package of correspondence remained unopened and undisclosed to me or others in the immediate family.

At the same time the correspondence was found, his Army Air Forces pilot's wings were found, along with additional Army Air Forces memorabilia, also perhaps forgotten, in a green metal box. It was a poignant end to the pilot's wings Bill worked so hard to obtain. As you will read, there were many times he thought he would not earn them. The cast aside pilot's wings also demonstrated that he had moved on from flying to his life's work as a historian.

In reviewing and editing the correspondence, spelling and punctuation corrections were made for consistency and clarity for the reader. The word airfield as currently used was changed to air field to reflect use in official Army Air Forces documentation from the 1940s, for example, Bainbridge Army Air Field. Sometimes the words "Army Air" were dropped to reduce repetition, i.e., Bainbridge Field.

Chapter 1

BEFORE THE WAR 1939-1942

In high school, Bill was an average student, but his Evanston Township High School (ETHS) teachers noted his leadership, dependability, willingness to admit mistakes, and his popularity throughout high school. Also, it was observed that his popularity sometimes interfered with his studies. Though responsible and well-liked, Bill displayed a stubborn persistence and a temper.

The summer between his junior and senior year at ETHS, the last peaceful summer before the war began in Europe, Bill spent traveling. He drove his mother's friend, Marion "Anne" Kappes, to Quebec. Always an observer with an opinion, he considered Quebec "too commercial." Afterward, Bill hitchhiked through New England, visiting relatives. In Westfield, Massachusetts, he visited the house where his father grew up. In New York City, he visited the World's Fair.

Bill was elected one of four senior class presidents for the 1939-1940 school year at ETHS. The school newspaper published a profile of the new class president. According to the article, in addition to this new position, he was treasurer of the Spanish Club and a baseball fan. The article noted that, "often he can be found arguing about baseball with Mr. Magill." Mr. (David T.) Magill was one of the high school coaches. Also, the article noted he was—and remained for life—a collector of good books. One of his favorites was *Mutiny on the Bounty*. Other interests included saving old coins, playing golf and sailing. Bill also told the student reporter that he did not like "sophisticated girls, bright fingernail polish and fast dance music." In addition to describing his hitchhiking trip to New England, the article also disclosed his plan to work his way to Honolulu on a freighter.[1]

Bill's friend, Jean Forster, had developed an affinity for languages starting with French at ETHS. Remarkably, fifty odd years later, she could still translate a book from French to English. Bill and Jean graduated from high school in the early summer of 1940 as the Nazis were over-running Belgium and France. Jean was academically advanced, so she graduated at the same time as Bill. Shortly thereafter, she enrolled at Swarthmore College in Pennsylvania.

Following graduation, Bill traveled south to Cuba, planning to sign on as a crewman on a tramp steamer and sail to Mexico. As Bill described it, the adventure did not go as he had hoped. Though he thought the countryside was beautiful, Cuba was not the romantic Caribbean Island he imagined. Penniless, he could not get a job on a steamer because there was a long waiting list for jobs. Furthermore, to get one of the jobs, he needed to be in the labor union and have experience. Bill possessed neither experience nor union membership. In a letter to his father, Bill revealed a stubborn streak that would assist in pushing him through future flying school and years of academic education; "... I promised myself that I would be gone for 2 months so I cannot come home until Aug. 22. I will hitchhike to Lakeland, Baltimore, New York, Syracuse, Cleveland and White Lake, spending some time in all those places—and that should take at least 1 month." (July 6, 1940, letter)

In mid-July, he spent several days in New York City with his Aunt Agnes and cousin, Bill Hubbell. They took Bill to the movies at Radio City Music Hall and a baseball game.[2]

After he returned to Evanston, Bill busied himself with a variety of odd jobs, such as "office boy," painting, washing cars and windows and doing yard work. The next summer, in 1941, Bill took a trip to Syracuse, New York to visit his Aunt Leila, whom he described as "very funny."

Later that summer, Bill wrote about the "Grose Expedition," which was "led" by "Dr. Grose," his younger cousin, Lucius Trowbridge (Trobe) Grose, who *did* become Dr. Grose, a professor of geology. When Bill wrote about this trip, his imagination was in high gear. The objective was "to bring civilization to the Babcocks." "Miss Louise," also a member of the expedition, was of course, his younger sister, who wrote an account of the trip. In reality, this was a one-week visit to assist their older sister, AA and her husband, Bob Babcock, who were building a cabin on Rainy Lake in Ontario, Canada, just over the border from Minnesota.

About seven years older than Bill, Bob was like a "big brother." He taught political science at Black Mountain College (BMC), an experimental liberal arts college near Asheville, North Carolina. In addition to his teaching duties, Bob participated in college construction and work on the college farm.

With this family connection to BMC, Bill applied for admission. On the application, he indicated his interest in English literature, composition, and farming. In his college application, he acknowledged that his grades in high school had been average, but after working a variety of jobs, including work in an acoustic tile factory, he felt ready to apply himself academically. Bill was admitted to the college and *even* received special permission to bring his pet dog, Rainey, "a toy collie, police dog mix" with him.[3]

Located on the shores of Lake Eden, near Asheville, North Carolina, Black Mountain College was founded in 1933 with thirteen faculty and twenty-six students. The college applied the educational principles of John Dewey, who believed that students do best when they are allowed to interact with the curriculum and take an active part in their own learning. A number of the faculty were refugees from Germany and eastern Europe, fleeing Nazi Germany. The setting was informal and, as Bill was to learn, the students assisted in building the college and maintaining its farm.[4]

Bill, accompanied by his dog Rainey, enrolled in Black Mountain College in the fall of 1941. He was "absolutely thrilled" to be at the college. Stories of Rainey's adventures around the lake and farm were included in his correspondence. Bill rode horseback around the college farm, often with Rainey running beside him. He liked horseback riding so much, he mused about joining the cavalry.[5]

Black Mountain College promoted an informal environment in which students and instructors lived on campus, ate meals and socialized together. Formal grades were not assigned, but the faculty wrote evaluations of each student's work. Bill appears to have had good relations with his instructors, who were down to earth and involved with the students. One instructor, Mary "Molly" Gregory, supervised the wood-working shop. Under her direction, students constructed tables, desks, chairs, benches, bookshelves and even the sign at the entrance to BMC. Under Gregory's instruction, Bill wrote that he was becoming a carpenter and building his own study.[6]

The experience at Black Mountain ignited Bill's lifelong interest in learning, which is reflected throughout his correspondence. He began his serious study of American presidents, history, and world affairs. In his letters, Bill enjoyed telling his family about BMC faculty and events. Bill was enthusiastic about Roland Boyden's American History class, and he immersed himself in subjects like George Washington. Early on, Bill was also influenced by Paul Radin, an anthropology professor and an expert on Native Americans. Radin was an interventionist in the war. He did not consider England worth saving but thought that "Hitler is worth beating."

That fall term Bill wrote a paper on Civil War Reconstruction and read two biographies of President Grover Cleveland for the history course. He judged one of them by historian Allan Nevins as "fairly good." Bill's judgment was amusing, since Nevins' biography, *Grover Cleveland: A Study in Courage*, won the 1933 Pulitzer Prize for Biography/Autobiography. Nevins would later write the forward to William Hanchett's biography of Civil War journalist, poet and soldier, Charles G. Halpine, *Irish: Charles G. Halpine in Civil War America*. Bill may have laughed at his youthful naivete if he had remembered describing Nevins' Cleveland biography as "fairly good."

Occasionally, Bill included news items from periodicals in letters to his father. As an example, a story in the *Chicago Tribune* dated October 27, 1941, pondered, "What vital interests of the U.S. can Japan threaten? She cannot attack us. That is a military impossibility. Even our base at Hawaii is beyond the effective striking power of her fleet." The United States soon learned differently on December 7, 1941, and went to war near the end of Bill's first college semester. Bill wrote that he was playing touch football when news of the attack on Pearl Harbor was broadcast.

In January 1942, accompanied by English and Drama instructor Robert Wunsch, Bill and three others, serving as student delegates, represented Black Mountain College at a conference on the postwar world at the University of North Carolina, Chapel Hill. There were delegates from thirty-two colleges at the conference titled "Youth's Stake in War Aims and Peace Plans." First Lady Eleanor Roosevelt was one of the featured speakers along with Arthur Sweetser, a member of the American Peace Commission after the First World War and a strong supporter of the League of Nations. Mrs. Roosevelt, always a strong supporter of youth and education, attended conference sessions and spoke at Memorial Hall on the second day of the conference, January 31, 1942. As described in several letters, Bill almost met Mrs. Roosevelt, but she turned away from him as he stood in line to see her. Later, in 1944, he "confessed" that as he approached Mrs. Roosevelt, he had stepped on the toe of Mrs. Addie Worth Bagley Daniels, the wife of Josephus Daniels, Secretary of the Navy under President Woodrow Wilson, and a Roosevelt family friend. Bill also wrote that Mrs. Roosevelt was asked if her husband planned to seek a fourth term as president and shared her reply.[7]

Think of the extraordinary timing of this conference—it was held in January, 1942, a month after the attack on Pearl Harbor. The Axis powers still held the initiative around the globe, but Americans were focused on war objectives and plans for the peace that would follow an Axis defeat. There was an undefeatable American spirit present.

Bill's letters often drew his family into his studies and sometimes solicited suggestions from them. For example, the budding historian indicated that reading about George Washington was easy, but he was having difficulty writing about him and how his character was brought out by the American revolution. He also asked for suggestions for a title for the term paper.

In multiple undated letters, he described activities and outings with Rainey. Like his dog Mac, who would wait outside the Evanston theater, Rainey would wait outside his classrooms. By early spring, Bill oversaw the new poultry division of the college farm after he acquired the first group of chicks. He noted his canine companion's puzzled reaction to all the chickens. Bill's correspondence about the college farm revealed his interest in farming and the prospect of making money raising chickens.

Throughout Bill's time at BMC, finances were always a problem. As previously noted, the Depression had hit his family hard. Despite BMC's arrangements to accommodate the family's financial situation, it was becoming clear that he could not continue at the college. Bill wanted to stay in school and promised his parents that he would hit the books even harder.

In May, shortly before Bill's twentieth birthday at the end of the term, his American history instructor and advisor, Roland Boyden, sent a positive letter to his father evaluating Bill's college work.

Throughout his college experience, the war dominated the news and impacted everyday life. Before Bill left in May, his brother-in-law Bob

Babcock departed BMC to work in the Treasury Department. In 1944, he was commissioned an officer in the U.S. Navy and went through Supply Corps training at Wellesley College, where his mother-in-law had studied.[8] Many of Bill's friends, including his music instructor, John Evarts, who spoke German, joined the U.S. Army. Boyden would become an intelligence officer in the U.S. Navy. In addition to leaving behind his interests in academics and farming, and because of an unstable housing situation in Evanston, Bill had to leave behind his faithful dog, Rainey. It must have been a sad scene. The war and family finances had intervened, and Bill returned home at the end of May.[9]

Chapter 2

MIAMI BEACH— ARMY AIR FORCES BASIC TRAINING

Bill left Black Mountain College and took a job arranged by his brother-in-law, John McFadden, as an elevator operator in Chicago's Palmolive Building.

In the days after the attack on Pearl Harbor, while still at Black Mountain College, Bill had speculated about joining the Army Air Forces, but nothing had come of it. Now, since continuing in college was financially impossible, he considered his military options. Because of his interest in boats and sailing developed during summers at White Lake, Bill liked the prospect of skippering U.S. Navy PT boats. Much later, he said that he spoke to Navy recruiters about this idea and was told "No" when he confessed, he had asthma. According to the story, he then visited an Army recruiting office and said nothing about asthma.

Available documentation shows that Bill enlisted in the Army Air Forces on Saturday, October 10, 1942. He reported to Fort Sheridan in Chicago on November 1, 1942, for processing into the Army Air Forces.

As with all new recruits, Bill's first stop was basic training in February 1943. As part of the Army Air Forces wartime expansion, the Miami Beach Training Center opened the year before in response to the attack on Pearl Harbor. In one of his first letters home, with perhaps prescient insight, Private Hanchett envisioned an air force separate from the army. Though he backed away from the idea at the end of his observation, he was on to something. What Bill observed, and became part of, had been years in the making among Army Air Forces brass, whose plan for a separate air force came to fruition after the war.

As Bill entered basic training, his father went to work for the George S. May Company, and Alice began work at the Northwestern University dental clinic, and later that year, started work at D.S. Lyman drug store. The May Company participated in business consulting and Will travelled around the country conducting job evaluations and advising business executives on management practices.

In addition to being a college student, and now a Private in the Army Air Forces, Bill was an uncle. Three of his sisters, Jo, Fran and AA, had young families. The previous year, Jo welcomed her fourth daughter and both Fran and AA had young sons. Sometimes in his correspondence, with a smile no doubt, he referred to his young nieces and nephews as "brats." With similar jesting, on the back of a photo showing him holding a dog who belonged to his sister Jo, mother of four young daughters, Bill wrote that he was holding Happy McFadden, his "favorite niece."

In Miami, Bill indicated that his fellow recruits were "swell guys." Basic training included military drill and ceremonies, physical training (PT), infantry weapons and marksmanship. The new recruits stood in ranks, marched, drilled and did PT on golf courses throughout the city. In PT, one of the exercises was the "Duck Waddle," a movement that persisted in Bill's memory through the years. To do this exercise the instructions said to "assume knees-bent position, hands on hips, retaining this position, walk forward." As all in the military do, Bill also performed kitchen police (KP) duty, scraping and washing pots and pans. It was not all drilling and KP, as he told his family in one letter, boasting that after he finished writing, they would be jealous because he was going for a swim in the ocean. Passing through Florida on his way to Cuba in 1940, Bill fell in love with the ocean and now he loved ocean swimming, especially after a hot day on a golf course drill field.

Correspondence From
MIAMI BEACH BASIC TRAINING CENTER

February 2, 1943, Tuesday

Dear Mother & Dad:

… The train trip was long—we didn't get here until 11:00 last night—and enjoyable, despite the fact that we weren't allowed to get off the train at any time. My voice was gone completely Sunday, but improved yesterday, and is OK today. I was very lucky to get *a lower berth to myself both nights!*

We left Chicago at 8:30 from the 12th St. Station. We went via Cincinnati and Knoxville to Atlanta, Jacksonville, etc. After arriving at Miami, we were herded together and stood waiting for an hour for trucks to take us to Miami Beach.[1] Once in the military zone, we had to wait until after 3:00 am before we were assigned to our rooms. Darn poor planning and typical GOP bungling. I am at a very nice, but modest for Miami Beach, hotel called "Coral Reef."[2] I am sitting on my bed, which is next to the window and can see the ocean right outside!

We got up this AM after a swell hours [one-hour] sleep and waited for almost two hours for breakfast. I have just returned from that favorite meal and have taken a shower, put on clean clothes, and am waiting for something to happen. I know no more about things now than I did in Chicago.

One of my new (and I think temporary) roommates has turned out to be a very good friend of Jack Hanchett [Bill's cousin] . . .

We were just given a 5-minute warning signal, so I'll close this.

You can bet I'll write again as soon as I get the time, and that I'm thinking of all of you and hoping everything is O.K.

Much Love.   Lovingly, Bill

The weather is perfect—the view terrific—the coloring powerful—it is just like a May day in Chicago. Everyone is going around in shorts only!

February 3, 1943, Wednesday

Dear All:

Please send mail to me at the address on other side. Things are beginning to pick up now, as we get organized. There are several drill fields, but I think most of the drilling will be on a golf course!

The weather continues to be great and I like it better, all the time.

Haven't been able to leave hotel in evening yet, so haven't seen John E. Evarts. [Black Mountain College (BMC) Music instructor, also now in the U.S. Army.] Don't put name of my hotel on envelope. Please. Hope everything is O.K. Write soon, por favor.

Lovingly, Bill

February 5, 1943, Friday

Dear Mom & Dad:

This outdoor life is wonderful! We are right on top of the ocean. I am tickled to death with the setup here and will be more so when things get straightened out. It seems these many cadets were just plunked down here with no definite idea of what was going to be done to us. We are stalling around, marching, standing in ranks etc. The food is not so hot. I have 4 roommates whom I like very much. Swell guys. I am writing this on the floor as there are no chairs or tables and we are not allowed to sit on the beds. You should see my tan! Haven't been able to see John yet but think I can Sat. No letters from home, but I know it's because of the confusion here.

Love, Bill

February 7, 1943

Dear Mother & Dad and everyone else:

I can't tell you how much I dislike writing letters in longhand. The thoughts come so fast that I can never get all I want to say about one thing down before I have to stop and say something else. Chances for a more intelligible letter than usual are good for today, because for the first time I have all the time I need and a good place to write: We have from 12:00 noon till 10:00 pm tonight free and I am writing in the recreation room of a nearby hotel, which has been furnished with writing desks, ping pong tables, magazines, etc.

Last night was our first evening off and I spent it, including dinner at an open Italian restaurant, with John Evarts. Had a wonderful time with him talking about BMC [Black Mountain College] days and going over things in general. He is working in the Classification office at the other end of the Beach, and though he says he likes his work and that it is very interesting, I know he doesn't, and it isn't . . .

He [John] is doing some "show" work & is going to play the piano at something or another tonight. I plan to go but it's pretty far so I may not. He played the role of Roosevelt in a half hour radio program, describing the career of that *great president* last week. I was very flattered that he was so glad to see me, and I think we'll probably get together next Sat. too.

Our hotel is right on the ocean. In fact, when we go out the backdoor, we don't use the front except at night, we go right on to the sand! My new room is in the back, or east, facing the ocean! It's a grand view, of course, and this room was one of the very finest. It's a bit crowded now, though. All of the other boys in this room are veterans like me and were also working in Chicago, but I only knew one of them. They're a nice bunch—most of the guys are at that.

We are still greatly disorganized. These thousands of cadets were just put down here and apparently no definite program had been worked out before. If you want my opinion, this large movement, which is entirely new, is all part of a plan to establish the Air Force as a separate branch of the service, but maybe not.[3]

We haven't settled down to a real routine yet, but our day always begins at 5:15 am and, last week, ended at 8 or 9. We are doing drill, exercises, etc., but mostly we just stand in rank.

Chow is fair only! The cafeteria has facilities to serve adequately 1000 less than it is taking care of, so you have a fair idea of how peaceful and unhurried our meals are. We eat out of our mess kits, by the way.

Today we had a huge parade for the Colonel.[4] He is little short of the Almighty around here and the soldiers tremble at sight of him, which, due to my close association with Eddy Shafer [unidentified], strikes me very funny.

The weather has been perfect. We wear only pants and shirts all day, and I've already got a sunburn that I know would make Wese [sister] turn green.

I received my check last week—it was the only thing I did receive—but I haven't been able to cash it yet.

I will certainly be glad to get some letters and the socks when they're done and the pictures when they've been developed. By the way, it is very important to include "Flight 446" on letters addressed to me. If you have written before, I'll get your letters sometime. This new number will cut out the delay. Correct address is on the envelope . . .

I'll send this Airmail, so you'll get the correct address as soon as possible. Meanwhile, lots of love.   Lovingly, Bill

February 12, 1943

My address is:
Pvt. Wm. F. Hanchett, Jr. 16135510
A.A.F.T.T.C. B.T.C. 9 T.S.S. 1129 (SA)
Flight 446
Miami Beach, Florida

As yet I have received *no* mail from anyone, except a swell letter from Jess [aunt] several days ago. Shall I blame you, or the Democrats? Send an issue of the *Sun*, por favor. Will plan to write Sunday. John E. [Evarts] and I are going to hear Lily Pons Sun. afternoon.[5]

As ever, Bill

February 14, 1943, Sunday morning

Dear All:

At last, we have settled into our regular routine. We get up at 4:45 am—eat chow, clean our rooms, and march the two miles to the golf course drill field before dawn. Then we strip to the waist and do calisthenics for half an hour as the sun rises and warms our backs. Then we "double time" it over the fairways, roughs, and through sand traps. This is the best part of the day for me! I like that sort of exercise and love the early morning...

I have learned that we will be here for only about 3 weeks more. We will then be sent to some college or university for technical training. I don't know where, or what.

Enclosed dad will find an editorial which he will do well to read. Walter Locke's column is a nation-wide syndicate. He is a member of the BMC advisory board and spent a weekend there last year.[6]

The weather is wonderful, and I have been swimming several times . . .

Just woke up from an hour's nap after having returned from a swell chicken dinner. The food, by the way, has come up to par now and is darn good . . .

I wish you could see my room. It has white plaster walls, a little hallway, leading from the main hall on either side of which is a closet and the john. Opposite the door and hallway are two big windows from which you can see nothing but the ocean, unless you look straight down when you can see the sand beach. The water can't be more than thirty feet away. I am on the third floor. The "Coral Reef" was very elegant in its day, they say, with maroon carpets etc., but now it is stripped of every bit of its elegance— including hot water.

There are always lots of ships passing by and it is interesting to watch them.

Thursday, two generals visited the camp, and we had a big parade for them. It was rumored that one was Gen. Arnold—chief of staff of Army Air Forces.[7]

I know it will make you all very jealous to learn that, as soon as I say "Lovingly, Bill" again, I will get into my bathing suit and go swimming and lie around on the beach for a while before coming in to get dressed and meet John Evarts for the Lily Pons concert. Ah! What a life!

Well, I don't need to say that I will be glad to get your letters. You might mention the delay to AA and anyone else who may have written me and wondered why they hadn't heard from me.

Very much love to everyone and an extra big dinner for Jeff [family cat] from me.

Lovingly, Bill

February 19, 1943, Friday night

Dear All:

Well, I've received some very startling and welcome news from home about home during the past two days. I'm tickled to death about your new work, Dad, but as yet I know absolutely nothing about it. I've heard from mother, Jo, Fran, and Wese since you started, but none of them said anything more than that you'd started. But that's enough for me. I'm anxious for details, however, and hope I'll get them soon. *A thousand congratulations! What an example of guts you have been!* The old "fighting heart!"

I've got some surprising news myself. It looks practically certain that I'll be leaving here the first of next week, or about the time you receive this! We'll probably head north (as if we could go any other direction), which is fine in its way, but how I'll miss the view from my window! Will be going to some college for the regular preflight technical training, which up to this time, has been given at field camps. It'll be fun going back to school, but I wonder how I'll do with work that interests me so little. We've had a bit of it here, lectures mostly, and it just doesn't excite me, but I'm not in the Army to be excited, am I?

We had several chilly days, for which we were totally unprepared in the way of blankets, etc. during the cold wave last week, so I hadn't been swimming for quite a while until yesterday. I tell you there is absolutely *nothing* like coming off a drill field all hot, dusty, and tired, and taking a plunge in the ocean. The waves are wonderful to dive through and ride on, and all in all, I think I like saltwater swimming much better than small lake swimming. Another thing I like is the daily sunrise over the water and some really beautiful cloud formations that come with it.

Have seen John Evarts every weekend so far and will see him for the last time (probably) Sunday evening. He's really a peach of a guy and though he hasn't said a word, I know he misses Black Mountain [College] terribly. You probably could not find a more complete change in ways of living than from BMC to AAF, and he had lived at the former for 9 years and been as some poetic student put it, the "heartbeat" of the college all that time.

Will have supper and go to the weekly vaudeville show put on by soldiers for soldiers. At this concert several weeks ago, he played a piece called "Collins Avenue" (the main street which is always full of marching men, honking taxis, etc.), which he made up as he went along!

Apparently, it was a big success. Did I ever tell you about his piano character sketches? He used to play an original piece which "sounded" like "Johnny *was*," and we could almost always guess who he was playing.

Now he is doing the sort of work I did all fall—and it was through him that I got the tip about next week's shipment—though it is a common enough rumor.

All our evenings aren't free, but I have been able to read *Pride and Prejudice*. I think I have enjoyed it more than any other book I've read . . .

Wese, thanks for your two letters, one written the night I left. I'm glad you liked *Crime and Punishment* and wish you could read Jane Austen next. Will you make a special point of giving my best regards to Barbara and telling her that Michigan stars have nothing compared to the *Moon over Miami*.[8]

I'll keep in touch with you, but really don't think it wise for you to write me until I get a new address or learn how long I will keep this one—my congratulations again, Dad—and love to all.

Lovingly, Bill

Chapter 3

COLLEGE TRAINING DETACHMENT 46— TENNESSEE POLYTECHNIC INSTITUTE

After about a month of basic training, Bill was assigned to take courses at Tennessee Polytechnic Institute (TPI) in Cookeville. Across the country, educational institutions cooperated with the AAF by providing new aviation cadets with academic courses in what were called College Training Detachments. Before the war, aviation cadets were required to have at least two years of college. When the United States entered the war and the demand for more personnel was critical, the educational requirements were lowered. Given the lower requirements, new cadets did not necessarily have the background in science and cultural awareness that the Army Air Forces required of officers.

Many colleges and universities had low student enrollment because of the demand for military personnel. So, after basic training, aviation cadets were assigned to over one hundred colleges and universities across the country for academic, military and physical training in College Training Detachments. College physical education teachers and coaches attended a training course at Maxwell Field to learn physical education/training unique to the needs of air-crew personnel. Marching to and from classes, aviation cadets attended academic courses in mathematics, physics, English, history, geography and military customs and courtesies. Bill's air cadet class, Class 44B, was the first to be trained under the system of College Training Detachments, where, in addition to academic and physical training, cadets were introduced to flying in a light, Piper Cub type airplane.

As he did at Black Mountain College, Bill enjoyed the courses at TPI, especially history and geography. Bill was "only slightly annoyed by a great deal of Army nonsense in connection with going to and from classes, eating meals, etc."

In early May, as President Roosevelt and Prime Minister Churchill began a series of meetings in Washington codenamed Trident, Bill's classes ended, and orientation flights began at TPI. In his first flight Bill had "a wonderful time." They flew over the college, and he said, "the country is really beautiful from up there."

By mid-May, Bill was going through the aircrew classification process at the large AAF classification center in Nashville. This was the stage where it was determined if the cadet would train as a navigator, bombardier, or pilot. Candidates who failed the aptitude testing or the physical requirements were washed out or assigned to other positions in the AAF. In an undated letter, but according to the text, written the day after his birthday on May 25, he wrote in large letters, "I made it! A/C Hanchett classified as pilot! *WOW*!" This letter ended months of speculation about which position he would be assigned to in the AAF. In closing the May 26 letter, conscious of his new status, Bill cautioned his family that he did not want to see any more correspondence addressed to Private Hanchett. He was now Aviation Cadet (A/C) Hanchett.

According to official records, eighty-five percent of Bill's 44B class went through the college training detachments. In November 1943, the Flying Training Command requested a report covering the effectiveness of the ten hours of flying cadets received in the college program. The War Department had ordered the flying requirement, not the AAF. The report concluded that the ten hours of flight training was useful in Primary Flying School, but Bainbridge Basic Flying School instructors did not feel that this training had any impact on the cadets in the school. Cadets themselves indicated confusion during Primary because of a lack of standardization in the college program. During the summer of 1944, the college training program ended.

Even though the Army Air Forces found that the College Training Detachments and the ten-hour flying orientation were not effective in the overall training of pilots, Bill enjoyed and profited from the courses offered at TPI, especially the classes that contributed to his developing interest in history.

Correspondence From
TENNESSEE POLYTECHNIC INSTITUTE

March 5, 1943

Dear Dad:

How does it feel to hit the road again, old boy? I've thought a lot about you and your new work, but until I received mother's letter today, I didn't know where you had gone.

I'm very pleased that you're up in Canada and am very anxious to hear just what you are doing. The pamphlet you sent me has given a good idea of the George S. May Co, Ltd. in Canada, but I don't know what your position is. The business sounds very interesting and worthy of a man of your talent and experience.

Is Winnipeg near Sault Ste. Marie? What sort of town is it? Do you have any time for relaxation, and can you find anything to do of special interest?

... I am beginning a course of several months study at the Tenn. Polytechnic Inst. [Tennessee Polytechnic Institute]. I am including two clippings from a recent college publication which will clarify our status here. Our program will include 180 hours of Physics, 80 hours of math, and I don't know how many hours of *map reading*, current history, and English. This will be extremely valuable training and is much more liberal than I had expected.[1]

I'm terribly happy to think of you going about your business without extreme rush or pressure, and I know it must be a tremendous relief to you. Gradually the problems that still exist will be ironed out and you, and all of us, will be able to enjoy to the utmost this new era which George S. May has opened up. The intensity of the old miserable days is over, and I know what pleasure you'll get in settling your obligations and getting solidly on your feet again. Your persistency and faith and goodness will be amply rewarded.[2]

Will close this now because we're being shown a movie about the war in the Pacific in a few minutes. We've seen several of these kinds of movies and they're darn interesting and informative.

I hope you'll receive this Monday and that you'll have time to write me soon. Best of luck in your work and have some fun, too.

As ever, Lovingly Bill

March 25, 1943

Dear All: (hope this includes Dad!)

. . . There is very little new to say about myself. Our days are full and much the same from day to day, but they are certainly not monotonous, and I am again experiencing the rather new emotion of looking forward to the beginning of each class and being sorry when 2 o'clock comes. From 2 to 5 is devoted to the military. After 6:30 we are more or less free, being confined to campus. This time I always spend studying on Tues. & Thurs. in the library, and on the other weekdays in the classroom of the particular subject which needs my attention most. I might add that this subject is Math . . .

It's 6:30 pm now and time for me to get over to the library. —Am back at the barracks again! Have to be in by 9:00 pm, Lights Out at 10:00, reveille at 5:15 am.

Am having a wonderful time (have I said that before?) and am only slightly annoyed by a great deal of Army nonsense in connection with going to and from classes, eating meals etc. Have made some good friends, two I like especially . . .

I'll be thinking of you Sunday and I know that you'll have a grand day. Write me about it! How does it seem to be home, Fat?

As ever, Lovingly Bill

Here is address for the Church: Pvt. -, Squadron B, Headquarters 46th College Training Detachment Tennessee Polytechnic Institute, Cookeville, Tenn.

April 3, 1943

Dear Dad:

Well, old boy, you're certainly covering territory and doing it deluxe, as well!

I was glad to get your letter and copy of the letter sent to mother and AA, telling of your experiences flying and the set up in Dallas.

Have heard wonderful reports about you and how you like the job, and nothing but an armistice tomorrow could make me feel happier . . . By the way, did I ever beat you in golf, or was I always "just about to"? Funny I never panned out in that game.

It seems we are having every weekend off—1400 Sat to 1600 Sun—and a 2-night pass on special occasions. This may mean that I can visit Black Mountain sometime. The bus schedule is very bad; it takes over 12 hours for the trip, but if I can make better train connections, I may go. The only thing that would stop me would be leaving so quickly and being such a darn sentimentalist. What do you think about it?

Monday, we begin Physics and drop English, and I imagine I'll have even less spare time than I do now. Physics will be difficult, I'm afraid.

The 1st quarter group, I am in the 2nd quarter, has begun flying and my group will too in the next few weeks. This will be exciting, of course. I hope you realize that it is by no means certain that I will be a pilot. My imperfect eyes and indefinite ears throw a big question mark in the way. I think I have a better chance for being a navigator, as the physical requirements are less strict. However, this is the most difficult job to get as far as academics are concerned, and my training here may not be enough to make me qualify, even if I passed the physical test. The navigator, of course, charts the course of the plane and is responsible for keeping it on the course. He is also a fully trained pilot, capable of flying his ship. This position is the most desirable from my point of view, but to be frank with you, I expect a long and uneventful career in the ground crew. Time will tell.

Incidentally, I have taken out a $10,000 life insurance policy, which costs me $6.50 monthly. You and mother [are] beneficiaries and will undoubtedly receive the policy in 3 or 4 weeks. It is effective immediately, however.

Well, Pop, will close now.   As ever, Lovingly, Bill

April 6, 1943

Dear Mother:

Today we entered the second phase of our program. We, my quarter, that is, have dropped First Aid and English, and have begun Physics, which we have 3 hours a day. This is darn stiff, and with the advanced algebra we are studying, our program is difficult and full. We also have a new math teacher, who couldn't help but be an improvement over the old.

Am just about to go to the library for the evening. Plan to do some reading on Modern Europe. Our lectures on this subject have clarified much about World War I and II. Hope you and Wese are having fun together.   Write soon. Bill

---

April 14, 1943

Received a letter from dad today telling me that he flew home from Texas and that he expected another assignment soon. It's a bit comical that I should join the Air Corps and he should do all the flying. Well, I hope to make up for lost time, starting next month.

I am enclosing 2 or 3 snapshots that were taken on a Sunday morning walk not long ago. There will be some more as a result of last Sun., and I will send them on when I can. You'll also find a schedule for our academic work during April, and I think you'll understand why I've been sending postcards recently.

I have made many friends, but three especially good ones. Don Dalton, who is in a picture with me, and I are seldom apart, and with the exception of Ted, I have no closer friend.[3] Recently a new squadron was formed, note change of address, and 80 of us moved to new quarters in the basement of the Engineering Bldg. The three mentioned above, and I, are all together and Don sleeps right below me. All in all, I think I like the new barracks better than the old. Don is the boy from Oak Park, who is very much like Bob Christy [an ETHS friend].

I have to admit that I am far from outstanding as a student of Algebra or Physics. The pity of this course is that it is so condensed and high powered that few in the class can keep up with the work. The classes are temporary and so the teacher has no opportunity to know the students and consequently the only marks turned in are those grades made on the weekly quiz, which, of course, is no way to tell how much a student is getting out of his work.

You can see how fast this work is being thrown at us by the fact that last Sat., after about 5 weeks of work, we had covered a whole college semester of algebra! The standard joke around here is that if you drop your pencil in class, you'll lose two weeks of algebra. Physics is also being taught in an advanced level.

Well, this isn't an excuse, but an explanation of grades that I'm afraid will be mighty close to the borderline in those two subjects. History and Geography are not difficult for me, and I love them as much as I always have. We're studying the 1st World War now, and it is fascinating... Lots of Love. As Ever, Lovingly, Bill

April 18, 1943

Thanks for your letter, Mother. It's all right about Jeff and I'm proud of the independence the little rascal has shown. I agree with you that his life has been much too sheltered like that of many others.

A couple of weeks ago I met the wife of the head of the Engineering Dept. Yesterday, she invited Don and me to dinner for today. We had swell food and a good time. It was the first time since Jan. 30 that I have used a linen napkin, and I sat in an easy chair! Believe me, it really seemed good.

Rain all day today and nothing much to say. Hope to hear from dad soon and trust that all are well. As ever, Lovingly Bill

Easter 1943 [April 25, 1943]

Hi Mom!

Seems strange writing to you at 1246 [Ridge Avenue, Evanston]!

Had a fine day today. Baptist Church in the morning, fried chicken dinner in the mess hall, 2 hrs. sleep, band concert on college quadrangle, and parade just before supper. It was a dress parade, bleachers erected, and several hundred, over 1,000 Cookeville citizens, lined the campus watching us go through our paces.

Thought of you and hoped dad was home to go to church with you and sing the *Hallelujah Chorus*. I missed that and you as I always do. Much love and get rested!

Lovingly, Bill

May 2, 1943

Dear Dad:

. . . Tomorrow, I begin the last phase of my work here. I am through with Geography and History and begin flying! The planes are small, light, and slow, but learning to fly them will be a good introduction to the larger planes. All together, I will have 10 hours of individually instructed flying time. This is the usual number of hours a person has before he solos, but I've not had the mechanical training so will not do it. The boys in the section ahead of me were very enthusiastic. They left for Nashville yesterday, so I am now in the next "graduating class."

During April in Physics, we studied Heat, Light and Sound, and covered the ground usually given in a semester's work. During May, my group will study Electricity. Physics is interesting and has opened a whole new world to me. We have a lot of problems to work, of course, and they have a very practical value: telling distances by length of time to hear an echo, and that sort of thing! Here is a problem that is typical (but more difficult) of the kind we work.

"How far above the surface must a cake of ice be carried to be melted by the impact of the fall if all the energy is changed into heat? Answer: 112,032 ft." (I couldn't get it!)

How do you like that one?

Had an interesting morning at the stables of the county fairgrounds. There are several horses in the stable there and I enjoyed fooling around a barn again. The horses are very fine ones and are used for show purposes or were. Two colts 2 & 3 years old have not been broken and the mare has gone blind in one eye. She won a great many prizes in her day and is still a beauty. The colts have lots of life and it's a pity the owner doesn't do something with them. They are just wasting away in the old stable. The jockey who showed us around was a typical southern negro with horses in his blood and it was a real experience to talk with him.

Last night I weighed myself—174 with summer clothes on! Have you put on any weight?

Well, Fat, will close now. A few minutes ago, was delivered a card from mother. I am far from enthusiastic about her staying with Fran and I hope the arrangement will be very temporary.

Let me hear from you again soon, because I love to hear about what you're doing and things about your work. Where do you work? Do you have a desk and of just what duties does your job consist?

Write as soon as you can and lots and lots of luck to you.

As ever, Lovingly Bill

May 2, 1943

Dear Mother:

Missed hearing from you last week, but know you're very busy making final arrangements and you must be tired as the deuce. [The family had to move to a new residence.]

Tomorrow, I begin the last phase of my work here. I drop History and Geography and Physics laboratory and begin flying! The planes are small and slow, but my 10 hours of individual flying instruction will serve as a good introduction to larger planes. After 10 hours most people are soloing, but I will not because I have not had any mechanical training.

The boys in the 1st group left for Nashville yesterday, so I am now in the next graduating class. Am sorry to lose my favorite classes, but at least my program won't be so darn full and flying will be fun, of course.

I'm enclosing some pictures which you can keep and also the ones which you sent to AA. The "dried prune" picture has been canned because AA suggested I was trying to look like Cary Grant. Jack Kauffman was a very good friend. It was his wife who was here and worked on the cafeteria serving line. Several of the wives do this. A nice arrangement because they can see their husbands, make some money, and help out the school. Jerry and Jack are swell people, and I hate to lose them. Both left yesterday . . .

Well, lots of love to you and the others, and please write soon. Where is the clock, my stuff, etc.?   As ever, Lovingly, Bill

May 5, 1943

Dear Dad:

Thanks an awful lot for the swell mirror, comb, & file kit! It's really a swell set! Have polished the mirror and it is very bright and clear; and golly I sure needed one!

Yesterday went "up" for first time. After flying around for 20 mins watching instructor's movements, he put his hands in his pocket and there I was flying an airplane! Did turns and banks. We fly very low, 1000 ft Tues., and so I could make out all details below. Country is very pretty from the sky, isn't it? How high do your planes fly? We will probably go higher soon. Tomorrow, I learn take offs. All turns must be *exact.* A 90° turn doesn't mean 95° and instructors are very strict about this. Write when you can and have fun during your off time.

Best of luck! Thanx again. Bill

May 11, 1943

... We're really busy now. Have a class in Civil Air Regulations from 7:30 to 9:30pm six nights a week, and so have continuous classes from 8:00am to 9:30pm!

Flying is wonderful and do I have a lot to learn! Am doing turns, stalls, spins, and short dives, and it's thrilling. You'd love it, Mother! ...

Bill

May 12, 1943

18 men are needed to fill a quota in Nashville and my name is on list to go, so leave here Sunday afternoon! You're no more surprised than I am.

Will probably stay at Nashville for 3 or 4 weeks, while being classified or eliminated. This is what counts! The real test! Am sorry to go before the rest of the boys, naturally, and to leave my courses unfinished, but it *will* be exciting to learn what my work will be for the duration.

Red Cross in Cookeville is taking care of me, as will not be paid before I leave, so don't worry about me. Will write again when I can. Lots of love to you and regards to the Weed boys [nephews Tim and Chuck] & Fran. Bill

---

May 15, 1943

Dear Dad:

. . . Will be leaving tomorrow and somewhat sorry to go. Am frankly expecting to fail because of eyes or something, but if I don't, things will be very nice! I did several take offs and made one very bad landing. I must have bounced 20 ft! Flying is very exciting and difficult, too. It is surprising to learn that there are more traffic regulations for planes than for cars. It's all very complicated, but fun. *Will* write from Nashville!

As ever, Bill

May 17, 1943

College days are over! This is a really large camp, makes Fort Sheridan seem small.[4] Have seen Jack Kauffman, who has been classified as a navigator, and received some rather encouraging news about my chances. However, I'm still sincerely doubtful and certainly hope you won't consider my feelings as modest. It's going to be tough!

Arrived Sun nite: bed at 11:30, up at 4:30 and K.P. all day! Expect to begin classification in next few days and probably will be here for several weeks.

If I don't write much for the next several days, it's because we have been advised not to. We are told to give our eyes as much rest as possible. Will save them for reading your letters only (and hope there will be many)! Where's dad? Did he get my card? Love.

As ever, Bill

[The letter below is undated, but refers to "last night, my birthday," so the letter was written May 26, 1943.]

I made it! *A/C [Aviation Cadet] Hanchett*! Classified as Pilot! *WOW*!

Tomorrow some of us—including WFH Jr.—will be issued new uniforms and any replacements of clothing we need. From now on, I wear brass on my collars and after leaving Nashville, will wear a cadet's hat, which will be given to me tomorrow. It's something like the one I wore in Chicago but has a wide blue band around it and instead of the round disc above visor, it has a propeller with a spread of about four inches.

The remainder of my time here will be spent doing things like guard duty, K.P., etc., and I won't be a bit sorry to leave. Expect it will be to Alabama, but probably not for two weeks or more.

Enclosed is an article from the detachment [46th College Training Detachment] paper at T.P.I. It is essentially true, but the horses and mules fought more like half-hearted Italians than the fierce Prussians. A/S [Aviation Student] Reilly, who wrote story, made them out to be.[5]

Not much news, except that I'm terribly thrilled with this appointment. I really meant what I said when I said I wasn't at all confident of qualifying, and so you can imagine how I feel now.

Mother, thanks for your fine letter of 5/24 . . . Lots of love to you.

As ever, Lovingly Bill

Don't let me see any more letters addressed to *PVT*. [Private] Wm.
Fr. Hanchett, Jr.

May 31, 1943

I'm very happy to say that I'm pulling out of here today,
unexpectedly soon. We'll undoubtedly end up at Maxwell Field,
Alabama, but there are all sorts of exciting rumors that have us
going to Santa Ana, California, Texas, etc.

I will be going to pre-flight school. I'll tell you what that is when I
know myself. For us who have had military experience, it will
probably be different from what it has been up to this time for boys
straight from civilian life. We are the first of our kind to attend pre-
flight, just as we were the first of the students at College Training
Detachments.

Received a letter from dad today telling me that he was going to
Oklahoma City and expects to remain there a month or two. He
mentioned that you might be able to come down for a few weeks. I
certainly hope you will. It would be lots of fun and be good for
both of you.

It has occurred to me that you might be able to take a detour to
Montgomery on your way down or back. It would be wonderful if
you could. We could spend the whole night and Sunday together if
we got the timing right. Usually, one is confined to the post for 2-4
weeks after arrival, and there may be other things to consider.

Ask dad what he thinks about this. It's quite a bit out of your
way—perhaps too far, but a nice idea anyway.

I'm reading [Wendell] Willkie's book, *One World*.[6] It is excellent. Willkie is internationally minded, yet he keeps that certain Americanism so many drop when they begin to think in terms of one world. When I finish—almost done now—I'll send the book home. Hope all of you will read it—you'll find it fascinating—and save it for me.

As a cadet, I make $75 monthly (*still* have not been paid incidentally and may have to wait until July 1-Feb to July!)

. . . I'll write again as soon as I arrive. According to Bob Wunsch, Rainey has lost her personality but is still a nice dog.

Lots of love to you, Mother—and all the girls and babies . . .

You can tell Fran that I do not hate the Japs or the Germans, and I never will.

I gave a speech in our English class at TPI—quite proud of it incidentally—about history. I said, somewhat more clearly than I remember stumbling along on the same subject at the dinner table at 2310 [Sherman Avenue, Evanston], that history has taught that man has not changed for the last few thousand years—though the world about him has—and that we must learn that peace will come only when we cease to think of good and right in terms of just over nations, ourselves, etc.

Dr. McGee liked the speech, but from that day on the other boys were convinced that I was a communist and called me "Red." Which proves that *whatever an American doesn't understand is Communistic*.[7]   As ever, Lovingly Bill

Chapter 4

PREFLIGHT AND PRIMARY FLYING SCHOOL

Aviation cadet training consisted of four distinct phases: Preflight, Primary, Basic, and Advanced Flying School. According to the Army Air Forces booklet *44B Preflight*, published in July 1943, aviation cadets were the "embryos of a great machine." The Preflight training program at Maxwell Field, near Montgomery, Alabama, included military training, drill and indoctrination, and academics in aircraft recognition, naval and ground forces, first aid, Morse code, chemical warfare, math, and physics. Bill immediately began to strategize on how he could save money so he could return to Black Mountain College (BMC) after he left the AAF.

Bill did not like the "continuous and unmerciful hazing by upper-classmen" that new cadets, known as "rats," received, and he told his father that he would not do it when he became an upperclassman. When they were not double-timing (running), Preflight underclassmen would march everywhere and observe strict protocols at meals. According to Bill, the food was delicious, ". . . but there is little pleasure in eating it . . ."

Bill toughed it out and became an upperclassman. Shortly afterward, he met Harriet Engelhardt, a recent graduate of Black Mountain College who had returned home to Montgomery. She later served in Europe with the American Red Cross. Some of Bill's happier times during Preflight were spent with Harriet and her family.

He graduated from Preflight and transferred to the Primary Flying School at Douglas, Georgia, where civilian instructors taught aviation cadets in primary trainers, which were open air, two-seater biplanes, PT-17s. Bill's civilian instructor was William B. Dillard of the Raymond-Richardson Aviation Company, a government contractor. Major Thomas W. Bonner was the commanding officer of the 63rd Army Air Forces Flying Training Detachment and Douglas Field.

When Bill first arrived at Douglas in south-central Georgia at the end of July, he was impressed with the food and the new construction—"bungalows of modern design." Bill thought it could be "a fine resort," "a country club." Located in a forest of Georgia pine, there was a reading room, and badminton and tennis courts. At first Bill naively observed, "... since we are to fly regularly here, and that [is] some considerable strain on us, the Army is concerned about our relaxation time ..." A few days later, as classes began and he experienced the emotional, as well as literal ups and downs of learning to fly an airplane, he admitted he had spoken too soon about the Army being concerned about giving cadets free time.

Beginning in mid-September, Bill repeatedly asked for information concerning the recent death of Miss Dodd, his supervisor in the high school cafeteria. Not many details were forthcoming from home, frustrating Bill, because he wanted information about a teacher who had been a positive influence on him.

Correspondence From
PREFLIGHT AT
MAXWELL ARMY AIR FIELD

June 5, 1943, Saturday night

... When we got off the train early Tuesday morning, the Cadet officers, wearing the sabers, met us with the remark, "This is Maxwell Field, Alabama. You won't see it for four weeks." And so far we haven't. Underclassmen are confined to their rooms in the evening (are not allowed to write letters, do anything personal— just study) and during all formations must walk at a rigid attention with their eyes glued to the back of the neck of the man in front of them. Anyone caught changing his vision is punished. Going to all formations we march the "rat line" at a rapid pace, and again look directly to the front. If you fix your eyes to one spot you get dizzy, so it gets so that you don't see anything at all.[1]

When in our rooms at night we have to be on our toes ready to holler "attention" when an upperclassman comes in to do some hazing. They do this often, too.

At meals all Cadets sit at attention on the last four inches of chair, using one hand only, and not speaking. To get the butter or anything else, we say, "Sirs, does anyone else care for the butter? Please pass the butter." This out loud and to no one in particular.

Well, there are lots more things we have to do, but this will give you the general idea.

At Nashville, Cookeville, and Miami, and at all Enlisted Men Camps, each man is allowed a food ration of $.49 a day. We Cadets are being paid on the basis of $1.00 a day for food, so you can see that our chow is exceptionally good, as good as any served at a good cafeteria before the war and probably better than what you can get anywhere now. We have beef, steaks, veal, etc., swell vegetables, and ice cream every day. This is fine with me, of course, but it doesn't seem right that we should eat so much better than soldiers.

I will be an underclassman for four weeks, and an upperclassman for four. I'm disappointed to say that I'll do no flying here, but once I leave here and go to Primary School for 8 or 9 weeks, I'll get several hours of flying every day. After Primary comes Basic & Advanced, for 9 weeks each, and then if I have stood well in my class, will be commissioned a 2nd Lieut. and have my wings!

I hope you realize that it is possible for me to "wash out" here, or at any other time, during my training. I'm not especially worried, because if diligence means anything I can tell you I'll qualify. But only the best, most natural fliers are selected, and the ones who just can't get the knack of flying are eliminated all along the line. I hope I won't wash out but want you all to be aware of the possibility.

We underclassmen, or "rats," get up at 4:30 am and have classes all morning.[2] In the afternoon we have drill and physical training, which is about the most rigorous given anywhere in the Army. We have an obstacle course that is no cinch and a 2-mile cross-country workout through ravines, up hills, through woods, cross creeks, etc. This course is known as the "Burma Road," and of course, we run all the way. The path leads through country that reminded me very much of Turkey Run. Before we leave Maxwell, we will run 7 miles without stopping. That's quite a ways.[3]

You may be interested to know that since my eye examination at Nashville, I've had my glasses on about twice. I read practically all of Willkie's book [One World] without them and go to all of my classes minus that bulge in my right pocket. A case of habit, I suppose.

Hope to get some letters soon. Pvts. [Privates] aren't given mail their first week, so expect to have a good haul Monday . . .

As ever, Lovingly Bill

June 13, 1943

The week has gone very quickly, but by golly it has really been tough. The month given to underclass cadets is about the toughest sort of training given in the Army. The physical part of it isn't all, though it is very strenuous. The main thing is that the upper-classmen don't give us any peace at all. We are on the double every moment. For instance, yesterday we ran 1 mile to the beginning of the Burma Road, ran the two-mile uphill downhill road, ran 1 mile back to barracks, and had 8 minutes to take off sweaty gym clothes, take shower—7 [cadets] to 1 shower—and get in formation. Anyone late is gigged. It's hard, but darn valuable and I'm getting in fine physical shape. Incidentally, I've lost some of those 174 lbs., which, apparently, were not as much muscle as I had thought.

Our rooming accommodations are quite nice. I share a room with 6 others. There is a double connecting bath with another room of 7. I like my roommates quite well. Two are Chicago boys, and we have a good time talking about the old city . . .

. . . What sort of a job will Bob have in the Navy? AA is fortunate to be able to go to Black Mountain for the duration. Quite a break for Rob [nephew] and Rainey [pet dog at BMC] and even though it will be sad for AA in many ways, I think she will be happier there than anywhere else.

An hour ago, I went to the weekly Protestant Church services. It was quite nice, and I was reminded of the many times I came up into the balcony late at church after having parked the car under the viaduct and taken as long as possible to walk the block and a half to Chicago Ave. Tonight there is going to be a classical music program at one of the chapels, which I'm anxious to go to.

Can take anything they can dish out, but this one day of peace is valued very highly by A/C Hanchett.

Still have not been paid but expect to be at end of month. Have several deductions, insurance, Red Cross loan, so will not have a great deal coming. It ought to be over $75, however.

We underclassmen are not allowed off post, of course, so have not been into Montgomery, neither did I get into Nashville. I remember being in Montgomery with dad.

Food is still delicious, but there is little pleasure in eating it. Most of the upperclassmen are OK, but some take delight in making things harder than they need be. This, mine, may be the last of the class system, but to the college training detachment, which will probably absorb Pre-Flight School altogether soon. Well, lots of love. Think of you lots and hope you can write often and soon. Regards to all.   As ever Lovingly, Bill

---

June 20, 1943, Sunday

Dear Dad:

... The only time during the day when we are allowed to write letters, or do anything personal, is between 9:00-9:30 PM. Lights out at 9:30 and so you can see we don't have very much free time.

Only one more week of being a rat. The hazing has lost its novelty and is more annoying than terrifying, as it was at first. There is so much nonsense in connection with it that I think it's of doubtful value. The idea is, of course, to teach prospective officers, who will someday be *giving* orders to *take* them without question. However, the upperclassmen certainly are not learning how to *give* orders and get the most cooperation out of their men, which I should think is equally important. I am not going to be a hazer. I don't think you have to yell at a person in order to make him get in step or adjust a hat to the right angle. There've been many times when I would have felt better, and more like acting like a prospective officer and gentleman, if the cadet officers had *told* me I was doing something wrong, instead of *yelling* at me. I suppose this is a very valuable lesson. I've learned a lot of them, by the way. The odd (and unfortunate) thing is that it's not the lesson I was expected to learn.

You have probably read my letters to mother telling about the food. You'd love it, Dad. Every night we have ice cream—as much as you can eat—and very often pie with it! Lots of iced tea, iced cocoa, punch (you know how I like cold drinks), and meat of all sorts. I don't suppose you civilians can get such food. The only complaint—my usual—is breakfast. It's eggs every morning, and I don't like mass produced eggs.

... What should I send home? I'd also be interested in how your problems are being solved, if you care to tell me. I know the old strain has been getting relieved.

The reports I get from home about you are very favorable and apparently you are doing sensationally well in your new job. Mother wrote something about a job you were offered in Oklahoma City and also that some other May [George May Company] men whom she met were "genuinely fond" of you and "didn't know what they'd do without Will." Dad, that's wonderful! I'm terribly proud of you and I'm so pleased that you no longer have the constant day to day worrying. By golly, that was hectic, wasn't it? You can't keep a good man down. What an inspiration your 11-year fight will be always.

Received a letter from Leila, who is sure she has mapped out the Allied strategy in the Mediterranean. She's in favor of hanging John L. Lewis—as I guess a lot of people are.[4]

Our academics are interesting. We are learning to identify all the important Allied planes and will learn enemy planes sometime. The main part of the program is the physical training, however, which is about the most strenuous the Army gives. The Morse code is darn difficult for me. I passed a 5 word a minute test yesterday but am not at all sure of myself and will have to do much better. Have you ever had code?[5]

Well, Dad, congratulations on your successes and lots of love for being such a swell father.

                                                            As ever, Bill

Wednesday [No date, estimated June 30, 1943.]

Dear Mother:

Nice stationery? Jean Forster sent it.

Today I am Barracks Guard, and as such miss all my classes and formations, and spend the time sitting on the screened-in porch, reading magazines, writing letters, and trying to be as inconspicuous as possible, so as not to attract the undesirable attention of upperclassmen, who are still here, by the way, and I guess this sentence is long enough. Anyway, it's a nice change from the everyday schedule!

I will be an upperclassman tonight after the Graduation Parade, which I will miss because of a dental appointment.

We have already begun our new classes. I suppose I've written that during June we studied: International Radio Code, Math & Navigation, Maps & Charts, Chemical Warfare, Aircraft Recognition, and a number of short courses. I got *100* in the Math final examination. This was quite a surprise, considering my past record in that subject. The exam was mainly on vectors, which I think are interesting, and figuring out wind-drift problems.

Code is a little more difficult for me, and I have started going to evening classes to get caught up. Don't know why I should have trouble with it.

One of my roommates, a Chicago boy, is interested in Black Mountain, so I sent for a catalog for him. While looking through the list of students in it, I discovered that one of the girls lives in Montgomery. She is Harriet Engelhardt, who left school before Fran and Wese got there. I called her up, of course, and we have a date Sat. night [other letters clarify their date was on Friday night], which will be my first time off an Army Post since May 16. Ought to be fun.[6]

I am mailing you our Pre-Flight book, which I think you will enjoy reading. I have marked one or two places.

Thursday [Continued from above.]

Am an upperclassman at last. Oh boy! Swell letters from you and Fran—also Ted [Edward "Ted" Long, ETHS friend] & Bill Hubbell [a cousin]. Must cut this short so as to get money order to you [by] Sat. Paid this morning! Hope you can keep enough to take care of personal expenses, household, etc., and please treat yourself to something special and let me know what it is. Will write Sunday.

Lots of love, old girl! Bill

July 3, 1943 [Saturday]

Dear Dad:

Am an upperclassman at last, and golly what a relief. Our "rats" are expected tomorrow.

Last night, had my first open post since May 16. Had dinner with Harriet Engelhardt, who is an old BMC student who lives in Montgomery. After dinner we drove out to their golf club and spent the evening talking about old times. A week from Sunday I'm going out with her again for a swim in the club pool.

Apparently, your job didn't last as long as expected so I won't write a letter till I know where you are. Hope mother can go with you somewhere soon. Good luck, Dad.

As ever, Bill

July 4, 1943 [Sunday]

Dear Mother:

Many happy returns of the day!

... I like being an upperclassman! Can sleep till the luxurious hour of 5:45, no more rat lines, or persecution complexes; no more nonsense. So far have taken a very inactive part in the training of our rats, and I'm sure I'll continue to do so.

Had a fine time Friday night with Harriet Engelhardt. We spent the evening at her country club. Next Sunday I'm going swimming with her out there.

There's not much doing in Montgomery and there are so darn many soldiers in town that you have to stand in line for everything. Not much fun there, but we have a nice recreational hall on post, which though crowded, is about the best place to go.

Today is the first sunny day we've had in a week, a swell day for golf. Wish I could have a game with dad. It rained so much last week that we didn't have any P.T. at all. I certainly will feel it tomorrow.

I hope to hear from you about AA. In what shape was the cabin?

Things are much the same with me as when I wrote last. This month will be my last on the ground, I'm glad to say. Am really looking forward to Primary.

Give my regards to Fran and the boys.

Again, *lots of love and a very happy birthday* [July 7th]!

As ever Lovingly, Bill

July 11, 1943

Dear Pop:

... This week we begin having 2 hours of physical training a day! Burma Road, obstacle course, and calisthenics. This will really be hard, but it will toughen us up if anything will.

Invasion of Sicily makes good reading, doesn't it? It won't be long! I hope, until we start hitting Europe. It will be a hard fight, we can be sure of that. Let me hear from you when you can.   As ever, Bill

---

July 15, 1943

Word from Don Dalton from Nashville. He washed out because of weak eyes—and I'm the one who wore glasses! (Haven't had them on in several weeks, incidentally).[7]

... Today we're going to the high-altitude chamber. We will be taken "up" to over 30,000 ft!—in the chamber, of course. This must be done slowly, and we have to wear oxygen masks. Will write Sunday.   Best of luck. As ever, Bill

---

July 19, 1943

... Thank you for the *Evanston Review*. It was swell to see it and read about the old town. I may be in Serviceman's section sometime! Because Public Relations Office here had gotten information about each of us to send home ...   As ever, Bill

---

July 25, 1943

Thanks for card and letter. Enjoyed both as much as usual.

Eva [unidentified] couldn't get down here after all, I'm sorry to say, but

Harriet got my roommate a date anyway and we had a fine chicken dinner on her lawn before the dance. Today I went swimming at the club and then had dinner at Engelhardt's again.

Leave for Primary this week and will be very glad to begin flying every day. After 9 months, it's about time!

Yes, Mom, have some very good friends here. None as good as D. Dalton, but my roommates are an especially fine bunch. They kid me a lot about BMC, and I am known as "Black Bill from Black Mountain." One of them has a Master's in Commerce. He is a New Yorker, who knows a good deal about dad's friend, Joe McWilliams.[8] Fran should ask Frank [unidentified] about him sometime . . .   Lots of love, Bill

---

July 25, 1943, Sunday

Dear POP:

A letter I wrote you last Sunday and sent to Minneapolis was returned yesterday. Sorry you didn't get it. Am afraid I won't be able to write for a day or two because we are very busy with final exams. Will leave here this week for southern Georgia. I don't cover the ground you do, but am seeing a good bit of the south at that.

Last night was our Graduation Dance. Dinner at Harriet's before with roommate and his date. This morning went swimming and had dinner at Engelhardt's again. It certainly seems swell to get off post.

Went up to high altitude last week. 38,000 feet! Got a bad case of bends in my leg. Will write more about it later. Quite an experience. Write me here, as mail will be forwarded. Hope things are OK.   As ever, Bill

[Written on opposite side.]

I will begin flying every day at Primary! Nice card from Aunt Leila. Jack H. [Hanchett] is in Birmingham. Too late to see him. Tom is a Lieutenant.[9]

Regards

July 27, 1943, Tuesday

Sorry I don't have time to make this more of a letter than a note but am very busy packing and getting things all set to leave this afternoon or tomorrow morning, we don't know which.

Don't know very much about Douglas, Ga., except that the town is very small, not more than 3,000, and the field has only about 300 cadets. As you know, it is Primary and we will fly every day. They say there is a high percentage of washouts, as high as 60%, and so it may be that I'll be back in the GI army, but I'll keep trying you can be sure of that.

I'm very interested in the financial reports you have been sending me, and hope the enclosed will take care of a few more petty things. They will certainly have to be petty.

Thank Fran for sending *Mud on the Stars*. It came at the right time, because I'll be able to read it on the train. I've read 50 pages and think it very good. Excellent, in fact.[10]

Am sending my class's Pre-Flight book to dad, and he will forward it to you. It ought to tell you lots of things about Maxwell I've never had time to write.

Have fun at Jo's and write when you can. Guess you can't at that, but I'll get you my address as soon as possible. I suppose mail would reach me care of AAFFTC [Army Air Forces Flying Training Command], Douglas, Ga. I know it would because the field is so small . . .

Say hello to Joanne and Carol [young nieces].

It's nice to use a typewriter for a change. Imagine you're glad I'm using it, too.

Lots of love, Mother. I think of you all the time.

As ever, Bill

July 28, 1943

Dear Pop:

Have sent a copy of my class's Pre-Flight book to you. Most of the writing in it is very high schoolish, but I think you will be interested in learning things about life here that I haven't written. The enclosed article about the high-altitude run is particularly good.

Am leaving here today for Douglas, Ga. and *Primary* flight training. Mail will reach me c/o AAFFTC, Douglas, Ga. *Class 44B*.

What is your job this time? I have *some* very surprising literature about Joe McWilliams. If you want to see it, let me know.

Hope you're OK!

Regards, Bill

Correspondence From
PRIMARY FLYING SCHOOL AT
DOUGLAS ARMY AIR FIELD

July 30, 1943

Dear Mother:

Arrived here [Primary Flying School, Douglas, GA.] yesterday morning after a rather uncomfortable trip. This is really paradise! You'd never think it was an Army post. The buildings are now bungalows of modern design. Larry Kocher might have built them.[11]

There are only 500 cadets here and the food is magnificent. Better by far than what we got at Maxwell, because it is not prepared for so many.

There are over 100 airplanes, neatly lined up along the take-off apron. The 250 upperclassmen have soloed, and we new cadets begin instruction Monday.

My room is at the edge of the airport, and I have a fine view of the hangars and planes from my bed.

The camp is in the midst of a pine tree forest and is an unusually pretty site. It would very easily be a fine resort.

Since we are to fly regularly here, and that means some considerable strain on us, the Army is concerned about our relaxation time. There is a fine reading room, and I have already started "The Magazine." There are also badminton and tennis courts. The whole thing seems like a country club.

The only worry is that there is a relatively high percentage of washouts. Many boys can't learn to fly, or can't learn fast enough, or are eliminated for one thing or another to make room for the best half. Time will tell.

Am sorry I didn't get your letter to Maxwell telling that dad had left S.A. [San Antonio] ten minutes before I did, because I had just sent my class's Pre-Flight book down to him. It will be forwarded to Evanston in time, I hope.

I was amused by Wese's letter, which you sent me. I hope she doesn't cry every time the sun sets!   As ever, Lovingly, Bill

---

August 3, 1943

I spoke a little too soon about our "leisure time," because now that we are in our regular schedule, there just isn't any. Classes, drill, physical training all morning, flying all afternoon. We are only in the air for an hour but must spend the other four hours in the "Ready Room," studying the different maneuvers and regulations. I am amazed at how complicated the business of flying a plane is.

Everything must be exact. Turns must be precisely 90°, not 95°, or 45°, not 50°, etc. Wings must be at correct angle when turning etc. I had no idea that there was so much to learn. When you're up in the air it's not a joyride. *It's the hardest work I've ever had.* The instructor is jumping on *you* every moment, calls you everything he can think of and makes you feel as intelligent as a jackass. Apparently, this is the best way to teach pilots.[12]

The planes are open two-seaters that look very much like World War I biplanes, except that they are new and faster.[13]

You can see that with my flight work, (on the ground and in the air) and my studies, (theory of flight and aircraft engines, right now)—I am plenty busy. And not only busy but having to fight like the devil to keep my head above water. This is hard. There's no fooling about that. I do like the field very much and my barracks are very summer campish. However, am afraid there'll be no reading outside my technical manuals. Guess the time has come when I've got to devote everything I have to my job; and that's exactly what I'm going to do!

We're required to keep an accurate account of the time we spend in the air and I need a watch. My old Ingersoll [watch] is all shot and I'll have to have another one. No chance to get a cheap one in Douglas so wish you'd get me a $3-$4 job and send it down as soon as possible. I want the *pocket type*, *not* a wristwatch and just about any cheap make will do. Hope you'll be able [to] drop in at Herb's next time you're downtown and get it, because I really should have it soon.

The cookies arrived in good shape yesterday and I thank you and Fran for them. A swell variety and all were delicious. It was swell of you.

Will close now as must hit the books. Got a 90 in a theory of Flight Test today and have *got* to keep up my average. Lots of love.

As ever, Lovingly, Bill

[Drew image of watch face.]

—as soon as you can. Buy the kids a milkshake with the change. Thanks.

August 8, 1943

Dear All:

The first week of flying is over, and I've got to admit that I don't like the stuff. That will probably surprise you, but it's not at all an unusual reaction at Primary. Riding in a plane is a lot different than flying one, and the business just doesn't thrill me. It's not even as much fun as driving a car!

Ground school is coming along in fine style. We have daily tests and my average is 93+. My flying, however, is rotten; probably greatly influenced by my attitude, which is certainly not the best. I have no doubt but that it works the other way, too. Anyway, I'll have to keep trying and hope that, if I can learn to fly, I'll learn to like it. If I wash out, though, I won't be anywhere near as disappointed as I once would have been, or as you probably will be.

I didn't have enough flying at Cookeville, (which is too bad) to know whether I liked it or not, and I thought I liked what I had because I thought I *would* like it or *should* like it . . .

Read in Walt Winchell's column not long ago that the May Co. had woken up to Joe McWilliams. I hope his association with [the] company is over by now and that it will have no bad effects on the business. He is really quite a character, Pop![14]

LATER

Have had a very nice lazy day, most of it spent on my bed reading the paper, Sat. Eve. Post [*Saturday Evening Post*], and Robert Frost.[15] It sure seems good to be able to relax and take it easy. We're on the go every minute during the week. Studies take care of about all of the evening . . .

John Evarts is now a Corporal and will soon go to a specialist school to study German, I think . . .

Will close this now. Hope to hear from dad this week, as well as from you.

As ever, Lovingly Bill

August 10, 1943

Furlough out of question. We just don't get them.

Dear Pop:

Envy your trip to Alberta. The scenery must be beautiful. Would like to get up there some day.

Things here are OK, but I'm not any sensation as a pilot. There's a lot to it and I may catch on soon. Am not sure when I'll solo, if I solo at all. Probably not for 10 days or 2 weeks, though.

Thanx for your swell letter. It's always good to hear from you and *I look forward to word from you!*

News is very good these days. It seems now that the war will be over the end of 1944! That's not far at all! Wish we could get going in Europe proper. The Russians can't be blamed for _____ [unreadable] and we certainly are indebted to them.

Am glad you had a "vacation" in Evanston but know you're happy to get going again.   Lots of luck, Love Bill

August 13, 1943

Dear Mother:

Am pleased to say that I've made some very good progress in flying, and as might be expected! Like it some better, though I'll still take a V8 [car engine] to a PT-17 any day. Guess I'm not hopeless, but certainly slow.

Went into Douglas for first time Wed. night, our one night a week off. Though only to ten PM, at that. Not much of a town so I'll probably spend weekends here. May not be able to make satisfactory connections to the coast, but hope I can, as it would be swell to get out of this place.

Do you remember Jim Hoel? I worked with him at game table at ETHS. He was shot down over Germany and is now a prisoner of war![16]

Hope the kids aren't keeping you too busy and I know you must enjoy being with them. Had a card from Sally [Jo], who seems to be having a fine time in Tucson. Lots of love, Mom, and for gosh sakes take it easy!   As ever, Bill

---

August 15, 1943

Dear Dad:

Thanx for your note and the pictures of the Canadian Rockies . . .

You'll be glad to hear that I've made some very good progress in flying, after a perfectly miserable start. I like the business a good deal better, too, and have the feeling that when I can get up there by myself, I'll like it even better.

The instructor is yelling at you every moment and you try so hard to do things right that it's hard not to become both nervous and confused.

Last time up, I made seven landings, one of them pretty good, but I think I'll catch on to the idea in time. The Army doesn't waste much of the latter with its cadets and most of those who washout, washout because they don't learn fast enough.

Am enclosing a picture of the type we fly. Get in an hour a day, except when the weather is bad, as it has been a lot lately. Wouldn't be at all surprised if I soloed the end of this week, or first of the next.

I haven't a chance of getting a furlough before next February, unless I washout before then. Then, however, I'll have a gold bar and a pair of wings to show you, so it'll be worth waiting for.

Don't treat the possibility of my being eliminated too lightly. A very high percentage of us will be and I'm *definitely* no better than average in this game, if that good.

The week's activities are very tiring. We have no time to relax during the day, and only a few minutes before lights out at night. Nothing at all in Douglas, so Sundays are spent out here by most of us. Had a fast game of volleyball this afternoon. There is a fine athletic field, with a large variety of games to play, but by golly I could really use a few days off.

Had a card from Denny Dennison [Joseph John Dennison, ETHS classmate], who is in transitional training with the B-24's. Do you know much about Army planes? These are the 4 motored "Liberator" bombers, used a lot in the Pacific and some in Europe. So far, I prefer medium bombers, the B-25 Billy Mitchell's [twin-engine medium bomber], and that's what I have stated as my preferences. At this early stage, the request doesn't mean much, of course.[17]

Well, old man, let me hear from you soon and lots of luck to you.

As ever, Lovingly Bill

Let me know about Canadian postage rates.

August 18, 1943

Dear Mother:

I knew Gene Reilly (Oak Park) at 166 Van Buren, at Miami, and especially well at Cookeville. He has been discharged because of sinus trouble and is now at home. He wants to meet all of you, and I have sent him your addresses.

I know you'll like him and give him a good time when he calls. He must be a bit low. He is the one with whom I listened to records at T.P.I. Thanks a lot.

Am due to solo at the end of this week, or the first of next. Am doing considerably better.

Hope AA will be able to see Aunt Leila, as I imagine she will.

Thanx for letter, Mom. Bill

August 20, 1943

Dear Mother:

Today, after my instructor and I had flown around for 40 minutes and made one or two practice landings, I was told to "take the damn thing up myself." And, by golly, I did!

I wasn't a bit frightened, as I had thought I might be, but *I have never been more thrilled!* It's really quite something to feel the power of the plane as you take off, and then to cut the motor as you come into land.

I circled the field three times, landing after each circuit and taxiing over to where my instructor was waiting. After a few corrections, or a lot of them, I should say, I took off again. Two of my three landings were fairly good and I think my instructor was perfectly satisfied. I know I was.

There will be three more supervised solo's and then I'll start going off cross-country by myself, practicing the maneuvers we have to know.

A large percentage of those who wash out, do so before they solo, so I've passed one obstacle. However, at the 20th, 40th, & 60th hour in the air, students are "checked" by instructors other than their own, and a large number are washed out on one of these checks.

Well, I've gotten this far and with luck I may go farther.

My attitude, as you can probably tell, has changed, and I think it will continue to be better as I get off by myself more often.

I am definitely not a born flyer and I seem to learn slowly, but this solo has done an awful lot to encourage me.

Will have to beat it now, but I wanted you all to hear the news.

Hope you're getting rested now, Mother, and lots of love.

As ever, Lovingly Bill

Dad has a picture of one of the PT-17s, and I hope you'll see it soon. That front cockpit looked *very* empty today!

August 29, 1943, Sunday

Sorry not to have gotten a letter off to you last week, but was kept busy right up to taps practically all week.

I've had several hours solo flying now. It's a real thrill to be up there alone, practicing stalls and spins and S turns, etc. I keep thinking that it can't be me. The most fun of all is coming in for a landing; cutting the throttle at 500 feet and gliding down to a few feet above the ground and then leveling off. You'd love it, Mom, and I can't wait till the time I can take you up.

That last sentence sounds much more confident than I really am, however. Sometime this week I have my 20-hour check. This is really tough, and I'm not kidding. Already two of my roommates at Maxwell have gone . . .

Several of the boys got some pretty raw deals on their elimination and the general feeling is that luck counts about 75%. Quite a number have gone; too many.

I was very happy to get your letter Friday and one from Wese and Fran earlier in the week. You probably don't realize how much those letters mean. The usual procedure is to read them 3 times right away, then carry them in [my] pocket until night when they are read *at least* twice more!

Mail call and lights out are by far the best formations of the day.

Sundays are very dull, but restful. Today I got up at 8 and ate breakfast, bought a newspaper and went back to bed to read it. Then I had a 45-minute shower and got everyone sore at me for singing *Rule Britannia* all the time. In the afternoon, went to the movies with two of the boys. Something is lacking, though the day was a nice enough change.

[Written on the left edge of paper.]

Well, hope everything is OK with all of you. How's the hay fever, Mother?

As ever, Lovingly Bill

September 1, 1943

Dear Mother:

I can't begin to tell you how pleased and proud I am about your job [at Lyman's Drug store in Evanston]. It's a very fine thing for you to do, and I know how much satisfaction you'll get out of doing it . . . I know the store and remember it as being very modernistic, and a pleasant place to work, too, I should think. It's convenient to get to, too.

Tomorrow, I have my twenty-hour check with a check pilot and am reasonably confident of passing it. I just hope that I don't make some obvious error, like heading downwind for forced landing practice, as I did today-by myself luckily.

From now on I'll fly 2 ½ hours every day and have a half hour every other day in a link [Link] trainer. You've probably heard of these and know something about them.[18]

Every few weeks the Army has us fill out preference forms concerning the planes we want to fly. If, at the end of our training, we are qualified to fly the plane of our choice, that's the one we fly. I have requested medium bombardment three times. I like the B-25, Billy Mitchell's. If you ever see pictures of one, you might be interested [referring to the B-25 twin-engine medium bomber].

Of course, all that seems a very long way off, but time has a way of passing quickly, and February will be here soon enough. I only hope I am still a cadet when it comes.

Will close now and get back to air navigation, which is most interesting, but complex to my simple mind.

Congratulations on your job . . .   As ever, Lovingly Bill

September 5, 1943

Today I spent about three hours cutting weeds and cleaning up around an old roadhouse, which the Cadet Corps is fixing up as a night club for us. They've spent a good deal of money and the place will be very nice. We certainly need somewhere to go on Saturday nights.

After work, seven of us went farther out in the country to a pond, the bottom of which has never been discovered. It is a very beautiful spot in a pine grove and the water is cold and clear.

We stopped at several negro farmhouses for water on our way out and in. At one farm I rode a mule. Much as I like flying, I'd still rather ride an animal than in an airplane, because it's alive, I suppose, and you can feel a sort of human relationship with it.

The negroes were quite impressed to learn that we were among the ones who fly over their farm every day, and we had lots of fun answering their questions.

Altogether, I think this was the best Sunday I've spent in several months.

I've got some swell friends down here and it's tough when any of the fellows wash out. One of my roommates from Maxwell [Field] flew a plane into the ground yesterday. He wasn't hurt, but is all through here, of course (carelessness on his part). The plane was totally wrecked.

Am glad to say that I passed my recheck and now don't have to worry until my 40-hour check, which I will probably have the week after this one.

It's lots of fun to take the ship out alone. We now have two solo hours to every dual hour. Naturally enough, everything goes perfectly when you're up there by yourself . . .

John Evarts is now studying German problems at the University of Illinois. He studied in Munich and has a fine background for the work. At last, he seems to have gotten into something worthy of him. Maybe you'll be able to see him sometime. I hope Jo could put him up some Sat. night. Know Jane would like to meet him.

When does Wese begin school? What courses will she take?

Well, lots of luck with your job. Think of you often.

> As ever, Lovingly Bill

Regards to Fran and the boys, Wese, Jane, Jo, etc.

> September 8, 1943

Dear Mom:

Thanx for your letter of the 3rd, which was especially good . . .

Isn't the news about Italy tremendous? The house of cards is beginning to fall, and I think more development will come quickly.[19]

Have a long letter from AA. The servant's quarters at BMC burned down to the ground. Seems as though there must be a tragedy to go along with the yearly "crisis."

> Regards to all, love to you, Bill

> September 12, 1943

Dear Pop:

. . . I have 36 hours in the air now and will be up for my 40-hour check this week. I was confident of passing my 20-hour check, but frankly don't know if I can make this one or not. A certain degree of precision is expected up there now, and I may fall short of the mark. We have several different figure-eight maneuvers, stalls, spins, etc. So far about 25% have washed out and every one of us lives in constant fear of being eliminated. The indefiniteness of it all makes us indifferent to what happens, somewhat, at least. We would just like to *know* one way or the other . . .

Had a good letter from Aunt Leila yesterday about her reaction to Italy's surrender.

Well, Dad, hope things are going well with you and your work, and that you'll write soon.　　　　Best of luck, As ever, Lovingly Bill

---

September 12, 1943

Does Jane still live in Evanston? The Cadet Club opened last night. It's really very nice, but there's not a great deal to do there. I went bowling and to the movies with one of the boys last night and to the movies again this afternoon, often sleeping until 11:00.

Did you ever get the picture of the plane I'm flying from dad? I have 36 hours now and am due for the much dreaded 40-hour check this week. All of us live in expectation of sudden elimination and it's gotten so we don't give a d— one way or the other. Don't know if I'll pass the check or not. Everything is so uncertain it's getting hard to concentrate on studies or be anything but indifferent to them. Am still in there pitching, of course.

Give my love to everyone and good luck to you in Wilmette. Have heard from dad.

As ever, Lovingly Bill

[Written on right side.]

Send *Review* re Miss Dodd.[20]

September 19, 1943

Dear Mother:

I was glad to get your card. I appreciate how busy you are and am very pleased you are liking the job.

I squeezed by my 40-hour check last week and yesterday I did my first loop. I have 50 hours now and am working on acrobatics. Already, I have enough time to get my private license as a civilian pilot. I've come a fair way, but I frankly don't know if I can get much farther. You couldn't understand it, but I'm very indifferent to success or failure. We all are, as a matter of fact . . .   As ever, Bill

---

September 26, 1943

Dear Mother:

Thank you and Fran very much for your swell letters . . .

For the past week I have been practicing Acrobatics. The loop is the most spectacular and the easiest to do. For tops in thrills there's nothing like flying upside down in a slow roll, especially in an open cockpit plane! I'm enclosing a picture of the ship we fly, because you've never mentioned getting one from dad. Students fly from the rear cockpit and the instructor talks through a tube, or rather yells through one.

The motor is 225 Horsepower, and the plane cruises at about 95 mph.

The plane in the background above the lower right wing is a Basic Trainer [BT-13], and is the ship I will fly if by chance I pass my 60-hour check ride Monday.

On Wed. and Thurs., I went on a cross-country hop, using the navigation we have learned so far. Flew in formation (though we weren't supposed to and we weren't really close together) and had a swell time. Both trips were about 80 miles and were made in less than an hour.

I'm enclosing an editorial from the post newspaper. It's the best of many of its kind that I have read. What do you think of it?

By the way, I wish you'd send down the *Review* telling of Miss Dodd's death. I'm very sorry to hear of it, because she had a big effect on me in high school, made me realize that there was something more worthwhile in life than the Chicago Cubs.

Our class is scheduled to leave here next week. About whether or not I will go too, I am as uncertain as I have been all along about the length of my stay here. If I do wash out, I'm pretty certain of being able to be a Bombardier . . .

Both Fran and Charley should read *USA* by Dos Passos. I realize more and more that it is true. In fact, all of you should read it.[21]

Incidentally, Jean Forster graduates from Swarthmore next month. If you can think of anything, except jewelry and perfumery, that would be nice to give her, please let me know right away. Repondez s'il vous plait.

What is Wese studying? I'd love to hear from her sometime, though I know she's busy with studies and Chandler's.

A year ago now, I was in Utah and had decided to join the Air Corps. I sure didn't realize what a headache it would be. If I get through as pilot or bombardier, it will be well worth it, however.

Danny Deaver wrote last week. He is an A/C navigator, now studying gunnery in Nevada. Don Dalton is in radio and at Scott [Army Air] Field, Ill., so I suppose he'll be getting home for a weekend sometime.[22]

By golly I'd sure like to get home for a while. If I were in the GI's, I'd have no trouble getting a furlough, but no chance as a cadet. I enjoy looking at the pictures I have of all of you and think of you very often. I'm pleased with all of you, much more so than I could possibly have been, say a year ago.

I'm delighted that you like the D.S. Lyman Co. and I know well how much it likes you.

As ever, Lovingly Bill

[Separate undated note may have been enclosed with above letter.]

Made a very bad mistake on my check today and must have a recheck Sat., Sun., or Monday. I used a road for "S" turns and figure eights where it went by one of our auxiliary fields, and that was all I needed to fail the check. Don't know if I'll pass the next one or not, but I certainly won't make the same blunder again. I know better than to do it, too.

Will close now and get to bed.

Lots of Love,   As ever, Lovingly Bill

September 26, 1943

Dear Dad:

Your swell letter of 9/18 was missent to Douglas, Arizona, so I didn't receive it until yesterday.[23] It was good to hear from you, Pop. I certainly look forward to your letters.

Last week I went on two cross-country hops, using what we have learned of navigation so far. Both trips were only 80 some miles and were made in about an hour. I flew in formation with two other boys, and we had a swell time dipping our wings to each other.

For the past 10 days, I have been working on Acrobatics and would like 10 more for practice before my check, which, unfortunately, is tomorrow. If you want a real thrill sometime, try flying upside down in an open cockpit plane!

If I pass my 60-hour check tomorrow, I'll go on to Basic the end of the week for 9 weeks in a Basic trainer. The plane is much more advanced, but I'm not at all confident of ever flying it.

As I told mother, if I wash out as a pilot, I'm pretty sure I'll be a bombardier, which runs a pretty close second anyway.

You asked about the degree of climb for an airplane. I've stood mine [PT-17 Trainer] on its tail a lot of times, but that's only for a short distance and the normal rate is *much* less. Our P-38 Lightning will climb straight up for some time and is a steep climber in any case.

Keep your eyes open for publicity on a new heavy bomber and a pursuit plane. Before the war's over, a fortress will be a light bomber! [Editor's note: fortress refers to the B-17 Flying Fortress four-engine heavy bomber].

You've been away a long time, but your job sounds congenial, and I know the country is. When you do get home, see what you can do about an unfurnished apt. I'd be tickled to death to help out as much as I can, so don't hesitate to ask me.

Well, Fat, best of luck to you. Let me know about what you are doing during your free time, which I suppose is about as little as mine. I think of you often and am pleased that you like your work so much.   As ever, Lovingly Bill

If I do leave this week, it will only be to Bainbridge, Ga, so write me here and the letter will be forwarded quickly.

October 1, 1943

Passed final check Monday, graduated Wed., leave for Basic tomorrow.

A/C ---
Class 44B
AAF Basic Flying School
Bainbridge, Georgia

Have sent home a picture of my instructor and his five students, all of whom passed. Hope things are OK.   Write soon. As ever, Bill

Chapter 5

BASIC FLYING SCHOOL— BAINBRIDGE ARMY AIR FIELD

At Bainbridge, Bill learned to fly a basic trainer, the BT-13 Valiant, a single engine, two-seat monoplane, known to pilots as the "Vultee Vibrator," due to its noise and vibration. Like the PT-17, this plane did not have retractable landing gear, but it did have an enclosed cockpit and a radio so that the student and instructor could communicate easily, rather than by hand signals and shouting back and forth. Basic pilot training included formation flying, instrument flight, aerial navigation, flying at night and cross-country. Aviation cadets received about seventy flight hours in the BT-13 before proceeding to advanced flying school, where cadets would specialize in either single-engine or multi-engine aircraft.

In contrast to his civilian flying instructor at Douglas Field, Bill liked his instructor-pilot, who had gone through the same aviation cadet program that he was in and, according to Bill, had more empathy for cadets.

Bainbridge was a much nicer air field and a little bigger than Douglas, according to Bill. He explained, "There is an Aviation Cadet Club and a very fine USO with a reading room and well stocked bookshelves. Also, current magazines and newspapers, maps on walls, etc."

Inching ever closer to the coveted pilot's wings, Bill hoped to fly twin-engine bombers. Already partial to the B-25 Mitchell medium bomber, he was now interested in flying the faster, more maneuverable A-20 Havoc light or attack bomber. Seeing the humor in his own speculation, he added that, ". . . it seems silly to be talking of what bombers I want to fly while I'm still in a BT, but we all have our favorites which we consider our own and we talk of them as if we flew them regularly . . ."

As training progressed, the idea of flying bombers evolved to wanting to fly the best fighter planes in the AAF inventory. Bill explained to his mother, ". . . I want a fighter plane that I can dance around the sky . . ." When he was making plans for his future as a daring fighter pilot, he could also admit his faux paus and laugh at himself. As an example, he described an incident when he accidentally deployed a parachute on the ground and was kidded about it by his fellow cadets.

Correspondence From
BAINBRIDGE ARMY AIR FIELD

[Written at top of page.]

Another new thing in the BT [Basic Trainer, BT-13] is a two-way radio set. We have to call the tower before every flight.

October 10, 1943

Dear Mother,

No chance to write you during the week, so I'll try and get caught up now.

This is by far the toughest place I've been, from the work standpoint, that is. The washout rate is not so great as at Primary, and barring any bad breaks, I'm reasonably confident of getting through.

We're up at 4:55, breakfast at 5:15, at 6:00 we march two miles to the flight line, and takeoff at 6:45, just as the sun is coming up. At 12:15 back to the Cadet area and lunch. At 1:05 classes begin. At 4:05 they end, and 15 minutes later we're dressed for PT (physical training). At 6:00 we have dinner, at 7:15 a standby inspection until 8:30 (first two weeks only). From 8:30 to 9:30 we study and gripe, at 9:35 we're asleep, and I'm not kidding!

Being a Cadet is not easy, by a long shot, and we have all sorts of disciplinary barbs sticking us all the time, because we're future officers etc. A G.I. soldier doesn't have to take a fraction of the nonsense we do.

The food is not what it has been, but no legitimate complaint about it, because every Cadet mess in the country is now on field rations.

My flight instructor is a grand fellow, entirely different from the one I had at Douglas, though Dillard was a pretty good egg, at that. The best thing about him is that he quietly *explains* what I'm doing wrong and doesn't scream and swear about mistakes. You probably can't imagine how rattled and nervous some instructors can get you, because absolutely nothing is sacred with them. There were many times when I hoped I'd be washed out at Douglas, and I told that to Dillard when we were all through and he asked me for suggestions. We got along pretty well together on the ground, but I couldn't fly with him worth a damn.

Lieutenant Beaver, unlike Dillard, went through all this Cadet rot and is much more understanding, consequently a better teacher.

These first two weeks we are able to get in very little flying time, as the instructor has to divide his attention between his six students, but we will solo this week and then we'll be able to get our three hours a day in the air.

October 11, 1943, Continued

Tell Wese I'm very pleased to have her picture. Several of the boys would like to meet her—and I don't blame them. Pretty smooth!

Couldn't finish this last night because a scheduled 8:00 inspection didn't come off until 9:30, leaving us all standing by our beds, unable to do a thing but get mad at officers.

I haven't been into Bainbridge and probably won't for some time. We are given every other Sunday off. Very generous, don't you think?

The step from flying PTs to these BTs is a really big one. In the PT [Primary Trainer, PT- 17] we had a very small instrument panel and had to divide our attention between only 3 dials. We now have over twenty things to think of, including prop pitch, landing flaps, three gas controls, two stabilizers, and many other things as unknown to the PT as they probably are to you.

Flying this plane will be quite something, because any other plane can only have a few new things—such as retractable landing gear— and the other changes will be largely adaptations of what we will have already learned to use.

Dad says he sent you a booklet about aviation cadets. I'm sorry it doesn't tell you more about our life. The BTs are shown opposite page 8, on page 2 & 3, and the AT [Advanced Trainer] I hope to fly in the next couple of months is on page 21 . . .

There's a good deal of unpleasantness here all right, but I must say I enjoy the intimate contact with the boys, *and* no matter how much I've ___ [unreadable], there are plenty of laughs, too . . . [1]

Regards to all and love to you.   As ever, lovingly, Bill

Please send this to dad, because I'll only be able to drop him a card this week. Let me hear from you about Miss Dodd.[2]

October 11, 1943

[Addressed to the YMCA Hotel in Pueblo, Colorado.]

Dear Dad:

I was very glad to get your long letter and am sorry I can't answer rt [right] now, but we have only an hour free in the evening and I've got to do some studying.

This BT is a *real* airplane and anything else I run into will be much like it, so learning to fly this will really be something.

Have sent home a letter telling about things here. They are really tough, believe me. It's swell that you've been able to see so much of Colo. [Colorado] and like the job so well. Awfully glad for you. Best regards and good luck, old Top![3]   Bill

---

October 17, 1943

Dear Mom:

Your card received—realize you're very busy, however I would like to hear about Miss Dodd! Can't you send down the *Review*. Would like to write to Phil Dodd.[4]

I am well and liking flying more every day. We flew today, by the way. BTs are quite different than PTs, and it's hard to get the hang of it, but I'm making good progress and don't expect much more trouble. Have had a little though.

I didn't go up to Fort Sheridan until Nov. 1—almost a year ago.

Letter from Ted Dreier [BMC instructor] and *cookies* from AA this week. Hope everything is OK, Mom, and you're taking good care of yourself. Think of you.

As ever, Bill

October 17, 1943

Dear Dad:

We had to fly today, so haven't had the usual free Sunday. We could sleep later this morning, though, and I got into Bainbridge last night for the first time, so had something of a weekend.

I was delighted to get your last letter and hear about your trip to the farm on the Arkansas River. I'll have to keep that section in mind, though for some reason I'm partial to northern Wisconsin, which I don't know awfully well, at that.

I'm mailing you a booklet about the base. It has many pictures of the BT, and I think you'll find it interesting.

Haven't taken the ship alone yet, but will have by the time you get this, I feel sure. The BT flies much differently than the PT. You have to use much more rudder and less aileron, and it takes a certain amount of practice to get the coordination right.[5] The last few days I've gotten the "feel" of the ship somewhat and my instructor says I'll solo tomorrow.

You may have read a letter I sent to Fran re a change in the Basic and Advance training programs. It was announced that before leaving here we would fly AT-10's, and before graduating from Advance we'd have B-25's, the Tokyo bomber.

For some reason, they've changed their minds, and the old program still holds and AT's will be flown only at Advanced.

I still like twin engine but am leaning from B-25's toward the faster, more maneuverable, A-20, which is a light bomber. It seems rather silly to be talking of what bombers I want to fly while I'm still in a BT, but we all have our favorites which we consider our own and we talk of them as if we flew them regularly.

Bainbridge is only slightly bigger than Douglas, but it seems to be much nicer. There is an Aviation Cadet Club and a very fine USO, with a reading room and well-stocked bookshelves. Also, current magazines and newspapers, maps on walls, etc.

It must be gratifying to realize that the Merrills [unidentified] are so pleased with the work you have done. Congratulations, Old Top!

Will close now and drop mother a line.   As ever, Lovingly Bill

Think of you constantly and would love to take you for a ride. I'll do it someday, all right. I promise to make it exciting for you.

Good luck, Dad.

October 24, 1943

Dear Mother and Wese:

If there is anything you need, tell me. Miss Dodd? [still inquiring about the recent death of Miss Mabel Dodd, ETHS].

I'm delighted to hear of your room and hope and feel sure you will be comfortable and happy with it.

Had from 4:00-9:30 pm free last night, so I bought some small things for you . . .

We flew all day today, which makes three straight Sundays of work. Am tired as the deuce.

Had fine steak dinner at Stephen Decatur Hotel last night. Think of you very much.

As Ever, Bill

October 31, 1943

Keep writing. Letters are the high spot of any day, believe me.

Dear Mother & Wese:

Your swell letters came today, and I was very pleased to get them. Glad you liked your surprises.

This is the fourth straight Sunday we have had to work, though we could sleep until 9:00 and the rest of the day wasn't so hard. My flight piled into trucks and went to one of our auxiliary fields, just over the Florida boundary line about 25 miles away.

There were planes there and each of us made eight graded landings with full flaps. The flaps have a considerable braking effect and so the glide down is comparatively steep. My landings haven't been very good so far, and I'm very pleased that I did pretty well today. My first two were not so hot and I had to give it throttle to get into the field, but I settled down and my last two were quite good, I think.

My air work is about average, no better than that, and so if I can get my landings better from now on, I'll be sitting pretty.

I was among the last to shoot my stages, so I flew the plane home. The evening was setting in and there was a grand sunset on my left. A very beautiful sight.

Had another one a few days ago. It was one of those cold & dark fall days with a heavy overcast about 3,000 ft up.

My instructor and I climbed up through the dismal weather and went through and above the clouds. Up there, of course, it was very bright and clear, and we spent some time hedge hopping along the tips of the clouds.

Now for your questions:

I can't think of anything you could send me, except an occasional *Review* and *The Chicago Sun*. I can get all the candy I want at the PX.

No, I don't feel rested in the morning.

Yes, I'm careful and will let you know the next time I rip off a wing on a chimney [being facetious]. Is that what you meant by a "bump"?

Wese, I was very interested in your letter and your attitude toward National.[6] My first impression is that you are undoubtedly getting more out of school there then you think you are. That you are not completely satisfied is an excellent sign, I think, because it shows that you are not content to take only what is given you in the classroom but want to explore the vastness beyond. That means you'll never stop learning.

But you may have one of my weaknesses in trying to learn too much at once and thinking it possible to digest more of subject by merely taking more of it. Can't be done.

The only thing I can suggest is that you take what National has to offer, *everything*, and continue your reading and thinking when you are graduated. As the commencement speaker always says, "graduation is not the end, but the beginning." Maybe that's why they call it "commencement."

National can make you a teacher and you can make yourself a good one. Don't shut yourself away from the school or the other girls, because those relationships are just as an important part of your training as the subjects you are taking.

You will have plenty of time for reading all through your life, so *don't hurry*; and learn each step well as you go along, because you're sure to stumble if you try skipping one or two in your eagerness to get to the top.

Your plans for the summer aren't worthy of you. This isn't the time to dash off to Mexico. I hope you'll spend the vacation doing some sort of war work, and I think you ought to. Bang, bang.

What's this about being mad at the warehouse and why are your books and the cushion still there? I suppose it's another financial problem. You should have all you need from the warehouse, so let me know how much you need to get things out. I'm enclosing $20 which should help.

Hope the tea for Jess [Bill's aunt, a younger sister of his mother] is going along OK. Give the old girl my love and thank her for her last letter. Know how much you are enjoying her visit.

I'm looking forward to February a thousand times as much as you. I suppose you realize that is when I am scheduled to get my wings and a gold bar [insignia of a second lieutenant]. Just three months! I'm not through yet, though. Knock on wood.

Am terribly pleased you like Lyman's, Mother, and I hope you're really not too tired after the day.

Good luck to you all and lots of love.   As ever, Lovingly Bill

You asked for it, Wese, OK?

October 31, 1943

[Addressed to the YMCA hotel in Pueblo, Colorado.]

Dear Dad:

Shot 8 landings at one of our auxiliary fields in Florida this afternoon. They were graded, and I think I did satisfactorily. Flew home as the sun was setting. Very beautiful and quiet up there alone. I love it! Sure hope I'll make out all right.

Have your program for the concert the other night. I would like to have heard those selections with you and also to have spent that weekend on the farm. How much longer will you be in Pueblo?

Glad you're having such good times, Dad.

Think of you often and *miss* you.   As ever, Bill

November 13, 1943

[Addressed to the YMCA Hotel in Omaha, Nebraska.]

Dear Fat,

Have had a swell letter about you and how well and happy you look. That's the best possible news for me . . .

My taste has changed from the bombers I used to want to fly, to the faster more maneuverable, single engine, low altitude fighter, the P-51 Mustang. Boy, will I be glad when I finish this Cadet business, if I finish it the way I want to! That will really be a relief.[7]

Understand you're picking up weight. Can you top my 167?

Best of everything, Dad. Bill

November 17, 1943

[Addressed to the YMCA Hotel in Omaha, Nebraska.]

Dear Dad:

. . . Yesterday I was practicing lazy "8s" and chandelles, when 3 P-47's dove in on me and began dog fighting. Most thrilling thing I have ever seen. One was directly beneath me, so I did wing over and came down right on top of him. We were so close, I could see him look up and smile! The P-47 is our best high-altitude fighter, the Thunderbolt. Do you know many planes? These were doing all sorts of flight maneuvers around me.

Think of you.   Good luck, Dad. Bill

November 21, 1943, Sunday

Dear Mother,

The only trouble with today is that it hasn't been long enough. There was a roll call formation at 9:30 this morning, so I could sleep until 9:25. After that two others and I walked over to the weather office on the flight line to complete a meteorology assignment. Then it was time for dinner, which was no worse than usual (my appetite is much better than the food), and then a nap and at three to the theater to see a favorite movie.

It's now after supper, and I'm sitting on my bed, where I spent all last evening, incidentally, reading detective stories. This is the second Sunday I have had free and, believe me, really put it to good use.

Tomorrow I am going to put in my request for *single* engine Advanced. As you know, I have, up to now, wanted to fly a medium bomber, but now I know I'd go crazy flying straight and level and so I want a fighter plane that I can dance around the sky. My choice is our P-51, North American Mustang, which is just about the world's best low altitude fighter used a lot on railroad hunts and strafing missions in Europe and elsewhere. It's a beautiful little ship, and I suppose you have seen pictures of it many times. Do you know many of our planes? You should.

Did dad bring home the booklet about Bainbridge? I want you to see what the BT-13A looks like. At Advanced I'll fly an AT-6, which is smaller, faster, and less clumsy than the BT. It has retractable landing gear and a constant spiral prop and is only a short step from the real thing.

I'm all through with night flying here, except for a cross-country of over 200 miles, which I'll have sometime this week. That's quite a navigation problem when you're not flying by radio, by the way (the night part of it).

Glad to get your card and hope you had a good time at Homewood [a town about an hour south of Evanston].

How do you like your job? I know you're pleased with the weekly check, but how about the work itself? Do you find interest in it and like the other employees?

I had a swell letter from AA and, for the first time, learned that she's going to Evanston in January and will take an apt. [apartment] when she can find one. That brings up something I've thought a lot about. When you begin looking for a place for her, I want you to keep an eye open for one for yourself.

My chances of getting through this seem pretty good, and if I do, I'll be making $225 a month, plus allowance, which might bring that up as high as $275. What a raise!

I'm very anxious for you to have a real home, with the clock and the piano, and nothing could make me nearly so happy as to make this possible.

Won't say anything more now but keep it in mind and we'll do something about it when the time comes.

Monday night [November 22, 1943]

Forgot to tell you a crazy thing that happened to me Sat. I had laid my parachute in the rear cockpit and was standing beside the plane. After a minute I picked up the chute, but the rip cord caught on the throttle, and before I knew what had happened, I was covered with the white silk parachute, which sprang out even without the force of wind! I have been kidded a lot about this. Have a lot more confidence in a chute now. Of course, mine had to be taken to the parachute dept. to be repacked.[8]

Jane has sent a *Sun,* which I'll enjoy reading tonight. I have also run across an article in *This Week* about Alaska, which has made me very conscious of the possibilities of Seward's ice box, for a farm after the war, I mean.

Well, I think about you very much and would like to be able to sing songs with your accompaniment again. Remember "Britannia" and "Evelina?" Also, Thanksgiving favorite—"Come ye Thankful People, Come."

Will mail this Airmail in hopes you'll receive it before Thanksgiving.

Still will be swell for all of you if dad is home. I hope he is.

We'll have no holiday here, but I'll give special thanks for such a perfect mother and family.   All my love, As ever, Lovingly Bill

Write when you find time, as I look forward to your letters more than you know.

[Written at top of letter.]

Cookies, cake, fudge. Do you have a telephone?

December 1, 1943

Dear Mother,

Your last letter was one of the very best I have ever received. I've read it many times and feel more than ever before that I've just been home for a visit. That's the kind I like, of course.

I also had a fine letter from dad, who told of his 14 hours sleep last Sunday! I got a big kick out of that, no kidding.

As far as Xmas is concerned, there is really not much you can do for me. There's nothing I'd rather have than mail, and I hope you all will follow that suggestion.

Some cheap editions (or our own copies) of a couple of books like *House of Seven Gables, Jane Eyre, Adam Bede,* etc. would be swell to take care of an occasional evening and Sunday. There's no sense in anyone buying me a good copy because I will have to send it home when I'm through with it. Couldn't carry it with me all the time, naturally. 25 cents Pocket Books could be passed on to someone else.[9]

I've thought a lot about what I could give you. Bainbridge is such a hole of a little town, there is nothing suitable there, and not in our PX either. If I sent money home to you and had *you* buy the gifts and give them for me, they wouldn't mean much. This really puts me on the spot, because I do want to give something to each one. Whatever I do send will be very insignificant and I will plan to make up for it to everyone when I get home. I'll have enough money to give everyone a good time and plan to do so!

Probably will leave for Marianna on Sunday or Monday. That's the last step toward the old wings and boy will I be glad to take it![10]

Will cut this short and cram for a final exam in meteorology, which I have tomorrow.

I'm much happier about your job since your letter. You have made some very interesting observations of people who come in, so I know you'll never be completely bored.

Much love Mom.   As ever, Lovingly Bill

I'm enclosing Tar's letter you asked me to keep and send. Found it in my locker.

December 1, 1943

[Addressed to the YMCA Hotel in Omaha, Nebraska.]

Dear Pop:

Got your letter today. 14 hours of sleep! That must set some kind of a record. Would like to do it myself. Today we had a hurdle landing stage (practice) at an auxiliary field. Had to clear a 15-foot hurdle and land within the next 300 ft. I did it OK a couple of times but bounced rather badly. This teaches us how to get into a short field.

Have passed my final checks and will go to Advanced [Flying School] in a week or so. It's single engine, I'm happy to say. That's what I wanted—a fighter plane.

Absolutely no chance for me to be home at Xmas but will make it on Sat. If you're not there, I'll go to you wherever you are.

Write again, much love, luck. Bill

Illustrations

Bill Hanchett, Second Lieutenant
commissioning portrait in khaki uniform,
February 1944.

William Sr. and Alice Trowbridge Hanchett, Bill's parents.

The Coral Reef Hotel, Miami Beach circa 1942,
as it appeared when the AAF used it for basic training.
Wikimedia Commons photo, public domain.

Aviation students at College Training Detachment,
Tennessee Polytechnic Institute, March 1943.
L-R: Bill Hanchett, Gene Reilly, and Don Dalton.

PT-17 Caydet and Douglas Field hangars.
Photo courtesy of Douglas 63rd Preservation Society, Inc., Douglas, Georgia.

Jean Haire-Forster, circa 1943.

Christina Kammerer Haire-Forster,
Jean's mother.

Arthur Haire-Forster, Jean's father.

BT-13 Valiant with Bainbridge Field, Georgia markings.
U.S. Army Air Forces photo, public domain.

AT-6 Texan.
Photo courtesy of San Diego Air and Space Museum.

Hanchett family golf outing during a leave home, Fall 1944.
L-R: Jane, Fran, Louise, William Sr., Jo, Bill, and Alice Ann.

B-24 Liberators over Tonopah Field.
Photo courtesy of Central Nevada Museum and
Central Nevada Historical Society, Tonopah, Nevada.

B-24 Crew #256 at Tonopah Field, June 1945.
Standing L-R: Co-pilot Bill Mellinger, Pilot Bill Hanchett, Navigator Pete Strbick.
Kneeling L-R: Engineer Robert "Red" Thompson, Radio operator Dean "McGrew" Levie,
Waist gunner Hugh Butts, Tail gunner Cal Howarth, Armorer-gunner Albert "Frenchy" Rouillard.
Missing: Bombardier Bob Field.

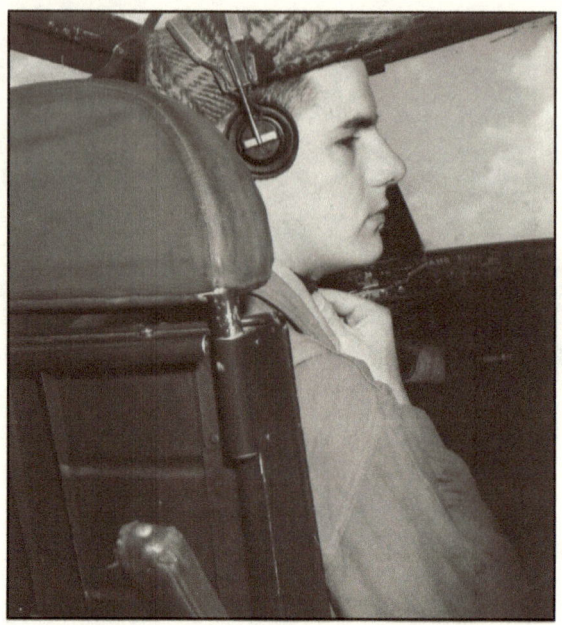

Bill Hanchett in B-24 cockpit, Tonopah Field, Nevada.

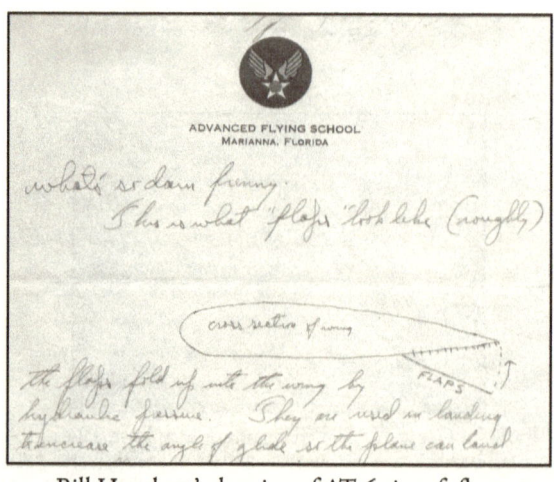

Bill Hanchett's drawing of AT-6 aircraft flap,
January 23, 1944 letter.

TABLE OF AIRCRAFT FLOWN BY BILL HANCHETT

The aircraft Bill flew are listed below. Technical specifications may vary depending on aircraft models.

AIRCRAFT	COMPANY	ENGINE	LENGTH HEIGHT	WINGSPAN	ALTITUDE CEILING	ARMAMENT
PT-17 CAYDET	Boeing	Single-engine Continental R-670 220 HP 7 CYL.	25 FT. 10 FT. 3 IN.	32 FT. 2 IN.	13,800 FT.	N/A
BT-13A VALIANT	Consolidated Vultee	Single-engine Pratt & Whitney R-985 450 HP 9 CYL.	28 FT. 9 IN. 12 FT. 4 IN.	42 FT.	19,400 FT.	N/A
AT-6 TEXAN	North American	Single-engine Pratt & Whitney R-1340 600 HP 9 CYL.	29 FT. 11 FT. 9 IN.	42 FT.	24,000 FT.	Two to four .30 CALIBER MGS.
B-24 LIBERATOR	Consolidated Aircraft	Four-engine Pratt & Whitney R-1830 1,200 HP 14 CYL.	67 FT. 2 IN. 18 FT.	110 FT.	30,000 FT.	Bombs: 6,000 LBS. Ten - eleven .50 CALIBER MGS.

Source: Historical Office of the Army Air Forces, *The Official Pictorial History of the AAF.* (New York: Duell, Sloan and Pearce, 1947).

Chapter 6

ADVANCED FLYING SCHOOL AND WINGS

"After a short bus trip" from Bainbridge, Bill arrived at Marianna Field in northern Florida. Marianna was an advanced single-engine flying school, training future fighter pilots.

He noted that the new "field was smaller and much more friendly than Bainbridge." He told his mother upon arrival that there would be a lot of "Acrobatics and cross-country trips." Service personnel have always been concerned with their meals, and Bill was no exception. He thought the food at Marianna was delicious, indicating "seems as though someone was making a fortune from our mess allowance at Bainbridge."

Cadets usually received a total of about 75 to 80 successful flight hours before graduating and getting their pilot's wings. Bill trained in the AT-6 (Texan) advanced trainer. The cockpit procedure was "bewildering," and he noted how sensitive the flight controls were on the airplane. The AT-6 cockpit and instruments were different and more complex than the BT-13. Among other differences, the AT-6 had retractable landing gear and was fitted with machine guns for gunnery training.

In his correspondence, Bill recognized that the cockpit procedure would get easier with time. Before a cadet could solo, he needed to pass a blindfold cockpit check. Constant flying practice was the routine at Marianna, and Bill persevered and grew in confidence as a pilot. Though he was not sure whether he would be a flight officer (like a warrant officer) or commissioned a second lieutenant, Bill told his family that he would have pilot's wings to show them in February after he graduated. Bill proudly noted that the receipt for the parachute he was issued said, "LT. WFH Jr."

As the anticipated graduation day approached, Bill earned the dubious nickname, "Flaps." One chilly morning he took off after ensuring that frost was removed from the wings. Climbing into the sky, he could not get any air speed greater than 90 mph. He knew that the plane would stall at 80 mph, so thinking that the mechanic had not removed all the frost from the wings, he declared an emergency, called "Mayday" and returned to the field. On the ground, the crew chief asked him, "Why in hell didn't you pull up your flaps?" Cadet Hanchett reported to the captain, who "laughed for a long time."

In writing about this incident, Bill explained that flaps, ". . . are used in landing to increase the angle of glide so the plane can land in a smaller place . . . What I did was the equivalent of driving a car with the emergency brake on." His nickname of "Black Bill" (derived from his Black Mountain College days) was changed to "Flaps" or "Mayday."

As he approached completion of advanced flying school, Bill was asked if he could speak French since the Army was training Free French air cadets. He had taken Spanish in both high school and at Black Mountain College. Bill was *still* unsure if he would be appointed a flight officer or receive a commission as a second lieutenant. He remained confident that he would receive hard-earned pilot's wings. Proudly, he announced to his mother, "8 days to go before Wings!"

Graduation Day was February 8, 1944, and he was proud to walk with the other graduates onto the stage of the Marianna Post Theater to receive his commission as a second lieutenant from Marianna Field commanding officer, Colonel John Persons, and his pilot's wings from the major who directed flight training. Graduation invitations and a press release to the Evanston newspaper were provided to the Hanchett family by the Marianna Field Public Relations Office.

In celebration, Bill went to Tallahassee on a short leave before his next assignment.

His discharge papers from enlisted service to accept his commission as an officer show that he was awarded the Good Conduct Medal for his enlisted service. A new chapter as an officer and pilot that included unexpected turns lay before him.

Correspondence From
MARIANNA ARMY AIR FIELD

December 6, 1943

Dear Mother:

Arrived [at Marianna Field] after a short bus trip. The field is smaller and much more friendly than Bainbridge, and I think I'll like it much better. The two meals I've had were *delicious,* too.

Probably won't begin flying for a few days. This is the last phase of my Cadet training, you know, and it will also be the most interesting. Lots of Acrobatics and many cross-country trips. Hope all is well. Received your letter before leaving this morning.

Thanx. Love, Bill

December 11, 1943

[Addressed to the YMCA Hotel in Omaha, Nebraska.]

Dear Dad:

Sorry, no time for a letter but want very much to thank you for your swell long letter of last Sunday. I like the sound of the Pueblo idea and would like to hear more about it sometime.

You'd be amazed at the cockpit procedure in the plane. Right now, I'm completely bewildered, but expect things to be easier in time. Before 6 hours flying, I'll have a blindfold cockpit check and have to locate and assimilate use of over 50 things!

My own [para]chute, one which I'll keep, was issued to me a couple of days ago. Receipt was made out to *LT.* WFH Jr! Also had a picture taken for gov. records wearing a gold bar! Barring the unexpected, looks like I'll get through OK. Meanwhile, they're really giving us a workout. We're on a 7-day week with 1 day off every 14. Busy as the deuce all day and lectures at night. Will write more soon, Dad. Hope you'll be home for Xmas, even if I won't. Lots of love, think of you.   Bill

---

December 11, 1943

Dear Mother:

Sorry I haven't had a chance to write you about things here and am afraid I won't be able to in any detail tonight. I do want to get this letter off with my present to the whole family.

Please use whatever you need of the enclosed check to buy a big turkey, mince and pumpkin pies, and other trimmings for the Christmas dinner at Jo's. Hope all who are there will have a good dinner and a Merry Christmas . . .

We are on a 7-day week here, with a day off every other week. I share a small room partitioned off in the regular tarpaper barracks, with two others, both of whom I have known since Maxwell Field.

The cockpit procedure in the AT-6 is bewildering. It probably will seem simple in time, but meanwhile I've got a tremendous lot of studying to do to get things right. I won't take the plane up alone for 5 or 6 hours. Before I do, I have to pass a blindfold cockpit check, in which I will have to locate and assimilate the use of over 50 instruments and gadgets.[1]

Will definitely get off another letter before the 25th, but you should have this now.

I am terribly busy all day and have lectures about duties of officers, etc. in the evening. Think of all of you more than you realize and am glad to hear from you. Much love and Merry Christmas.

As ever, Lovingly Bill

Food is delicious—seems as though someone was making a fortune from our mess allowance at Bainbridge.

December 15, 1943

Dear Dad:

It has been raining all day and been very cold, so there's no P.T. and I have a chance to write you instead of taking an hour's calisthenics.

The above [referring to airplane graphic on the AAF stationery] is a fair picture of the AT-6. Actually, the plane is not so stubby and is more streamlined. I think you can see it is a real plane. Notice the retractable landing gear.

That is something we didn't have at Basic, and we also didn't have a constant speed prop. As I wrote you in my card, the cockpit procedures seemed tremendous, but I caught onto it before I expected to and soloed from my third dual ride. I was one of the first in my squadron to do so and from now until I graduate, I'll have only 3 or 4 dual hours.

The [AT] 6 is very sensitive in the controls, and it seems you only have to squeeze the stick and wiggle your toes to go into a turn. Haven't had much time in it yet, but can tell I'm going to like it an awful lot.

Sometime in January about half the cadets in my class (there are 307) will be chosen to go down to Eglin [Army Air] Field to have aerial and ground gunnery training for two weeks. I hope very much to be able to go, because with that training my chances for a fighter plane assignment would be much better.

Class 44B is scheduled to graduate on Feb 8, so when I go home, I'll have a pair of wings to show you and will be an officer, either a 2nd LT. or a Flight Officer.

I hope you'll be home for Xmas. I couldn't send you individual presents, so I have sent mother money for a Christmas dinner which I hope everyone will enjoy. Wish I could be there, and you know how I'll be thinking of you.

Sunday, I have to order my officer's uniforms. We have a $250 allowance for this. (As a flying officer I'll make $225 a month! Not chicken feed, is it?!) Prices for uniforms are very high, and we are told the $250 is barely enough for all we need.

I'm glad your job is lasting through the quiet season, and I'm very interested in your idea of going into business in Pueblo [Colorado]. It will be swell when you and mother can be together again.

Think of you lots and am crazy to see you in Feb. Have a good time on Christmas. Lots of Love, As ever Bill

The plane cruises at 155 and is redlined at 240. It is *very* maneuverable. Landing over a hurdle (as at Basic) is not the same as hedge hopping, and I haven't done any of that. Acrobatics are done above 3,000', spins at 7,000'.

December 19, 1943

[No salutation in original.]

I just woke up from a 12 ½ hour sleep! Boy oh boy, give me more nights like that one.

It is about 10:30 and I only have a few minutes to write, because we eat in an hour and then have to go to the flight line for the afternoon. I don't mind at all, because I only wanted to sleep anyway.

I think it is swell about your trip to Omaha, and I wish you could stay there the whole week and come home with dad. But you sure will have a swell time, both of you.

Got a notice from the post office that I have a package there but haven't been able to pick it up yet. I also have presents from Tar, AA, Leila, and Fran in my locker and so will have fun opening them Xmas morning. Thanks a lot for whatever you've sent.

Well, Mother, have a good time with dad and know that I'll be thinking of you both and wishing you every good Christmas greeting. Next year we can be sure the star will be shining a lot brighter.   As ever, Lovingly Bill

---

December 25, 1943

Dear everyone,

You'll probably be surprised to hear that I am in the hospital with the flu, but am feeling much better now and expect to be out soon.

A couple of the boys brought over all your packages I have been saving last night and so everything was all set this morning. I can't thank you enough for the presents. They're wonderful, and I'm tickled to death with everything.

As you may have guessed, I'm using my new pen now and it works like a charm. Must try to make my penmanship worthy of it. It's a grand set, and I'm crazy about it . . .

Jane, I am halfway through with *God Is My Co-Pilot*. It's a fascinating book. I feel well acquainted with Col. Scott, because I've read several of his confidential reports in our War Room.[2]

I'm very pleased to have *Jane Eyre* and *Adam Bede*, Wese, and will begin one or the other tomorrow. It's nice these books have come at a time when I'll have a good chance to read them through.

The Church sent me some stationary and a small flashlight, which I needed for night cross-country trips . . .

I also have a book of cartoons on *"How Not to Fly"* from Leila, and 101 best cartoons from AA, and some postal cards from the Groses.

This isn't the best place in the world to spend Xmas, but I had a whale of a lot of fun opening all the presents after breakfast this morning and everything is piled at the foot of my bed now.

I'm anxious to hear from each of you about your day, especially about your time with dad in Omaha, Mom. He has the wrong idea about the 2 weeks aerial gunnery at Eglin Field. That won't delay my leave at all. It's part of the training course, but everyone won't get to go. I'm hoping to be able to, because it will greatly increase my chances for a good assignment . . .

Last night I had planned to go to the post chapel for Christmas Carols but heard them over some radio down the corridor instead. It was the first time this year that I'd heard the carols.

In a few days we will be all through with ground school as Cadets. Have had the final navigation exam and I got a ninety but can do better.

December 26, 1943, Sunday

. . . Am about done with *God is My Co-Pilot*, and this letter.

Think of you all very often and many thanks for the swell gifts. Love all the kids and *Thanks again.*   As ever, Lovingly Bill

---

January 2, 1944

Dear Mother:

A Xmas package arrived yesterday from Jo. Darn good fudge, and I'm eating some now. As you see, I'm using my new pen. It is really a beauty, though I wish it had a clip so I could carry it in my shirt pocket.

Don't get excited about seeing me in Feb., because if we don't get some better flying weather, we may have to stay here and fly during our "leaves." That would be a rotten break, but all we can do is hope. My future training is wholly dependent on my assignment, but it won't last a year. My God, I've spent 15 months already. Write you soon and lots of love to you and all the others.

As ever, Bill

January 5, 1944

Was Cadet Officer of the Day yesterday.

Dear Mother:

I'm afraid this has bad news. Prospects for a leave in Feb seem pretty slim. Ordinarily, Cadets always get their leaves after graduation, but our class is having trouble with the weather (all winter classes do) and the gov. [government] seems to have some extra plans for us.

The report now is that after we are graduated in Feb, we will stay here as officers and fly P-40's. That may take 10 days, or as long as six weeks. If the latter, I think furlough possibilities would be pretty good.

It's a darn shame and all of us have looked forward to and planned for those 10 days. Well, that's the - - - - - - Army, and there's nothing we can do about it. This all isn't final. Nothing is definite in the Army, but this is what now seems most likely.

Now for some better news which I haven't written you yet. I have been appointed to the Gunnery Squadron and so will go to Eglin Field [Florida] for gunnery in a few weeks. Down there we will shoot at a sleeve towed by a plane and at a ground target. The AT-6 has four 30 cal. [caliber] machine guns, all fired (as you probably know) by pressing a button on the stick.

I'm crazy to be able to talk to you about flying, I bet you'll have a lot of silly questions. Incidentally, I'm not getting enough mail! Help! Help!

This week, my Squadron has moved over to the Instrument Instructor's Headquarters, and we are flying on instruments with a hood shutting in the cockpit. In Basic we learned to control the ship in this condition, here we are learning to fly the beam, picking out the correct heading by bracketing.[3] It's damn difficult stuff, but again I am comforted by the fact that everyone thinks so and is sure he will flunk the check to be given, and which has to be passed . . .

Hope AA will write soon about her three uncompleted phone calls down here. Where is Bob? [Babcock, brother-in-law in the Navy] Lots of love to everyone—and don't feel too badly about Feb. I'll get home someday. As ever, Lovingly Bill

The P-40 I'll fly after graduation is the plane flown by Col. Scott and about which he wrote in *God is My Co-Pilot*. The real stuff, no less.

January 10, 1944

Dear Mother:

There's a rumor going around that we *will* get our leaves after all. I probably won't know until graduation, but now there seems to be some ground for hope. My fingers are crossed from now on in!

Have ordered just about all my uniforms now; $150 worth in 30 minutes Sat! I wish you could spend as much for clothes.

I'm looking forward to news about dad and AA. I am very pleased about the possibility pop mentioned in his last letter. Hope it works out.

I did a slow roll with my canopy open a few days ago and lost both my cap and my earphones! How are things with you? Heard my Offenbach ballet on the radio last night. Think of you.   Love, Bill

How're things at Lyman's?

January 12, 1944

Dear Mother:

I'm all through with the instrument squadron! I passed my check yesterday and now will be a rated instrument pilot when I graduate! I'll explain the beam procedure sometime. Sweating it out under the dark hood at 150 mph, can make it darn confusing.

The food we're getting is absolutely delicious, and there are at least three times a day I'm glad I'm not a civilian. Begin night flying next week. Having formation and Acrobatics now. Would like to hear from you when you get a chance.   Love to all—Bill

January 16, 1944

Dear Mother & Dad:

Took two very interesting trips this afternoon. One into Alabama at 2,500', the other a triangle around this area at 500'. That is very low for a cross-country and at 150 mph things really tear by! Saw a very nice house and barnyard on the side of a small lake. An ideal spot. Shades of the future!

Think it's great you plan to take an apt. and get out the furniture. Hope you can get what you want very soon. I'm really very pleased about dad's new work.

It was really dark last night, and there was absolutely no horizon. After takeoff you *had* to go on instruments till you turned back toward the field.

By the way, when is AA's baby coming? This month? Am glad to hear Fran is making progress, want to see that soon. Must be a beaut!

Write when you can. Nothing like letters from home.   Bill

January 16, 1944, Sunday

Dear Mom & Dad:

Your last letter, Pop, was the best news I've had for a long time, both because of the job stuff and because it won't keep you away from home as much as the May Co. did.

Night flying last night, about the darkest night I've ever seen. There was a heavy overcast at 1,500', so all we could do was shoot landings. I shot eight, all of them without using the plane's landing lights or flood lights—only smudge pots along the runway, they weren't smooth, believe me.

Fly again this afternoon. It's clear now, so probably will get in some Acrobatics. Ceiling has been around 3,000 [feet] for a week, so have had formations, but not much else.

Dad, I'm very pleased about your new job. It definitely is a step forward and seems to have swell possibilities. Congrats! Your weekend with all the family together again sounds good to me.

As ever, Bill

January 23, 1944

. . . Am sending you a booklet on MAAF [Marianna Army Air Field]. Not all pictures are of Cadets, of course. There are some swell shots of the AT-6.

Dear Mother & Dad:

This is a beautiful, warm Sunday, perfect for a long walk, but I can't get off the post so I may walk to the other side of the landing field and back. There is a dirt road around and it is not bad at all for an hour's hike.

Listen to this crazy thing I did a couple of days ago. I was on the first flight and was due to take off as soon as it got light enough to fly. The morning was very cold and there was frost on all the wings and props. This is a very serious hazard to flying, so I made sure a mechanic rubbed it off.

Then I strapped on the plane, warmed up the engine, checked the mags [magnetos-power for engine ignition], and taxied out to the runway, and took off. Everything was going along perfectly and I was sitting "fat and happy" until just after I pulled up my wheels and realized I wasn't getting any airspeed. I became unhappy immediately.

The engine was running all right, but I gave full carburetor heat anyway. I began to break out in sweat, but no matter what I did I couldn't get over 90 mph, which isn't a safe speed. Plane will stall just under 80.

Then it occurred to me that the mechanic hadn't got the frost off, and if so, I had better get down while I could. I was only at about 700′, but I turned back toward the field, picked up my mike and called "mayday," which is the air-to-ground "SOS." The tower was just as frightened as I was and gave strict instructions to all other planes to hold their position because of an emergency landing. I was given clearance for a downward landing and when I set the plane down safely, I felt sure I was going to get the D.F.C. [Distinguished Flying Cross].

Much relieved, I taxied back to the ramp and as nonchalantly as possible explained my difficulty. I got a great satisfaction in seeing the admiring looks of several mechanics who climbed up on my wing, but you can imagine what I got when the crew chief looked at me and said "why in hell didn't you pull up your flaps?"

I reported to the Captain right away and he got a big kick out of it and laughed for a long time.

[Written at top of page 2 of letter.]

In the bulletin picture titled "Night Watch" you can see flaps down on the plane at the left, if you look closely at the trailing edge of the wing.

By this time, you are probably wondering what's so darn funny. This is what "flaps" look like (roughly) [see drawing in Illustrations] the flaps fold up into the wing by hydraulic pressure. They are used in landing to increase the angle of glide so the plane can land in a smaller place. We didn't use them here for takeoff, and of course, never use them in flight.

You can see how when used in level flight, they would slow down the plane tremendously. What I did was the equivalent of driving a car with the emergency brake on and bringing [it] into the nearest garage to see what was the matter!

Well, anyway, I learned enough to check my flaps on the ground from now on. The boys don't call me Black Bill anymore. It's "Flaps" and "Mayday." [Black Bill refers to a nickname because of his association with Black Mountain College.]

I've often thought "flaps" would be a swell name for a dog with big ears.

I flew for a couple of hours last night. Took a X-C (cross-country) past Crestview and back. Tonight, I have another trip 100 miles beyond Tallahassee and return.

These trips don't amount to anything, and they're not nearly as much fun as the daytime ones. You can't see anything, and about all you can do is sing and you can't even hear yourself sing. At least it helps you [stay] awake.

We're only 16 days from graduation now. One of the fellows has had a tough break. He was shooting night landings at night (of course). He leveled it off too high, stalled out, and fell on a wing tip. That sounds like a much more serious accident than it really is. "Ground loops" happen quite often. Anyway, this poor guy, who is damn swell (from Asheville, N.C. incidentally) has to have check rides with about every Capt. [Captain] & Major on the field and will be darn lucky if he gets through.

Dad, a few days ago I sent you some literature on your old friend,

Joe McWilliams. *The New Yorker* report is especially good and I hope you'll read it.

Fran has written that you're going to take one or two more jobs with May [Company], until Cargill gets things organized. Hope it all works out as you expect it to.

One week from today, Jan. 30, will be a year from the date I left home.

I have a letter from Ted Long [ETHS friend], who is a midshipman at Harvard. Bob Long is also there but leaves for sea duty Feb 1.

Dick de Varennes [ETHS friend] graduated with 44A [AAF Class], but I don't know if he is single or twin engine. Did Wese happen to ask him? Glad to see he got his leave.

Don Dalton [friend from TPI who washed out as an air cadet] is in radio school at Scott Field, Illinois. He hates it and is unhappy there, but at least he gets to Chicago once in a while.

The gunnery schedule has been changed. It will not be given until after graduation, and then to a smaller number than first chosen. The field is Eglin Field, Florida, not Elgin Field, Illinois, darn it.

I've been very happy to think of you two seeing each other so much. I sure would like to have one of those dinners at Lyman's too.

What's new about another apt [apartment]? If you should need any help for the storage bill, please let me know.

Guess I won't be able to take that walk, cause it's getting late and I have to prepare my drawing for tonight. Map ain't much good at night, so we draw out our course line, navigation lights, big cities, radio beams, etc., on a piece of paper and use that instead.

On X-C [cross-country flights] drawings or maps are strapped on my knee.

Think of you all terribly much and am more anxious than you know to see you.

Lots of love to you both,   As ever, Lovingly Bill

January 30, 1944

Dear Mother:

. . . I'm looking forward to dropping in at Lyman's too, Mom, and I think chances of getting home the middle of Feb are quite good.

The graduation ceremony is on Feb. 8, and I am mailing you an announcement. With luck, I'll be able to get a train leaving Montgomery [Alabama] on the 9th. I can make fairly good connections from there but will have a deuce of a time going that comparatively short dist. [distance].

That's unusual because this afternoon I flew 700 miles (round trip), which is almost the total air distance all the way to Evanston! On this trip I got up into Georgia and across to Alabama, coming close to Maxwell Field and passing the negro training fields at Tuskegee.[4]

I have got in just about all of my time. Still lack 3½ hours of navigation, 6 hours Acrobatics, 3 hours formation, and 1 or 2 miscellaneous. Weather permitting, I'll finish this week; must, in fact.

Yesterday was our first complete day off since the 1st of Dec. We have had a few free afternoons, however, and flying here is so much more interesting than it has been at my other posts that free time, except in the evenings, does not mean as much as it used to. I'd just as leave fly [*sic*] as do anything else during the day.

I went into town yesterday, found nothing to do, and came back. I went in every store in town (the whole dozen of them) and could not find anything to read—nothing at all.

Most of our evenings are free now so I do have time to myself—but there are lots of things to do! Am caught up on my sleep and feel swell.

8 days to go before Wings!

Lots of love to you, especially, and to all the others.

As ever, Lovingly Bill

February 1, 1944

Dear Pop:

Thanx for your letter and card. From what you say of Sedalia, I imagine it is very much like Douglas, Bainbridge, and Marianna. These towns are dead as door nails, and when you add a few hundred, or thousand soldiers, the situation isn't improved any.

Well, it hardly seems possible that a week from today I will be an officer and wear a pair of wings. Last night I learned the good news that I will be a LT. and not a flight officer, which is an inferior rating. About 10% of my class were made F.O.s [Flight Officers]. They wear blue bars and are on about the same level as Warrant Officers. Two of the boys I've known well for 9 months got Flight Officer ratings. I consider both outstanding and it sure seems they got a raw deal. And, of course there are others who shouldn't be LT's who will be.

Some more good news is that I am pretty sure of getting a leave.

Probably everyone will, except those who are going to be instructors. I hope I am safe from that fate . . .

Still more good news, but this is still in the rumor stage. Many of us (how many I don't know) will be sent to Westover Field, Mass. [Massachusetts] for transition in P-47's (the famous Thunderbolt). Westover, I believe, is at Springfield, which means I could drop in on the Jim Hanchett's for an occasional home cooked meal, and also that I would be up where there is something doing.

As far as gunnery and P-40's are concerned, I don't know what is going to happen, and won't until graduation day, or the day before. That schedule was all messed up when the policy of giving it during Advanced was changed. I won't know anything about anything until the 8th. If you want me to telegraph you when I learn about my leave, send me an airmail. I don't know if you can change your plans, or not.

Tomorrow, I have to go down to Tyndall Field [Florida] and go up to 38,000' in the [altitude] pressure chamber. I had this at Maxwell but got a case of the bends and so have to do it over again. If I have trouble again, they probably will put me in some rotten job like being an instructor, or a job with the ATC [Air Transport Command] where most of the work is below 25,000. That's one swell way to see the world, but darn it, I want a fighter assignment. My final requests went in today:

1. Single-engine fighter—P-51, P-47
2. Twin-engine fighter—P-38
3. Dive bomber—A-36

But these preferences don't mean a thing. They take whoever they need, for whatever.

But by golly, I'll be so darn tickled with those wings I don't [care] if I have to tow targets![5]

Am just about through flying. Have a few hours of Acrobatics, need a few formation [flying] to get in, then I'm all done. Ought to finish Friday.

I have all my uniforms and they fit very well. Some very nice-looking clothes.

How are things progressing with Cargill and Zalin [employer]? Hope everything works out for the best.

Will close now, old man. Let me hear from you about where you expect to be, and keep your fingers crossed for my leave.

Lots of love,   As ever, Lovingly Bill

February 7, 1944

Dear Mother:

By the time you read this you may have received another telegram saying definitely whether or not I'll be home, and when.

This is the situation: my instructor told us that one of his six students was going to be made an instructor. The other five received their orders today and are leaving for home tomorrow. That means that it is practically certain I will be the instructor (the others are to fly P-40's).

All I can do is stay here and get in a lot of sack time and wait for my orders to come through. They will come in a few days, maybe even tomorrow. At any rate it will be before the 16th, when these barracks will be used by the incoming class (44D).

It's hard for me to say how disappointed I am about this assignment. I have really wanted to see some action in a hot ship, but for the next few weeks or months, I guess I'm destined to teach some dumb cadets stalls and spins. Of course, you understand I may not be an instructor, but I'm convinced I will be, probably at Basic.

About three weeks ago, my name appeared on a list with about 40 others, all of whom were called into the captain's office and asked if they spoke French. I don't know any more than you do why he asked that (it may have been a trick to get us to report to him, or he may have wanted instructors for some French cadets.) Anyway, the same 40 and I did not get orders, and so it seems very likely that we will be instructors, as about that number are to be chosen from 44B.[6]

I still may get home this month, maybe very soon, maybe not for a long time. It's all very indefinite and I'm sorry as the devil I'm not one of those leaving tomorrow. But when I do get home will have such a bang-up time, we won't mind the wait!

In three hours and fifteen minutes, my Cadet Days are over and technically I will be a civilian until 0830, when I will be commissioned a 2nd LT. in the Army of the United States! It seems impossible that this day has come. I certainly never thought it would when I was parading around Miami Beach, sweating away at Maxwell, and definitely not while being cursed at by Dillard at Primary!

Lots of parents are here, but it's good you didn't attempt it because transportation is so bad. If it had been better, I would have invited you down as a graduation present to myself.

You can imagine how excited all of us will be when we get up and put on our officer's uniforms for the first time tomorrow. Boy, we've really worked for those bars and wings, too. Most officers go through a three-month course at Officer Candidate School. The cadet course lasted 9 months!

I'll write you soon about the graduation ceremony, as I will have plenty of time, unless the orders come Tues. or Wed. Will have nothing to do here as an officer, no flying, studying, or anything. Pretty soft. I'm tired of it already.

I'm glad to hear that AA and Ann (without an "e", I hope) [newborn niece] are well. Ann, of course, will be as much a tomboy as her mother.

Am crazy to see all of you and am keeping my fingers crossed.

I may have to take an instructor's course for a few weeks, or I may go directly to my new field, or I may be assigned to teach here, or etc.

Hope to hear from you soon about where dad is now. Sent the telegram so he could make plans accordingly.

Hope you are well and all that. Lots de amour [Colloquial French for "of love"]. As ever, Lovingly Bill

P.S. Incidentally, it would be a terrific blow to my pride to receive any more mail addressed to "A/C WFH52" address me (LT. W-) care of Cadet Headquarters, MAAF.

Am enclosing one or two of my officer cards.

February 8, 1944

Dear Mother:

Here's today.

We woke up at 6:00 am and were too excited to go back to sleep, though we didn't have to fallout until 8:30.

At 8:30 we formed in 4 squadrons of platoons, the 290 members of 44B, and, led by the band playing the Army Air Forces song, marched proudly, and I mean *proudly*, to the Post Theater for the graduation exercise. I've never felt as I did during that march. There I was with a new uniform and gold bars. Civilians and soldiers stopped their work to watch us, and don't think my old chest wasn't sticking out six inches more than normal.[7]

The parade was the best part of the day. The ceremony was little but a short address by the Colonel to the visitors, telling something about the Cadet course. Then we filed up on the stage, and as our names were called off, shook hands with Colonel Persons, who gave us our commissions, and walked over to the Major in charge of flight training, who gave us our wings and shook our hands.[8]

When that was all over, the Commandant of Cadets got up and said, "Officers dismissed." We then let up a howl and began kissing and shaking hands with everyone and pinning on their wings. As soon as I walked out the door, I was saluted by a somewhat mercenary Sgt., who was anxious for the dollar given by new officers to the first soldier who salutes him. He made quite a haul, but I assure you I was more than glad to contribute my bill.

The rest of the day we went around with big smiles on our faces, getting a million papers signed and "clearing" numerous departments.

In the afternoon I received Fran's telegram and thought I'd put a call through for the fun of it. I got almost immediate connections. My call was to Mrs. C. F. Weed [sister, Fran]. She was not at home, but Mr. Weed *was*, so naturally I said OK, expecting to talk to old Chas [Charles Frederick Weed-sister Fran's husband].

Nevertheless, I was glad to talk to the old man. He is the first person who has known me at home that I have spoken to in many months. I got a big kick out of his opening remarks, which was "my God, Bill, why didn't you wait until night and save 15%!" He was very obliging, and I was glad to talk to him.

Nothing new about my orders. Have no dates whatsoever, except to read the bulletin board every day between 11:00 and 2:00. Will probably go to Tallahassee for the night tomorrow. Nothing to do in Marianna . . .   As ever, Lovingly Bill

Headquarters
Office of the Public Relations Officer
AAF Pilot School (Advanced-Single Engine)
Marianna Army Air Field
Marianna, Florida

Mr. and Mrs. William F. Hanchett
1246 Ridge Ave.
Evanston, Ill.

Dear Mr. and Mrs. Hanchett;

Today your son received the silver wings of the Army Air Forces and his commission in the Army of the United States.

The graduation exercises were impressive. To your son it meant recognition for his many hours of study, the concentrated, and at times exhaustive, efforts to train his mind and body, and gratification of his ambition to fly in our country's service. It wasn't easy - - -, but he did it! To those of us in the AAF Training Command it meant that your son is equipped to complete the task assigned him so that he and millions more can soon return home.

The inclosed [sic] story of your son's graduation has been forwarded [to] the *Evanston Review*. When it is published, we will appreciate your forwarding a clipping to us. For your convenience a self-addressed envelope that requires no postage is inclosed [sic].

Permit us to extend our congratulations..........We're proud of him too.

Sincerely yours,

R.L. Craig [signature]
Captain, Air Corps
Public Relations Officer

Headquarters
Office of the Public Relations Officer
AAF Pilot School (Advanced-Single Engine)
Marianna Army Air Field
Marianna, Florida

NEWS RELEASE—

William F. Hanchett, Jr. this week received a much coveted pair of pilot wings and was commissioned a 2nd Lt. in the United States Army. This event marked the completion of one of the most rigorous courses of training prescribed by the Army Air Forces Training Command.

Lt. Hanchett entered the Army Air Forces last year as an Aviation Cadet and was sent directly to the classification center at Nashville, Tenn., where he was chosen as potential pilot material. From there he went to an Army Air Forces Training Command Pre-Flight School where he underwent arduous toughening-up exercises and study. He received his primary and basic flying training at various training fields in the Southeast and was then sent to the Army Air Forces Advanced Flying School at Marianna, Florida, for two months intensive course in single engine flying tactics and operations.

Lt. Hanchett is the son of Mr. and Mrs. William F. Hanchett of 1246 Ridge Ave., Evanston, Ill. He attended [LEFT BLANK] high school at [LEFT BLANK] and Black Mountain College, Black Mountain, N.C. (University or College) where he was a member of [LEFT BLANK]. Prior to entering the service he was employed by [LEFT BLANK].

Chapter 7

INSTRUCTOR-PILOT SCHOOL—
RANDOLPH ARMY AIR FIELD
AND RETURN TO BAINBRIDGE

The day before graduation, Bill was disappointed to learn that he was to be assigned as an instructor-pilot. He preferred assignment as a P-40 Warhawk fighter pilot like some of the others with whom he had trained at Marianna Field.

Before he started flying school, while in preflight, Bill experienced the bends at 38,000 feet in his first high altitude chamber test. As noted previously, Bill underwent a second high altitude chamber test. His correspondence does not reveal the results of the second 38,000 feet high altitude test, except to say that he was not assigned to fly fighter planes.

Of the three airplanes he had flown so far, the AT-6 had the highest ceiling at 24,200 feet. At the end of Advanced Flying School, he thought he might be assigned to fly the P-40 Warhawk fighter. While the P-40 had a ceiling of 32,400 feet, the more advanced fighters Bill *really* wanted to fly, like the P-38 Lightning, the P-47 Thunderbolt and the P-51 Mustang had ceilings at 40,000 feet and above. Getting the bends at 38,000 feet precluded him from flying "hot ships" like these, so Bill was disappointed to be assigned to instructor-pilot training at Randolph Field, known as "the West Point of the Air" at San Antonio, Texas. Throughout his pilot training, Bill, like many others, daydreamed about the various airplanes he hoped to fly. Now he was in one of the "rotten jobs" he did not want. From another perspective, when the Army made him an instructor, the assignment introduced him to what became his career in teaching.

Randolph Field opened in October 1931 to serve as an Army Air Corps "consolidated training center." According to the U.S. Air Force official history of aviation cadet training, Randolph was the "city on a hill" for the Army Air Corps. Though most of the buildings at Randolph reflected southwest Spanish architecture, the base headquarters building, referred to as an early Art Deco design, was nicknamed the "Taj Mahal." In 1943, Randolph included the Central Instructors School, which turned out instructors for primary, basic, and advanced flying schools.

In this course, Bill ran into a high school friend who was also in the instructor's training program. His friend was washed out. Even though he held his own in one of the toughest schools in the Army Air Forces, Bill felt restless. He still wanted to fly combat planes. In frustration, on the ides of March, he wrote to his father, "... Heard from my three best friends all through Cadet Training. One is co-pilot on a Flying Fortress [B-17 bomber], the other two are flying P-40's [fighter], and I'm struggling away in the rear of a Vultee Vibrator. Rotten luck, believe me ..." (March 15, 1944, letter)

On a brighter side, Liz Parker, the secretary at BMC, reported to Bill that Rainey, his former pet dog, held her tail higher now that he had pilot's wings. Bill was pleased to pass on this news to his parents. (March 19, 1944, letter)

Instructor-Pilot

From Randolph, as he expected, Bill returned to Bainbridge, Georgia as an instructor-pilot. Bill wrote his mother that he had graduated from instructor school and that he was returning to Bainbridge. "... Ever heard of it? Six months ago, I went there as a dumb cadet. Now I am going as a dumb instructor, but there has been progress at least." (March 21, 1944, letter)

Still wanting to get into the war, he told his mother that he had applied for fighter pilot training but did not hold out much hope. By early April he was, "in full swing with my cadets."

The letters Bill wrote as an instructor-pilot showed he cared about the cadets assigned to him. He saw his cadets making the same types of mistakes he had made as a student in the BT-13. He said he liked his students, and they were anxious to please him. The cadets even liked his jokes. When he had to wash out a cadet from training, he felt bad because he knew they were trying hard to succeed.

Instructor-Pilots taught six or seven cadets at a time, classroom and in the air training. As an instructor-pilot there was a great deal of flying—eight or more hours a day in the air. As the instructor, Bill oriented each new student to the "flying area" which included the six Bainbridge auxiliary air fields, restricted areas and other landmarks. After "elementary air work" cadets progressed to Acrobatics, like executing Chandelles and Lazy Eights. Teaching Acrobatics for four hours at a stretch had Bill feeling like a "milkshake."

Each morning, the cadets would meet with their instructor in a semicircle. Bill described a typical briefing: "After exchanging salutes, I tell them who I will ride with and what I plan to have them do. Before solo we concentrate on things like forced stalls, forced landing practice, spins, and climbs and glides. Then, after the morning lecture (half hour of questions, etc.) we all go out to the plane. I get in the back seat and act indifferent and the cadet who rides first climbs in front and fumbles around trying to get the engine started before I ask him what the devil he is waiting for."

There was informality among the instructor-pilots, including the officers who led them. By the end of April Bill was referring to a Major, whom he had feared as a cadet, by his first name, Jim.

Despite Bill's busy schedule, Black Mountain College was never far from his mind, so in May he flew up to North Carolina for a nostalgic visit with faculty, staff, and with his dog, Rainey.

Departing from his duties as an instructor-pilot, Bill described participating in an infantry exercise with seventy-four other airmen. He was, after all, in the Army, and the philosophy was that everyone is an infantryman first. In early February, a "War Orientation" program had begun at Bainbridge. About twenty-five percent of personnel at a time participated in the monthly program, which consisted of lectures, films like *Swim to Live,* and a bivouac which included marching in a simulated theater of operations, defense against chemical and air attacks, pitching tents, field messing, field sanitation, and night operations.

This exercise took place only five days before the Allied invasion of Europe in Normandy, and Bill wrote about it the day before the American Fifth Army liberated Rome. In charge of six enlisted men, Lieutenant Hanchett was assigned to locate and assault an "enemy" machine gun nest. Instead, he and the others "got a kick out of capturing a deserted outhouse," which served as a sentry box.

It is interesting that Bill, who noted the invasion of Sicily, and the surrender of Italy, and wanted to get into "Europe proper," made no mention of the Normandy invasion. On the other hand, his sister, Fran, did have a memorable reaction to the invasion of the European continent. In Chicago, as she was driving with their nine-year-old cousin, she became so excited when news of the invasion was announced over the car radio, she did not pay attention and ran a red light. Pulled over by a police officer, she started talking and joking with the officer. When she explained what happened, the officer, also excited by the invasion news, let her proceed without a ticket.[1]

One of Bill's friends at Bainbridge was First Lieutenant Samuel H. Baron, a Chemical Warfare Service officer who shared an interest in history. During a walk, Bill and Sam witnessed German Prisoners of War working on a Georgia peanut farm. One morning during a gas mask training exercise, and with command approval, Baron threw tear gas into a barracks, which caused quite a commotion and resulted in him being very unpopular with the troops. Shortly after this, Baron left Bainbridge and eventually served in Europe in an infantry division.

Correspondence From
RANDOLPH ARMY AIR FIELD

February 20, 1944

Dear Mother, Dad, & etc.:

Arrived here this morning on schedule. A few of us went directly to the Gunter Hotel, where we washed up and put on clean clothes, and then took a bus the 18 miles to Randolph Field.

Have spent the afternoon filling out papers and papers, getting settled in my room, unpacking, etc., I am in a very comfortable room with three others. One I know. He is Newell McCartney, from Evanston. The other two seem like nice chaps, too.

Most of the movies about Randolph have dealt with Cadets and if you remember any of them, you know what sort of a set up the

Cadets had. The buildings are all permanent and Spanish in architecture. The Cadet detachment has folded up, and all their old buildings are now used by the C.I.S. [Central Instructors School], so you see I have a pretty nice place to live. And the best sack I've had in the Army! Officers rate two sheets. But I think that while we're here we'll be considered more as over-paid cadets than officers. The fellows who left just before my class came in were sent all over the country; some to Arizona and California. Some even to Bainbridge.[2]

Will let you know more about things here when we start going full steam . . .

My leave was a tremendous success, well worth waiting a year for, and don't think it doesn't make me happy to think I won't have to wait so long for another one.

Much love to everyone, especially you know who (or whom, as the "case" may be).

As ever, Lovingly Bill

March 5, 1944, Sunday evening 2000

Dear Mother:

Today was our half day off and I spent the whole morning in bed, which isn't strange since I didn't get back to the barracks till 3:00am.

I had been hoping all week to hear & see the *Barber of Seville*, which was being given in San Antonio. Couldn't make reservations by phone and there were no tickets available when Newell McCartney [ETHS friend and fellow instructor-pilot student] and I got there. We did hear parts of the overture from the outside, however.

My flight instructor has been criticizing me for being tense in the air and sent me up for a check with the squadron commander yesterday. Apparently, the latter thought there was some hope for me, because I have been assigned to a new instructor.

Already, several boys have been eliminated and more go each day.

My new instructor thinks my trouble may be due to concentrating too much on the instrument panel. When I fly next, he is going to have me cover up some of the instruments.

Instructors must have a lot of precision and polish in their work, and I may not have developed these qualities sufficiently yet. I will try hard to meet the requirements, even though I hope, in many ways, not to . . . The student officers have a very nice lounge in the Gunter Hotel and steaks are good in a nearby café.

Our time is completely taken up by flying and ground school and when we fly in the afternoon, the evenings are very short because we don't have supper until 1930 (7:30pm). This week we'll also be flying at night, which is always a pain in the neck . . .

Have crawled halfway through the *House of Seven Gables* and am thoroughly bored by it. It may pick up when I finally hear what the mystery behind [who] Clifford is.[3]

I think of you often . . .   Lovingly, Bill

March 11, 1944, Saturday

Dear Mother:

. . . I think my flying improved last week, at least I am not as tense as I was. My new instructor was right, apparently, when he diagnosed my trouble as flying both instruments and contact at the same time. Whenever I go up with him now, he has two of my key instruments covered and hollers every time he sees me looking at the others.

I don't think I had a pure personality clash with my first instructor. I liked him very well, and I think he liked me, in fact, he gave me a ride to town this morning.

Requirements have gone way up with our class and will be as strict from now on. Before we're through, I wouldn't be at all surprised if 50% of us are eliminated. Newell McCartney has "gone" already, and so have many more. Most of these will get good assignments, so don't feel too badly about it . . .

Night flying isn't necessarily more dangerous than day flying. If you go to sleep on the controls, it doesn't matter whether it's dark or light out.

It's no fun flying this Vibrator [Consolidated Vultee Valiant, BT-13] from the rear cockpit. Visibility is rotten and being behind the center of gravity, you don't have the feeling of being the ship's master, as you do in front.

Lt. Wetzel turned out to be in my squadron and only lives two doors down the hall. We have a few mutual friends, too.

Well, best of everything during the week, and much love to you.

As ever, Lovingly Bill

March 15, 1944

Dear Dad:

Fears of not qualifying are hardly groundless, but I'm improving and have about a 50-50 chance! Flying from the rear cockpit takes an entirely different technique.

Heard from my three best friends all through Cadet Training. One is co-pilot on a Flying Fortress, the other two are flying P-40's, and I'm struggling away in the rear of a Vultee Vibrator. Rotten luck, believe me.

Have been having bad weather the last few days and have been enjoying the extra rest and free time. The "tenseness" comes from flying with an instructor; I am absolutely at ease solo or with another 2nd Lieutenant. Can you see how that works? Eagerness to do well, I suppose.

Write soon again, Fat, and lots of luck to you. Hope you get home soon.

As Ever, Bill

March 19, 1944, Sunday night

Dear Mother:

Spent the morning flying formation. This is not especially difficult and is quite a bit of fun, even in a BT-13a. There were lots of bushy cumulus clouds in the sky today, and we had a good time flying around and over them, but everything was much better in that wonderful little AT-6.

This has been a fine week for me from the letter viewpoint. I heard from almost every member of the family and got a number of other letters besides. One was from Liz Parker, the BMC secretary. Wish you'd tell AA. Swell of her to write, gave me the latest news about how high Rainey holds her tail now that I have wings, etc.

AA will be interested to know that Derek, the colt we used to watch running in the rye field, has been sold. I remember how he used to throw back his head and bend his knees when he ran.

Also thought of my weekly Sunday morning walk down the valley with Rainey. Today would have been a great day for it, clear and cool, for a change. We've been having rotten weather, but it's welcome because we get some free time.

I've finished *For Whom the Bell Tolls*. [Ernest] Hemingway's characters are real all right, but I haven't been able to *see* them in either of his books I've read, and I haven't been made to feel the "great" love in either story. I liked Jordan's conversations with himself and think they were the best part of the book. Am reading *Between Two Worlds*! Tell Frances.[4]

By the way, if you can send me any jockey shorts (don't forget type and *brand*) size 32″ (or 34″) I wish you'd send them down. Can't get any down here and could use a couple of pairs.

Bought a new pair of shoes from Air Corps Supply. They will be swell for everyday and flying use and I can save my $8.50 boys for best.

Tell the girls I appreciated their letters and will answer them soon. Thanx again for yours. Hope you have a good week. Getting much sack time.

Lots of love, Mom,   As ever, Bill

March 21, 1944

Dear Mother:

I'm glad to say that I have been graduated. I was never sure of this and there have been many times when I was convinced, I'd be eliminated. Anyway, I passed.

Leave tomorrow afternoon for Bainbridge, Georgia. Ever heard of it? Six months ago, I went there as a dumb cadet. Now I'm going as a dumb instructor, but there has been progress, at least.

Address me care of BAAF Bainbridge, Ga and I'll write when things get settled. I think I arrive BAAF Friday.

Lots of Love, Lovingly, Bill

March 21, 1944

Dear Dad:

Am happy to say that I squeezed by this course and am leaving tomorrow for Bainbridge, Georgia.

I was definitely a border line case but think I will be able to handle the job. In many ways I'm glad to be going back to Bainbridge. I won't have to learn new traffic patterns and flying areas, and I will get a certain satisfaction in returning as an officer to the field I served at as a cadet.

I don't know if there is a BOQ, but I rather think so. If not, I'll have to live in town, which would be more expensive and inconvenient. But it would be nice in other ways . . .

Your bowling scores are good for not having practiced in so long. I haven't bowled since I've been here. Will hate to leave San Antonio for Bainbridge, as there is quite a difference in the two places.

I've been thinking of taking up the guitar. Wonder if you *can* actually teach yourself with the aid of one of those books. I will have more time to myself from now on and would like some way to "make music." A mouth organ might be more practical, but it would be hard to accompany myself and it seems a shame to let my rich baritone go unheard. Someday I'm going to take piano lessons.

I am now glad to be an instructor, because my "term" will be for only a few months, and I will be a much better pilot at the end of that time and will have a very good experience in dealing with other people and teaching them to fly.

Glad you're in a successful job. Hope you can get home soon. Address me BAAF, Bainbridge, Ga. Am going by Pullman and will arrive sometime Friday evening, I believe.

Good luck!   As ever, Bill

Correspondence as
AN INSTRUCTOR-PILOT
BAINBRIDGE ARMY AIR FIELD

March 26, 1944

Dear Mother,

Back at dear old Bainbridge! Arrived here very dirty Friday afternoon and, after taking a hotel room and getting cleaned up, reported to the adjutant.

I was assigned a room in the BOQ. It is a large room with 5 big windows, plenty of drawer and locker space, writing tables, and three other officers. One is the same officer who gave my class lectures on the radio range system. He seems very nice, but I've had little to do with him so far, and the others are away.

The Officer's Club is nearby and is a swell spot. There is a swimming pool about 200 yds. from my door, and I expect to take lots of morning and evening dips in it. An orderly makes my bed every morning and leaves my shoes nicely shined. I don't think this is going to be so bad, though there is not one instructor here who wouldn't give his right leg to be somewhere else.

Have spent all my time to date signing different forms and going from one office to another. You have no idea how much paperwork there is involved.

Have an interview with the Colonel tomorrow, will fly for a day or longer with the Advisory Board, and then be assigned students.[5] [Cadet class] 44G came in today and it is likely I'll start off with them. I hope so, anyway.

Have seen most of the instructors I knew as a cadet, but haven't run across Lt. Beaver, who was my instructor.

My trunk has not arrived from San Antonio and so I have to wear my greens, which need cleaning and are terribly hot. The temperature is way up in the 80's and the sun is very bright. Good old South Georgia.

Life is certainly not going to be cheap as an officer. I pay $1 a day for food, $45 a month for my room and there are dues and special expenses at the Officer's Club.

The cadet area looks about the same and brings back memories of Ernie Gyurits and what now seem happy times.[6] The mess hall has been remodeled and the food down there has improved 1,000%.

I'm going to take a short nap and will write you later on. Mail will be forwarded from San Antonio.

Hope everything is OK. Lots of Love, 　　　　As ever, Lovingly Bill

---

March 27, 1944, Monday nite [sic]

Dear Mother,

Didn't get a chance to finish the letter to you.

My baggage arrived today, so I'm settled and at last am wearing clean clothes.

The trip from San Antonio was A1 except for the ride from Montgomery here. I had an upper to Montgomery and enjoyed myself, though I prefer a car to a train any day.

Do you know Mr. or Mrs. Harold Gould, Noyes St. Evanston? I am living next to Gould's brother-in-law, Lt. Connery [Conary], who is head of the navigation dept. in the cadet ground school. He wants to fly up to Chicago with me sometime.[7]

Will finish this so you'll hear from me Wednesday. Somehow, the front on my [watch] face became cracked, so I have to send it to Jane to have it fixed. Am being treated like a million dollars.

Lots of love. Hope everything is OK.   As ever, Lovingly Bill

---

April 2, 1944

Dear Mother:

Thanx for your letter which arrived yesterday. I'm sure the shorts will be forwarded from Randolph, and I thank you for them, too.

One thing I need very badly, but which I'm afraid you won't be able to send, is an alarm clock. If you can get one, please do send it quickly. Don't forget I can never get too many letters, cookies, etc.

Have finished my first week of instructing. I'm always surprised when I hear myself lecturing to my six cadets, and am amazed at how funny my jokes have suddenly become.

I flew all day yesterday, getting in almost eight hours in the air, all of it with these stupid students who make exactly the same mistakes fifty times in a row, just as I used to do. And don't think I didn't get shaken up a bit by uncoordinated turns and rough spin recoveries.

My cadets are Jacot, Jackson, Jajich, Ingram, Ingham, and Iversen, and they seem very anxious to please me.[8]

Have come down with a chest cold and am trying to get rid of it today, as I'm hoping to solo Jacot and Ingham Tuesday and want to ride with them tomorrow.

Otherwise, I'm fine. We're having lots of rain, and the Flint River is higher than ever before. It's very interesting to see the flood from the air.

Am getting along very well here and like the C.O. of my flight very much. Put my name on a list requesting fighter training, but don't expect to hear anything for a long time. There is a rumor that this is going to be made a twin-engine school, in which case my chances would be better.

I'm awfully glad when I hear that you have spent a morning or afternoon at one of the girls' houses. Hope you'll be able to see dad soon. Will not write him as he probably has left St. Joe [St. Joseph, Missouri]. Hope Wese likes *Hull House*.[9]   As ever, Lovingly Bill

---

April 5, 1944

Dear Dad:

Your airmail arrived today. I have not written before because I've been expecting to hear that you've been home and are en route to Calgary, or someplace.

I am in full swing now with my Cadets. I have seven now, six whom I've had ever since they arrived at Basic from Primary. Two of "my boys" are about ready to solo and may do so tomorrow after I shoot a few more landings with them. One, I am afraid I will have to wash out. He just doesn't have what it takes but is trying so hard I feel badly about it.

I like the Cadets, and I think they like me. In the morning, I come out of the instructor's dressing room and the Cadets meet me in a semicircle. After exchanging salutes, I tell them who I will ride with and what I plan to have them do. Before solo we concentrate on things like stalls, forced landing practice, spins, and climbs and glides. Then, after the morning lecture (1/2 hour of questions, etc.) we all go out to the plane. I get in the back seat and act indifferent, and the Cadet who rides first climbs in front and fumbles around trying to get the engine started before I ask him what the devil he is waiting for.

Most of the rides last an hour and I usually ride five times a morning or afternoon, and rarely stir out of my seat the whole time. I only fly half a day and, except for three hours of PT a week and two lectures, I have the rest of the day off. I have grade slips to make out, but they seldom take more than an hour.

It's over a mile from the BOQ to the flight line and I'm thinking of buying a bike for going back and forth this summer. One would be very convenient to have and would help keep me in shape, but the only one I can get is pretty darn expensive.

Incidentally, PT for me means tennis, swimming, baseball. Oh hum.

Congratulations on your raise. It seems hardly possible to me that you've been with May [Company] for over a year. You are obviously doing fine work, though it's too bad you don't like the Co. better.

I was interested to hear about the basketball tournament. Vultee Aircraft Corp. is the company that makes the plane I'm flying.

There's nothing to do here in the entertainment line, but so far the time has gone quickly enough. The flying is a little more tiring than you would think as it is quite a responsibility in being up with Cadets who insist on putting the plane in unusual positions. It certainly keeps us on our toes. I fly all day Easter, which is too bad, but have Saturday off!

Dad, I hope you'll be getting home soon and that if you don't, you'll find something interesting to do when you're not working. I think of you often and wish I could be with you.

Best of everything,

As ever, Lovingly Bill

Write soon.

April 6, 1944

Dear Mother:

This will have to be a short letter and I'm sorry it can't tell you that I've sent you a box of Whitman's or a pair of stockings. Neither can be bought in Bainbridge, and as a matter of fact, I didn't know Sunday was Easter until day before yesterday.

. . . Last year I went to church in Cookeville, Tenn. The minister was stamping his feet and wiping his eyes all through the sermon. He had quite an effect on himself.

Saturday, I have off but fly both morning and afternoon Sundays. Have written dad a letter about the instructing, so will not repeat myself. It's not a hard job, though it is darn tiring to stay strapped to that seat for five straight hours while dumb Cadets rack it all around the sky. Haven't soloed any of mine yet but expect to tomorrow and Sunday.

I have to have three hours of PT a week (instead of six as a Cadet). Can play baseball, tennis and get credit so that's pretty nice. Also, must get ten hours of Link Trainer this month, which will be very valuable for me.[10]

I am pretty sure of being able to fly my own plane home this summer. One of the other instructors has flown to Chicago twice. I'll leave at dawn and get up there for a late lunch—spring salad, ham sandwiches, chocolate milk.

My cold has disappeared, and I'm feeling OK again. Did not have to lose any flying time either.

Am afraid I'll have to wash out Iversen. He's trying hard, so I hate to do it, but he just doesn't have the stuff. Ingham is becoming a sweet flier, and the others are about average. Jackson is a little weak.

Had breakfast this morning with the commanding officer of my flight when I was a Cadet. Seems funny.

I wonder if you will have to work Sunday. I hope you'll be able to see the girls sometime during the day. Sally [Jo] sent some pictures . . . which I'm awfully glad to have. I have all my family pictures in "menus" [Bill's humor] on my dresser.

Thank Wese for sending the book. Will read it tonight. It looks very interesting.

I send you lots and lots of love for Easter, Mom, if nothing else.

As ever, Lovingly Bill

April 17, 1944

Dear Mother,

Went to the Post Chapel yesterday, which makes the first time since last July in Montgomery that I have been to church. I enjoyed the music and singing a great deal but was unimpressed by the sermon. I'm all for churches without preachers and without Sunday evening get togethers.

After church, I took a date to Bob Ketchum's apartment for dinner. Austin (I call his wife that because she's so small) had a swell dinner for us, and I helped fry the chicken and mash the potatoes.

We finished dinner about four, went downtown for bowling, then back for lunch, cards, etc. It really was one of the best days I have had in the Army. Bob K and I are good friends, he also is an instructor, and Austin has given me the key to the house, figuratively speaking. It seems good to be able to have this sort of friendship.

Austin expects a baby in the fall and is sure I will be a great help when the time comes by reason of my experience with pregnant sisters. She was very impressed by what I was able to do for AA at Black Mountain.

We're still on a double schedule, and I'm pretty darn well shaken up and tired at the end of the day. The eight hours in the air isn't so bad in itself, it's just that the Cadets are so very rough on the controls.

Today, I gave one of my boys a spin, out of which he had to recover in a dive. He started to pull up from the dive, I kept the stick forward until I got enough speed to do a loop. After I pulled it through the Acrobatics, I picked up the microphone and yelled "who in hell told you to recover from a spin that way?" He turned around and with a very worried look on his face said "but, Sir-"

My students are almost through with their elementary air work and I'm starting them on Chandelles and Lazy eights. During the course of the hour-long rides, I usually throw in some Acrobatics to keep them interested. The BT doesn't handle nearly as well as the AT-6 and is not as powerful, but you can have lots of fun in it anyway.

This seems like a funny request, but sometime soon stop in at Lyon & Healy's [music store in Evanston] and see if you can get me a fairly good harmonica and a book telling how to play it. I can think of no way I would rather spend my evenings than learning to play a musical instrument and the harmonica seems most practical. If you have a better suggestion let me have it, if not let me know the cost of the thing as soon as you can.

The brownies have come and gone and were even better than usual. Thanx a lot also for your letters which I look forward to every week.

Wonder if you'll have any luck with an alarm clock? Hope so. Pop dropped a card saying he was leaving St. Joe and so I hope you saw him yesterday.

Am finding my bike darn useful and a lot of fun. I get a lot of good-natured kidding about it. "Will I check them out in two wheels?" etc.

Well, lots of love to you, Mom, don't work too hard and don't forget the harmonica. Bainbridge has nothing of course.

As ever, Lovingly Bill

April 23, 1944, Sunday

Dear Mom:

Well, another week has gone by, but quickly. Today, I didn't have to fly until 12:30 so I slept until about 9:30 and lay in bed for two hours reading *Dodsworth*. It is an *excellent* book.[11] Then I had dinner at the Officer's Club and bicycled to the flight line. Gave two air work rides and a formation ride and then flying was called off due to an approaching storm. I had to fly on the outskirts of the storm and, despite all I've read of flying in and near storms, I was amazed and a bit frightened at how the plane was tossed about by updrafts and downdrafts. Ships have actually been thrown up and down thousands of feet in a few seconds, though, of course. I ran into no such violence. It was hard enough, however, and the Cadet in front was really scared.

Last night, I spent another evening with a date at the Ketchum's and as usual with them, had a fine time. I was free yesterday afternoon and got a little sack time, after which I went for a swim in the pool. Pretty soft, eh? This summer I expect to run over for short dips before breakfast.

We're no longer on double schedule. Now, as normally, we fly in the morning and afternoon on alternate days. When I fly in the morning, I get up at 0515 and am on the line at 0600, lecture to my boys on the day's work until 0630, and then takeoff. Flying is over at 1230. In the afternoon we begin to fly at 1245 and are done at 1900. Most of the time I never get out of the plane, though sometimes I do, to stretch, while the next cadet to ride gets settled in front. The other five cadets meet the ship and walk the wing tips to the taxiway. Sometimes I have them bring me out a candy bar and coke. Until yesterday, I was leading my flight in number of hours, but are now in second place.

... Remember our Dickens project which sort of fizzled? Sinclair Lewis understands the American "way of mind" and I think you'd be very interested in *Dodsworth*!

Well, old lass, this will have to do for now. You ought to get a bike to ride to 400. Must be a long walk, but not unpleasant in the spring.

Write me all the news as usual. I really look forward to your letters.

Lots of love,   As ever Lovingly Bill

April 26, 1944

Dear Pop:

I have your two airmails, and as usual am interested to read of your work, though just what "job evaluation" is, I am not sure ...

I have been transferred to another squadron and am now serving as an instructor in the same flight [B Flight] I was in as a Cadet. Many of the old instructors, including mine, Lt. Beaver, are still there, and the squadron commander who was someone to fear in the old days, is plain "Jim" now.[12] All of the instructors, the C.O. and asst. C.O. are fine fellows, and I get along with them very well.

Because I was transferred, I had to leave the boys I soloed last month (first of this month) and now have a new lot of six fresh out of Primary. Yesterday they came down to the line and we crowded around the plane, which is really something to them, while I explained the instruments and controls. Then I started the engine for them and helped each one start it afterward.

Today, I gave them their "dollar rides;" I did all the flying, taking them around the flying area, pointing out auxiliary fields, landmarks, restricted zones, etc. Tomorrow, they begin to learn to fly the BT and it is my job to prepare them to solo by 10 hours.

Mother has sent me a "tonette" which is a musical instrument, and I don't know how else to describe it. It is a cross between a whistle and a clarinet and I've spent several hours playing it. Already, I have "mastered" *Old Black Joe* and *America*. It's an awful lot of fun and *it's music*. One of its best features is that it will play sharps and flats and I've sent to the Co. [company] in Chicago for a book of instructions and a book of classical music, especially arranged for Tonette. It's really just what I wanted.[13]

Well, Fat, up at 0515 tomorrow, so to bed now. Will let you know what progress I make with my new boys.

Let me hear from you soon. Best wishes, old boy, and good luck.

As ever, Lovingly Bill

May 7, 1944, Sunday

Dear Mother:

. . . I have been transferred to B Flight, the same one I was in as a Cadet. That meant that I had to start again with boys just in from Primary. Yesterday I soloed the fifth and last of my six new students.

It's really quite a responsibility to send one of the boys up by himself. If anything happens, it's the instructor's fault. The procedure for soloing is this: We have spent about five hours (one-hour at a time) practicing stalls, spins, forced landings, and other elementary maneuvers and then we start shooting landings at one of the auxiliary fields. Comes a time when I think the Cadet might live through some solo landings, I climb out of the rear cockpit, slap him on the back, and send him up alone for three landings.

Afterward, when he taxis up beside me with a big grin on his face, I look bored and try not to show that I'm pleased and very much relieved.

The funny part about it is that I will never trust those boys to make a good landing and when I'm in the plane, I'm always right on the controls with them. Yet I send them up by themselves.

Thursday I was control officer in the portable tower, which is placed right out beside the runway. As such it was my duty to regulate traffic by means of radio, and for my three-hour shift, I was boss over every plane landing and taking off. Roger.

This is darn interesting work, and I can tell that my flying has improved tremendously. Am building up a great deal of time, too.

Well, will close and hope you are having a good time with pop and that you will have a good week at Lyman's.   As ever, Lovingly, Bill

Getting a lot of enjoyment out of the Tonette! Extra $1.50 is for book sent to Jean. Her birthday is this month, but don't know date [the date was May 13]. Sent a present in March by mistake!

May 23, 1944

Dear Mother:

Hope you'll excuse me for being a poor correspondent this week.

Three packages arrived from Evanston today, but I'm saving them for Thursday [for birthday on May 25]. Thanx in advance . . .

Am flying formation now, finishing up the cadets who will receive the last half of their basic training in twin-engine ships. I think I am "permanent party" in Flight B, and I certainly hope so. Lt. Thompson, the C.O. [James Thompson], says he hopes so, too.

Today, Lt. Phil Labor, a Filipino whom I see a great deal [Bill and Phil trained together at Douglas Field, Georgia], and I were flying on each of Lt. Hendrix's wings, with our students, of course. Hendrix is the asst. C.O. and led us through some merry rat races (in trail). All very much fun, but against regulations . . . [14]

Don't count on me in June. August seems quite likely, however. After this class is done, I probably will have to take an instrument course, which will delay my leave until after the next class.

Was pleased that dad was home for a week and will be glad if you send his new address soon.

Still get a lot of pleasure out of my Tonette, though I'm not sure the others in building 683 enjoy it as much as I do.

Thank you again for the packages, and may I thank you for the typewriter?

Lots of love, and don't work too hard.   As ever, Lovingly Bill

Have spent the evening here (at the club) reading the *Reader's Digest* and *Time*. A very nice spot, with a big screened in porch and comfortable chairs. Ah!

May 28, 1944

Dear Mother:

I've just gotten out of bed, having slept for 10 hours and read for two, and now I have just time for a note to you, before eating and getting down to the flight line by 1230.

Your swell package arrived on May 25 . . . The typewriter will arrive this week, I presume, and please tell Wese I'm delaying my thanx to her until I can pound them out, and also my impressions of *The Little Prince*.[15]

I'm terribly pleased for you that the Groses and Jess and Cayo will be in Evanston soon. I know how glad you'll be to see your sisters again [Bill's aunts, Carolyn Grose and Jessie Pope, and his cousin, Cayo Pope] . . .

Well, must get dressed and go up to the club for dinner. Will be through flying about 1930.

Much love and many thanks for your birthday thoughtfulness.

As ever, Lovingly Bill

Are you a Dewey man, or is there someone else you'd like to see defeated by FDR? Let me hear about your politics, someday.[16]

May 28, 1944, Sunday evening

Dear Dad:

I was very glad to get your letter on May 25 and the package from you and mother, which arrived on the same day. Thank you very much for both.

I'm surprised you don't like district #1, as I should think you'd see far more interesting places than in the "Dust bowl," and anyway at this season Michigan must be much more comfortable than Nebraska.

As you see, I am writing at the club, where I almost always spend my evenings. There is a very nice and fairly large screened-in porch, furnished comfortably with easy chairs and reading lamps, which overlooks a patio with more chairs and tables and the swimming pool . . .

Tomorrow morning, I begin the instructor's instrument course, which will prepare me to teach instruments. I had thought I wouldn't get this course until between classes, but since I'm getting it now, there is at least a possibility that I can get home toward the end of June. I'm not counting on it, however, because lots of things can happen. Anyway, for the next two weeks I'll be flying with the Instrument Board half the day and my Cadets the other half.[17]

Taught four hours of Acrobatics today and I feel like a milkshake. Acrobatics are anything but fun after the first hour.

Well, Fat, will finish this now and hope to hear from you soon. As you can tell I'm leading a miserable life here. Oh hum, guess I'll take a swim.

Very best of luck and my love to you.   As ever, Bill

Am now back in my room. Jack Shimko, my roommate, is working on a model of a P-51. He has a P-38 hanging from our decking. Does excellent work. A precision craftsman, if I ever knew one, and a swell guy, too.

June 4, 1944

Dear Dad:

. . . Thursday night [June 1st] I was detailed to go on bivouac. About 60 enlisted men and 15 officers had to go, (it is a weekly affair, but not weekly for me).

We were led on a 7-mile hike with packs, and finally arrived at our campsite in the woods. This was about five PM and we had a good meal of stew, eating out of mess kits the way I did in Miami. After mess we put up our tents (I shared one with a Filipino LT. I know well) and chewed the fat until dark. [Bill shared a tent with Phil Labor.]

Then the major called all the officers to his tent and explained the tactical problem we had to work. He had a rough map of the area showing woods, ditches, lakes, and the enemy positions, as well as the location of our own troops.

I was in charge of six men and was supposed to hunt out a machine gun nest in one corner of the woods, wipe it out and then proceed to the main objective.

While I was leading my men down a ravine, the chemical warfare dept. tossed a tear gas bomb at us, and you can bet we lost no time in putting on our gas masks. We managed to survive this obstacle and had to cross a pasture on our bellies in rocks to get to where I expected to find the enemy.

Well, we got to the enemy's woods and very quietly, most of the time on our hands and knees, combed the area for the machine gun nest. After over an hour and a half of this, one of the men reported seeing "a sentry box-like-building which looked suspicious," so I gave orders to surround it.

I then crept around and made sure each man understood what he was to do when we stormed the building, and then gave the signal to attack. Well, we dashed up to the sentry box, expecting to have stones or pebbles thrown at us, but met no opposition. In fact, all we found was two empty holes!

It was getting late and close to the time for me to meet the others and support the main drive, so we had to give up the search for the machine gun nest, which turned out to be in someone else's section. Nevertheless, we got a big kick out of capturing a deserted outhouse. Needless to say, I slept exceedingly well, despite chiggers and wood ticks.[18]

Well, Pop, I want you to know how I enjoy hearing from you and would like very much to hear that you are enjoying yourself, which after all is the most important thing in life.

The absolute best of everything to you. Good luck, old boy.

As ever, Bill

June 12, 1944, Monday

Dear Mother and all:

As you might be able to tell, the typewriter has arrived and is being put to use. Thanks awfully for sending it and for having it packed so well. I hope the money I sent for that purpose covered the charges . . .

The trip from Ft. Lauderdale to Daytona was made along the coast all the way. We had very good beam connections, which is fortunate, because it was raining practically all the time and the visibility was very poor. We came from Daytona to Bainbridge at night, but the weather was good and the trip not difficult.

Tomorrow I am going to have an interesting experience. A pilot was needed to ferry some PT's [Primary Trainers] from a field south of here to Tuscaloosa, Ala. And I was given the chance to go. It will only be for one day, which is too bad, because I'm given an extra $7. for doing it. I haven't flown a PT since I was at Douglas and sweating through rides with that SOB Dillard, who I bet is a nice guy after all. Am anxious to see how it feels to fly the old thing again.

Am going to get off a letter to dad. No, guess I'll wait till tomorrow and tell him about my ferrying job at slightly less than $7 for a few hours flying. Regards to all the family and my love to you.   Bill

June 13, 1944

Dear Dad:

As you may have learned from the letter I sent mother yesterday, my roommate and I flew down to Miami for the weekend last Saturday. We traveled down the western shore of Florida, almost on top of the beach to Tampa. There we stopped for breakfast and refueling and set out across the state toward Fort Lauderdale, passing along the southern shore of Lake Okeechobee.

Coming back, we went straight up the eastern coast to Daytona Beach, and after a stop there, during which I tried several times to reach the Evans's, we cut over to Bainbridge, passing between Tallahassee and Thomasville. This part of the trip was at night, but I was already familiar with that part of the country, so didn't miss much. Coming up from Fort L. it rained most of the time. We were flying at only 1,500' and the visibility was very poor. We passed several cargo planes, C-47s, on the way to Miami.

Today I had another interesting experience. One of the Primary schools [Dorr Field] near Arcadia, Fla., is being closed and pilots were needed to ferry the PT's to another field. I was given the chance to go, and of course, went. I was flown down in a BT, stopped for lunch at the field at Arcadia, and brought a PT back here in the afternoon. Tomorrow I am to fly it up to Tuscaloosa, Ala. and will take the train or bus back from there; all these expenses very adequately taken care of by the USA. As a matter of fact, I will make nearly $7. a day extra and travel pay.[19]

Coming up from Arcadia, I flew directly over Lakeland and looked as hard as I could for H.B. Craven's house but was unable to find it. Have dropped him a card about it. So, in the last few days I have seen a great deal of the state of Florida. Saturday down the west coast, Sunday up the east coast, and Tuesday right up the middle. Most of the land is wasteland, there being miles and miles of nothing but brush and swamps. This is especially true down by the Everglades, as you know, but is true to a lesser degree of all Florida away from the coasts.

I am still taking the instrument course and this ferrying job is cutting in on my time, so I probably won't be through in time to get up to Chicago. However, I haven't given up hope for this month and it's not impossible that I can manage to fly up there, but they put so many obstacles in the way of long cross countries for pilots with less than a year's rating, that I may not be able to make connections.

Well, Pop, I'm looking forward to hearing from you and want to apologize again for the misunderstanding of a couple of weeks ago when you made the trip home expecting to see me. I think of you often and am always glad to hear about your job, and also your political views. As the war begins to develop and we get more of an idea how it will progress in the future, I become more convinced how much we need good old FDR in there during the crucial next few years. I don't think Bricker has a chance.[20] Dewey would make a formidable opponent, but what sort of a President?

Very best of luck to you as always, and special love for Father's Day.

As ever, Bill

June 26, 1944

Dear Mother:

I wrote you in my last letter that there was a good possibility of my taking a trip to Pittsburgh with Jack [Shimko]. Unlike the other good possibilities with which you are familiar, I did make the trip and had a perfectly marvelous time.

We took off Thursday afternoon at four and arrived at Pittsburgh, which is near Jack's home, shortly before midnight. At 0130, I caught a train for Philadelphia and got there at nine Friday. Went to Jean's [Forster] office building and we had a talk for an hour . . . After lunch, we took a train to NYC, did some window shopping along Fifth Ave. and met Calamity [Jane] at her hotel at seven. By the way, walking down the Ave., we just happened to run across Linda Willard, who left Evanston eight years ago. We all recognized each other instantly.[21]

. . . Jean and another girl have rented an extremely nice apartment in Germantown, and taking advantage of my right arm, they decided that Sat. was moving day. So, Jean and I loaded ourselves with all sorts of junk and went to her new place, which is really very nice; living room stocked with books and records, dining room, bedroom, kitchen, and bath . . .

Goodnight and love, Bill

June 26, 1944

Dear Dad:

. . . My roommate, Jack Shimko, with whom I flew down to Miami, has over a year's rating as pilot and so can take trips over 500 miles. He was going to his home in Pittsburgh for the weekend, so I went along and took the train to Philly.

Our first stop on the way up was in western Tenn., at Tri-City Airport, which is near Johnson City and two other towns. We arrived there about dusk, and after refueling, took off for

Pittsburgh. The visibility had been poor on the way up, but our view of the Appalachians as we crossed them was impressive. Now we were above the mountains, but hills went up as high as 3,000'.

About half an hour out of Tri-City, we ran into a thick overcast. Radio ranges are scarce around there, so it would have been impossible to go above and keep up with our navigation. The overcast was close to the ground, and because of the nature of the terrain it would have been too dangerous to fly underneath at night. There was only one thing we could do, and that was to fly right through the middle.

I have had a great deal of instrument time under the hood in an airplane and in a Link Trainer, but never before have flown instruments under actual instrument conditions. And believe me it was a real experience. I lowered my seat as low as possible, so as to have an easier view of the instruments and also to be less likely to be blinded by lightning flashes, and did the flying, while Jack was in front trying to keep track of our position by radio fixes. The overcast lasted for about an hour, but the storm for only 10 or 15 minutes. Needless to say, we got out all right and ended up just west of Pittsburgh. There it was a simple matter to turn on the old beam and go right on in.

Pittsburgh is very impressive at night. There are many chimneys ablaze, and I was given a new conception of the greatness of our production [capabilities].

We arrived there Thursday night. Friday night, the tornado passed one mile from the field. Sunday, when we took off, we could see very clearly the path it made when it passed through a small town.

On the way home, we took a detour and went out and buzzed Jack's house in Windber, Pennsylvania. We did rolls above his home and flew very low over it and waved to his family out in the yard.

Coming home, we had ideal weather conditions. Most of the trip was at night, and a bright moon made it a pleasure to fly.

Dad, I was glad to get your letter re[garding] income and expenses and agree completely with all you say about being fortunate to have the work, etc. I just feel that you are being cheated of something that is rightfully yours, and hope that sometime soon, something will happen so you can live with mother as you should. That is more important than anything I can think of, except the necessity of reelecting Roosevelt. Am sure you will work equally hard in both causes.

The Republicans will probably make damn fools of themselves in Chicago, and it would save them a lot of trouble if someone gave them all a push off Navy pier.

Hope to hear from you soon and believe me, I'm making every effort I can to see you before long. Very best regards and lots of luck to you. As ever, Bill

---

July 10, 1944 10:00

Dear Mother:

Haven't written you for much longer than usual, and I'm afraid this can't be much of a letter. Have been more busy than usual, but expect things to become normal by the time you and dad get here, and I can't wait for that.

I was awfully glad to hear your voice the other night, and those of several McFadden's the night before.

Ken Allen came down to see me Sat. night. We spent Sat. evening together, but I had to fly Sunday morning and so we only had half of Sunday. I don't think I know anyone with a better mind than his, and the Army is helping him in some ways. He has developed a case of arthritis and is on limited service with the Finance Office at Fort Benning. He has put on over 30 pounds and looks much better for it.[22]

Twice a week, all the officers on the post have to go to a War Orientation lecture given at the post theater, and that's where I have to go now. So long.

July 10, 1944 (2015)

Back again. I've been wondering, and especially since "entertaining" Ken Allen for one weekend, if you know what you're going to find here. The evenings we can take care of very nicely at the club or in your hotel, but what you are going to do during the day when I am flying is beyond me.

The club will be at your disposal, and of course so will your hotel, and at least you will be well pleased with both. But about all you can do in either is sit and talk and will you be bored? I know how grand it will be to be with pop again, but you shouldn't waste more than a couple of your days together down here. Maybe that's all your plans include, and for your sakes, I hope so.

. . . Have had two letters from Leila, one in thanks for my picture which I sent her. She says I look OK and can't understand why I should be for Roosevelt. I will take great pleasure in canceling her vote, or dad's, can't decide which. How about yours?

Well, Mom, will stop rambling on. Keep me informed about your plans, the days you expect to be here, etc. If you take my advice about only staying two or three days, try to include a weekend!

Love to all and you know how much to you.   As ever, Lovingly, Bill

---

July 30, 1944

[Letter below written after his parents visited Bainbridge.]

Dear Mom:

I suppose dad has a new assignment and you are back at Lyman's and things have settled back to normal. They have with me, but not quite, because I have the fun of remembering the times you were here and the places I showed you; like my room, the lounge, the flight room and line, the theater, etc. Golly, but it was fun having you here!

. . . We have a new instructor in our Flight to replace poor [name deleted], so now I have only four students, which makes things much easier, because now I can ride with them all each day. We are flying instruments now, and this is my first class instructing them. I fly in the front seat for this phase of the training, and the student in the rear with a hood inside the canopy. I will give each cadet 17 hours of instruments, and after that will start Acrobatics, formation, night flying, and cross countries.

My trip to Washington-Chicago fell through, as you can see. Next week I am Officer of the Guard, so will not be able to go anywhere then either, but I can promise you I'll get up there this summer or early fall.

It has turned out that you came down at the best time, because they have kept me busy during my "free" half day, studying the carbine [M-1 carbine, infantry weapon], and Monday I have to fire the darn thing. Also, the weather has returned to normal. The days are hot and sticky, but the nights are not bad at all.

There was a dance at the Club last night, but it was held in the lounge because of rain. I went, but got tired of dancing with other men's wives, so came home relatively early, and slept till noon. Went to the movies with one of the weather officers (not one of my roommates) this afternoon, and Jim Gould and I bowled this evening.[23] In fact, I've just come from the alleys. Will make no mention of my score, so you can assume I broke no records.

Thanks for your numerous cards and your letter. I have one today from dad, enclosing several uninspiring articles and one very good cartoon which I will send to Leila. It has a little poem, which points out that "Uncle Joe" was once "Bloody Joe." [Refers to Joseph Stalin of the Soviet Union.] That's one thing that worries me. Should we be so unreservedly happy about the Russian advance into Poland? That's just where they were going before they were at war with Germany.

Won't let dad forget the $5.00 bet we have on the election, and if you or any other member of the family wants to take that sort of a wager, I'm on!

Give my best to all at home and my love to you.　　　As ever, Bill

---

August 6, 1944, Sunday

Dear Mother:

This will be a short letter because I am Officer of the Guard today and must get back to the Guardhouse. I have just finished dinner at the Enlisted Men's Mess. The food was on a par with that at the club, but not served as nicely, of course.

We have been having more rotten weather and so are far behind our flying schedule. To make up for it, we had to be down on the line yesterday afternoon and this morning, but it rained both times so we could do nothing but play cards. My luck has continued to be good, and this morning I won $1.10. I haven't lost a thing yet. Shall I be a professional gambler instead of a beachcomber?

This afternoon finished *Oil!* by Upton Sinclair. Where did you get the idea I was reading *Personal History*? It was *Autobiography of Lincoln Steffens.*[24]

. . . Didn't write you that Jack Shimko is now a first Lt. He got his promotion the day after you left. He and Bill Recktenwald, who is one of the weather officer roommates you didn't meet, flew up to Pittsburgh Friday. I couldn't go because of the flying schedule, and then I didn't fly.

Jack said Jim (the 4th horseman) and I could have his car while he was gone. Jim used it Friday, and last night Sam Barron [Baron], who is the Chemical Warfare officer I introduced you to the last night and who also now has his first, and I drove to Thomasville and ended up with two very nice girls at the Officers Club at the P-39 Base, where there was a dance. The club is not so large as ours, but is equally nice, and dancing was indoors.

Was very glad to get your long letter and one from Fran and Jane. AA has finally given up all pretense of writing twice a week and has announced (by postcard) that she has "decided to plan" to write to me on Tuesdays. The Republicans are also going to reduce taxes, and rationing, provide jobs for all returning soldiers, balance the budget, and prevent war by means of peace forces.

Really must go. Send you much love as always. Think often of your visit here.

As ever, Lovingly Bill

August 8, 1944

Dear Pop:

. . . Thanks very much for your two letters and clippings. Some I agree with completely, but you know about the others. I don't exactly fear Russia, and yet I guess I do. Anyway, it is certain that she will be occupied with internal matters, to a large extent, after the war, and not as active in Europe as she might otherwise be. I am not against Communism if that's what the people want, but I don't want to see Russia, or England, or America, forcing their type of government on the liberated countries, and I certainly would object to Russian claims to the Baltic states and Poland. Since she fought for and won them before the war, do you think she will consider them her natural booty? We would find it hard to refuse Russia the spoils of war, should she ask for them.

Stalin thinks of Russia, Churchill of the British Empire, and Roosevelt of the relations of all, because he realizes that *this is the way to look out for America.*

. . . Got in some practice landings from the back seat last night. Haven't flown in the back at night since I left Randolph and was surprised at two fairly good landings. Decided I wouldn't try anymore and risk losing my confidence!

Capt. Thompson, who has been the C.O. of B Flight for so long, left last week for B-29s! I have taken up a collection among the fellows in the flight, and when he comes back for the day on the 14th, will present him a box of cigars, or something, from "the boys." Temporarily, at least, Lt. Hendrix, the one you met the night of the dance when it was so noisy, is taking charge. He is much stricter than Thompson and can't get the same amount of work out of the instructors. I personally like him. Our trip to Chicago has been postponed again, and if we don't start getting consistently good flying weather, I probably won't have any weekends at all free, we are so far behind schedule.

Well, Pop, I have to go now. I send you every good wish and hope that you can find some way to entertain yourself in Columbus. Think of you more than you know. Best of luck and love to you.

As ever, Bill

August 20, 1944, Sunday

Dear Mother:

The letter I promised to write during the week didn't materialize, and I apologize. Have been spending most of my evenings at the club with Sam Baron. He is a really brilliant guy, a Jewish Socialist who graduated from Cornell with top honors might well be. He reminds me a good deal of Bob Babcock [Bill's brother-in-law]. I'm surprised that he seems to have taken an interest in me, and I don't know of anyone from whom I could profit more by being with. Anyway, the evenings have gone fast, and I didn't get around to writing to anyone.

. . . I was able to get my grade slips written before the scheduled time for us to stop flying. I am having better luck with these students than I have had before. The chief difference has been in my relations with them. At the first of the class, along the time when you and dad were here, I was pretty darn tough on them and left no doubt in their minds that they were going to have to work for me. But recently, I've been able to loosen up and become more friendly and the boys really respond to the treatment. The trouble with cadets is that when they get to a new school, they're worried and concerned about how hard their instructor is going to be on them, and not how well he will teach them.

Today we were flying formation, and my Cadet twice took his eye off the lead ship, something he had been told a hundred times not to do under any circumstances whatsoever. He washed canopies for two hours.

Capt. Thompson has been transferred to bombers and I think eventually will get B-29's. We were all sorry to see him go, as he was considered the best Flight CO on the field. I collected $25 from all the boys, and we gave him a box of cigars. Hendrix took over the flight for a few days but is now back as Asst. CO and another first Lt., recently transferred from another Basic field, is the CO. Hendrix is a very dominating kind of guy, and he really runs the show.

I do remember the green Indian rug and think it will fit in nicely. I'm accumulating a lot of impediments, but as long as I don't get transferred, it'll be OK. The records are swell to have. Since getting the player I have bought Beethoven's *Ninth Symphony*. It's really about the only set I've got that isn't incidental music.

Fran has sent me *Days of Our Years*, and what I have read in it has been fascinating. Steffen's autobiography has affected my thinking more than any other single book. One quote I especially like: "Freedom of speech is the right of any proper citizen to say anything whatsoever that everyone already believes."[25]

I am very interested in the girls' political activity and hope they will find someone to replace that dope Day as well as Church. Then in '46 all of us can work on our pal Curly. My subscription to *Time* has now taken effect, and in addition to it I see Baron's daily copy of *PM* and his monthly *Protestant*, both of which denounce Ford and other anti-Semitics in every issue. Dad and Leila have been keeping me in touch with the Conservative press, so I'm all set for news.

I am unable to account for the many letters I have received from Fran and AA during the last two weeks. I expect the "touch" daily.

Also, Mother, can you make any suggestions for dad's birthday? If you are planning a "family present," I would like to be included. By the way, there is quite an article in the latest *Post* about George May. I presume he has seen it.

This isn't much of a letter. Phil Labor . . . and I ride to and from the flight line together on our bikes, usually passing our squadron of Cadets marching. The flight room has been painted a light gray and the lockers have been moved around somewhat in the Officer's room. It's fun to know that you have seen all these places where I spend so much time. The plants are doing nicely, and the wandering jew has grown new leaves. The cactus is getting top heavy.

I send you a lot of love and hope you and Wese are having good times together, as I know you are. Regards to all.   As ever, Bill

---

August 27, 1944, Sunday night

Dear Dad:

It's been several weeks since I've written you, but that's because you don't stay in one place long enough. Hope you'll be in Jerseyville [Illinois] when this arrives. I got your address from mother yesterday, and suppose I'll hear from you the first part of the week.

I am enclosing several articles from New York's *PM*, which I think you will find interesting. I see *PM* often and think it is a darn good paper. There is more reading material in one issue than in a whole month of *Tribunes*. As far as clippings from you are concerned, keep on sending the ones you consider especially good. I will do the same for you, and that way we both can maintain somewhat of a balance in our newsgathering. I am reading *Time* regularly. They are for Dewey but are trying to be fair about the campaign. The war news is well presented, and though several days behind the papers, it is more reliable than the papers and the accounts of battles aren't "padded" the way they have to be in a newspaper.

We flew all day today, or at least were supposed to. I got up at 0515 after four hours of sleep, and when I got down to the line, we had a very low overcast and there was no flying at all until after lunch. But we had to stay down in the ready room, anyway. Of course, we played cards. I have set a limit of $1.00 for my losses. When I get up, or down I mean, to that, I quit, so the game is never very expensive for me and it is always a lot of fun. There are games going on for much higher stakes, but I stay away from them, because I have too much to do with the money to throw it away.

There was a dance at the club last night and I took a civilian girl who works on post.

Seems very unfair that I am able to go to dances while the others are out in the fox holes. But I didn't ask for this job, and I may as well make the best of its many good points. According to Drew Pearson's column "Washington Merry-go-round," the Army is planning to release the men on a point system. One point for every month in the service, so many points for every month overseas, eight points for a wife and per child etc. It seems like a fair system. The demobilization will be a long-drawn-out process, and it is wise to have it so, don't you think? AA says she is expecting Bob shortly after Xmas! I think we'll be lucky to be out in 1946.

You remember me talking of Ernie Gyurits. He is the one with whom I used to have steak dinners on the porch at the Stephen Decatur [Bainbridge hotel]. I got a letter from him last week. He is a bomber pilot, B-17, out of England and has been awarded the DFC [Distinguished Flying Cross] and the Purple Heart! At the time he wrote, he was leaving for a rest in Scotland.

Another very good cadet friend writes from England that he is flying the "ship I've always wanted to fly," which I know is the P-51, because we used to talk about it.

Muffie Vaughan writes from Black Mountain that Rainey [pet dog] has moved to New York State with the business manager's family. His name is Orr, a new man. I'm just as well pleased, because down at the college she had many friends, but no one who really looked after her. Every dog should have a master.

. . . Was out for a walk in the country with Sam Baron yesterday and wanted to bring home a small bush I saw. He thought that was "going a little too far," so I didn't. We got caught in the rain and took refuge in some peanut farmer's house. He has 175 acres in peanuts. This year peanuts are selling for $180 a ton, and he gets about a half ton to the acre. That makes $15, 840 gross, and probably close to $10,000 net. He wouldn't be able to harvest the crop if it weren't for the German prisoners. He pays them $.80 a day and says they are real workers. I was surprised at this and said if I were a prisoner of the Germans, I'd do just as little work as possible. But it seems these boys have a quota of work to do, and when it is done, they have earned their $.80 and are through for the day.[26]

This was obviously a wealthy farmer and while his house was a fairly large, freshly painted one, those of his neighbors were the unpainted shacks you see so much of down here. The income of the south may have picked up tremendously, but the greater majority of it is still going to those who have always gotten the breaks.

By the way, the pre-war value of the peanut was as low as $35 a ton, which would reduce this somewhat fabulous income by about a sixth; or do you know your mathematics too?

Heard from Leila last week. She also sends me clippings, but most of them are with foreign issues and Argentina. She has admitted that she is "not at all sure she'll vote for Dewey," which is revolutionary! The fortune poll has so increased my confidence that I will remind you of our $50 bet on the election.

Wese has sent me Wallace's book [Vice President Henry A. Wallace], and I am anxious to learn something about old Hank. Really don't know much about him, except that I instinctively like him because of the *Tribune's* frequent remarks about him.

Well, Pop, I'll put a close to this letter. I hope your work in Jerseyville is interesting and that it is a "good" job. Jerseyville probably doesn't have the cosmopolitan air of Bainbridge, but you can find something to do, I'm sure.

Write soon, and my very best regards to you, old boy.   As ever, Bill

Have not yet played golf, but have circled the course many times and identified the spot where I lost my ball, where you couldn't get out of the rough, etc.

The peanuts are bought, and the oil is what is used. Peanut oil.

September 9, 1944

Dear Fran:

Thanks for your last letter and the two pamphlets about the Independent Voters League. I don't want to join at this time, but I'm enclosing a check for $10, which I'm sure will be decisive in Day's defeat. At least, I hope so.

I have finished all but a dozen or so pages of *Days of Our Years*. It is excellent, though as a narrative rather disconnected and rambling. The insight to European affairs is the thing, however, and in this it is comparable to Steffen's picture of America. I was especially interested in Van Paassen notes on the war in Ethiopia and on the colonial administrations of the French in Africa. So, the "good" people aren't any better than the "bad" people but are *good* because they are *good* in their relations with us, or because we profit from relations with them.

And that's a point I like. I want to vomit when I read and hear the war discussed in terms of Right vs. Wrong. And it's true that that's how most of us see it. Why dammit, if we were Right, there wouldn't have been a war in the first place. The Germans would have seen Hitler as an ambitious fanatic and wouldn't have followed him, the Balkan states would have had no reason to risk national suicide, nor would have Japan, had it been simply a matter of choosing between right and wrong. The trouble with us is that it is impossible for us to conceive ourselves as being wrong, and when an India and a Turkey hesitate to commit themselves, we still do not see that it is because the choice is often between a known evil and an unknown evil.

Japan wished to dominate the East, to "end the white man's rule" there, and why shouldn't she? I want to fight any nation which wants to tell other people how they will live and what they will think, (that is "wrong"), but I wonder if the natives in the Malay states, and the Dutch East Indies (perhaps not the Philippines) give a hang who exploits them, the British, the Dutch, or the Japanese, and even if they might not actually prefer the latter! We read of German and Jap barbarisms, and they are truly horrible. We do not read of French colonial tyrannies, British colonial tyrannies, and Dutch and American tyrannies. We are asked to wage a war against tyrants. I know I don't have to tell you that when civilization goes to the East, it is not to raise the standard of living for the natives.

In this war, Hitler and Japan's war lords are only incidental. The real war, and I guess this is true of all wars, is between those who own the riches of the world and want to keep them, and those who don't own the oil and mineral fields and want them. And the tragedy is that the people really don't give a damn who owns the riches. I like that story about Marshal Petain, who after the last war comforted a mother who had lost her son, by saying, "His death made it possible for us to have Alsace." And she replied, "They can have Alsace, give me back my son."

OK, then it's the big boys we fight for, their interests we protect. Of course, it was necessary to stop Hitler, but wasn't he a natural product of financial imperialism, the Brits, the French, and our own? And it seems inevitable that all we'll do after this war is to cut off the leg, and let the cancer keep on growing. Perhaps that's a trite analogy, but to follow it up anyway, we could say that in 1918 we cut off merely the foot. And to keep from making "the same mistake" this time we're going up to the hip.

But we're not doing anything but suppressing the source of war, and such suppression is hypocritical face-saving, and just exactly as tyrannical as the tyranny we are fighting to suppress.

It's swell to get your occasional letters and I sure am glad to hear of your political activities. You know how I approve of them. I hope old Chuck isn't having continuous trouble. You're making a wise move in going to Colo., if you and he are going to suffer by staying in Evanston. I think I'll live in Evanston, at least for a while. It would be so much fun to live in it and hate it at the same time and think of all the people you can shock!

Right now, I'm beginning a book on Russia. *The Soviet Power*, by the Bishop of Canterbury.[27] Said to [be] very good.

Well, Fran, this is rather a long letter for me.

I want you to give old Tim a clip under the chin for me, and the same for Chuck, who I suppose is walking all over the town. I had hoped to get home this weekend, but as has happened before, I was disappointed. [Tim and Chuck were Bill's nephews.]

I hope to hear from you soon. Give my regards to old Chas and to all the Babcocks . . .

Love to you.   As ever, Bill

September 9, 1944, Saturday

Dear Mother:

. . . Sam Baron has requested and been granted a transfer into the infantry. He leaves next week and has left me two albums of music. One is Beethoven's "Emperor Concerto," the other Franck's "Symphony in D Minor." The arrangement is that I am to keep them until he writes that he does want them, or that he doesn't want them with him. If the former, I send them on; if the latter, I send a check for both sets. And it is a very good buy.

As I told dad when I called him last night, I have until next Wed. free, or thought I did until about 15 minutes ago. Naturally, I put in for a cross-country and seemed reasonably certain of being able to get up to Chicago. At the same minute, the fellow I was going up with couldn't go, which meant that I would have to submit another request, which was out of the question, since they have to be sixty hours in advance of takeoff time.

I was disappointed at not being able to get home, but that has happened before. So Sam and I decided we'd go up to Albany tonight and catch a fast train over to Jacksonville, there to spend our time listening to street cars and other big city and well-loved noises, and to go swimming and lying on the beach. We were to leave at 5:30. At 1:30 I got a call from Operations, saying that I was on orders to go on another ferrying trip, so there went my second plan for a pleasant few days.

I have to report down to the line at 4:00. Because it is raining hard, we will take the train down to Arcadia, Fla., a ride of six to eight hours, I'm sure. If it weren't for the weather, we could fly down in one! At Arcadia, I'll pick up a PT-17, and fly it to Douglas, Georgia! And seeing Douglas, and perhaps Dillard will still be there, will be the only fun connected with the trip. I suppose it will be the train back from Douglas, so I probably won't arrive here until late Tuesday. The new class begins on Wednesday.

The latest latrine rumor is that BAAF will close down Dec. 1. Such rumors have been going around ever since I've been here, but we do know that the Eastern Training Command is closing many schools, and since we're one of the few left open, it seems reasonable that we may be one to close. This would undoubtedly mean that I would have an opportunity to get into [a] tactical outfit, though perhaps not a single engine one, since the emphasis seems more and more on heavy planes. And this emphasis will increase when we transfer our air fleets to the Pacific.

I hope you at home are not too optimistic about the war's end. I don't see how it can possibly be over, with Japan, that is, before the end of '45. And demobilization is going to be a slow process, too. But you can tell Fran I'll be home in plenty of time to help her with the elections in 1946.

. . . I hope you'll excuse me. Have to throw some things into a bag for this darn ferrying trip.

As far as hay fever is concerned, I have not had any since I was a child. During August I had a very slight cold, which made itself apparent at bedtime, but not during the night, but now I seem to have shaken even that off. Glad your hay fever is bearable.

Also, glad you're back at 2413 [Hartrey Ave.] and settled down to something like normal.

Lots of love to you as always and keep on writing.

As ever, Lovingly Bill

September 10, 1944

[Addressed to the Mayfair Hotel in St. Louis, Missouri.]

[Editor's note, on this date, as Bill was involved in a ferrying trip, General Eisenhower gave his approval for another kind of ferrying trip in which three allied airborne divisions were dropped into Holland the next week in Operation Market-Garden.]

Hi Pop!

Am on a short ferrying trip, so didn't get those few days off after all.

Swell to talk to you the other night.

Hope things are OK. Back at BAAF Tuesday night.

As ever, Bill

September 11, 1944

Arrived here 0300 this morning. My flight CO and I took out a room and slept till noon.

Weather is bad up the line and we may have to stay here today and leave tomorrow. Out to airport now.   Bill

Chapter 8

B-24 PILOT TRAINING AND
THE 1944 PRESIDENTIAL ELECTION

With the impending closure of the Bainbridge Field Basic Flying School, Bill's days as a BT-13 instructor were waning and he was assigned to B-24 Liberator transition training at Maxwell Field where he had completed preflight training. The upcoming presidential election was also on Bill's mind and became the topic of a spirited debate with his father and others. Bill's strong opinions come through clearly.

The B-24 was developed by Consolidated Aircraft Company in San Diego, California, which would become his future hometown. The B-24 was a four-engine heavy bomber with a ceiling of about 30,000 feet, an altitude which Bill could tolerate without getting the bends. The airplane was about sixty-seven feet long with a 110 foot wingspan. With a crew of ten, it had a longer range and could carry a heavier bomb load than the B-17 Flying Fortress. Unlike the B-17, the B-24 had tricycle landing gear, a twin tail, and a reputation as a difficult airplane to fly.

At Maxwell Field, Bill and other new B-24 pilot trainees were welcomed to the transition school by Major General William O. Butler, First World War veteran, a balloon (airship) pilot and later, a bomber pilot. Before serving as commanding general of the Army Air Forces Eastern Training Command, Butler served in the Aleutian Islands where he commanded the 11th Air Force.

Before any introductory flying, there was ground school for about a month which according to Bill, included an "... intensive course of engineering, studying everything about the B-24 ..." Bill logged many hours in the air as an engineer. After flying BTs and ATs, the B-24 was a new and challenging experience because of his limited technical background.

He did have some time off for fun, which he spent seeing movies like

Maisie Goes to Reno with two of his favorite actors, Ann Sothern and Ava Gardner.

In late October, he completed ground school and transferred to Courtland Field in northern Alabama where a B-24 flight training program had been established two months earlier. Bill was glad that he had 720 hours overall flying time, because some of the others in B-24 transition training had only 200 hours flying time. His time as a BT instructor-pilot was paying off.

The B-24 flight training at Courtland was intense. That fall Bill would have agreed with a 1944 study about transition training to combat aircraft that stated B-24s were difficult airplanes to fly. Bill noted that it took great physical strength to fly the B-24. He stood at 5 feet, 9½ inches and weighed 168 pounds as documented by a 1943 Army physical. Later in life, he attributed varicose veins in both legs to the exertion required to operate the brake and rudder pedals.

In addition to flying and family matters, as well as an interest in politics and current events, his correspondence covered a variety of topics, people, and even presidential pets in the news. The impending presidential campaign held Bill's interest and attention. The bitter campaign was in full swing, and Bill and his father parted ways on politics. Bill supported President Roosevelt, and his father supported Republican Governor Thomas E. Dewey of New York. They even had a small wager on the outcome of the election.

After the election, Bill passed the blindfold cockpit check on November 19, and he felt more comfortable flying the Liberator. He described flying with more ease and expected he would be given his own ship and crew in January, 1945.

In late November, Bill was looking forward to a long-range multiple day training flight coming up the next month, during which he would fly over Chicago on his way to New York City. He wrote that he would fly over the house in Evanston and would "dip my wings a few times" so that family members would know it was him.

Even though he was learning something new and challenging, Bill expressed a growing disillusionment with the Army. He had just seen the movie *For Whom the Bell Tolls* and was impressed that it was "more Hemingway than Hollywood," but he was critical of others in the theater who were "unappreciative and actually disappointed." To punctuate his frustration, Bill described how an unnamed major had given an impossible order concerning the storage of bulky flying clothes.

In early December, he proudly announced to his father that he was officially checked out in the B-24. At the same time, to his mother, he discussed more domestic things like his health, the upcoming Christmas holiday and seeing the new movie, *Thirty Seconds Over Tokyo* about the Doolittle air raid on Tokyo in April 1942. He commented how he and his fellow pilots criticized the inaccuracy in movies about flying but noted hopefully that maybe this movie would be different. Unfortunately, he did not share his opinion of this movie.

Meanwhile, the war progressed. In mid-December the Germans launched an offensive in the Belgian Ardennes Forest that became known as the Battle of the Bulge. In letters during this period, Bill reacted to the massive German attack and was concerned that the war was far from over.

Even as he was studying hard to learn the B-24, there was talk about transferring into B-29s, the Superfortress. To differentiate the B-29 from the B-24, the B-29 was called a *very* heavy bomber. In January 1945, while on an instrument training flight, he landed at Maxwell and toured a B-29. He was so impressed by the long tunnel between the forward crew compartment to the aft crew compartment, that years later he described crawling through the cramped space.

Correspondence From
B-24 PILOT TRAINING AT
MAXWELL ARMY AIR FIELD

September 24, 1944

Dear Pop:

Thanx for your letter. The clippings have arrived. It'll take more than that to make me vote for Dewey.

Have written mother about the setup here. We are going to take a five-week engineering course about the B-24, and during that time won't do any flying.[1]

Several B-29's are on the field. That is really a gigantic plane, and I'd a whole lot rather be in it than beneath it. It can do a lot of damage. On Wednesday it was wonderful to see you and play golf again. As ever, Bill

---

September 24, 1944, Sunday

Dear Mother:

I have delayed writing so that I could tell you something definite about the program here. Yesterday afternoon a lecture was scheduled in one of the Post theaters. and I thought that, at last, I would learn what it was all about, but it turned out to be nothing but a welcoming speech by the Commanding General.[2] So, there's not very much I can tell you.

This is a first pilot school. There are a number of Captains and 1st Lieutenants and other 2nd Lts. with experience in the class, but the bulk of the fellows are just out of Advanced, and among these I have met two of my former students and have talked to several more who were in B flight and knew who I was.

Apparently, we will do no flying for four or five weeks but will go through a rather intensive course of engineering, studying everything about the B-24. After that, we will fly it for about six weeks, and then be sent to an air force. Our tactical officer has told us that graduates are almost always given a seven-day delay enroute when leaving here, so it seems likely that I'll be home in December sometime.

I have sent you a picture booklet of Maxwell Field and in it you can see the Cadet barracks. Our BOQ is just like it. The buildings are one story stucco affairs, with a screened porch running the whole length. Each building is divided into about eight good sized rooms, and four or five officers live in each room. My three roommates are all from the south, and already I find myself asking them what date it is.

The processing hasn't taken all my time the last few days, so I picked up *Moment in Peking*, by Lin Yutang.[3] It is very interesting, but so far not especially significant. It does give a picture of Chinese life and later on I think it will deal with the revolution, which is why I am reading it.

. . . Last night I saw my favorite actress, Ann Sothern, in *Maisie Goes to Reno*.[4] I got a lot of laughs out of it and had a good time.

. . . Thanks for your letter and the note from Wese. I'll have to set Mrs. Burckhardt straight on my rank. She and Leila seem to think Syracuse is midway between Chicago and the south, but it was nice of her to suggest a visit anyway.[5]

Guess I'll quit now and get back to *Peking*. One thing the book has done for me. It has made the Chinese live [for me]. News from China must be very bad, because the newspapers aren't printing any of it. Think of destroying those air fields we worked for so many years to build and develop!

By the way, there are several B-29's on the field. They are gigantic, and very streamlined. The fuselage is shaped like a bullet. There has been talk (there always is) that after the 24's, we'll get into 29's.

Well, it's good to be able to think of you and Wese in your comfortable rooms, and I do think of you and all the others very often.

Lots of love to you.   As ever, Bill

September 27, 1944

Dear Pop,

Have been here a week today . . . Monday our classes began, and now that the real work has started, things will move along a lot faster.

As I wrote you and mother, I won't be doing any flying until this five-week engineering course is over, but I will be doing a lot of flying as Engineering Officer in the B-24 until that time. The whole idea is to get us familiar with the mechanics of the plane and its flight characteristics before they put us in that left-hand seat. Obviously, they are in no hurry to train us, this is the first class worked [*sic*] on this system, and so we probably will benefit from thorough instruction.

I'm enclosing several articles for you to read. Half of them are about FDR and the little man [Thomas Dewey], and the others are illustrations of why I said I do not trust the United States more than England or Russia. But I would be more inclined to trust it with Roosevelt reelected than I would with Dewey as President, because there are an awful lot of reactionaries who want nothing more than a Republican administration, and even if not many of them seem to be prominent in the GOP, they would all benefit and more would undoubtedly "come out."

I wonder if you saw Dewey as you expected to. I think he stands an excellent chance of carrying Maine. Don't you? I hope you heard Frank's [Franklin D. Roosevelt] speech last Sat. I didn't, but I read it. Boy, he sure gave it to Dewey. And Dewey lost his temper trying to answer back![6]

Well, Dad, it's almost time for lunch and I've got to go. We have the morning free today but fly till late tonight. You'd think they'd give us the morning off *after* we flew at night. They must have some Republicans making out the schedule!

Let me hear from you again soon, and very best of luck to you.

As ever, Bill

September 27, 1944

Dear Dad:

I think the enclosed editorial is worthy of a special letter. It was from tonight's *Montgomery Advertiser;* a southern paper, granted, but the facts quoted are undeniable.

The Republicans are claiming the Democrats made no attempt to prepare us for the war. As the editorial *proves*, the Republicans prevented Roosevelt from carrying out many of the measures he wanted to take toward preparedness. And they called him a "war monger" (as you know very well) every time he took some step toward defense.

The story that the Democrats are responsible for our military status at the beginning of the war is a perfect example of Hitler's Theory, "the bigger the lie, the more likely people are to believe it." Roosevelt mentioned this in his speech Saturday.

Think you ought to send the editorial to mother and Wese.

I have received my ballot and have definitely decided to vote the straight Prohibition ticket. I have always been an admirer of Ida B. Wise and think that with such a fine, far-sighted platform as offered by the Prohibitionists, the world stands a good chance to live in peace and prosperity. The Republican plan, no doubt, runs a close second.[7]

I did not have to fly tonight, so came home from the line early. It is now 2030 and I think I'll turn in and get some sack time. Have an hour of calisthenics at 0630 tomorrow . . .

As ever, Bill

October 1, 1944

Dear Fran:

I won't write much of a letter, because I'm anxious to get back to a book I'm reading, and I haven't much time left tonight.

You'd like the book, by the way. It is *Revelry*, a novel of the Harding administration by Samuel H. Adams, who is an authority on the period.[8] The book is light reading with clever dialogue and a good picture of Harding. Very entertaining and it gives a good insight to the way politics (and Presidents) are made.

Real reason for writing is to wish you a happy birthday, which I do.

Tonight, at the movies, Dewey was soundly "booed," which is surprising, because the little dope only said he was against unemployment!

Regards to AA and Chas [brother-in-law] and all the kids . . . write again when you can and tell me about things with you and also your political activities.

Happy Birthday, old lass.   As ever, Bill

P.S. Have written a 4-point outline (outline only) of how capitalism leads to fascism. Ha!

October 2, 1944

Dewey is loudly booed in Post theaters. I don't think he made such a hot impression on his trip.

Dear Pop:

I have your letter and Dewey's speech, which I had read. If Dewey believes everything he says, he will probably vote for Roosevelt. The Fala affair is rather silly, but after all the charge against Fala *did* have to be answered and I think FDR showed good taste as well as good humor and who brought it up anyway?[9]

Yesterday I went to a football game between Maxwell Field and Fort Benning [an Army infantry training center in Georgia]. Both teams were made up largely of pros and ex-college stars, so the game was on a high level. We lost 26-0. Thursday night I went to a game between Auburn and Howard colleges. Though a college game, the players were very young and the game not especially good . . .

As ever, Bill

October 2, 1944

Hello Mother:

We were supposed to fly yesterday afternoon, but I was lucky and was dismissed, so I went to a football game in town. Also went to a game Friday night between two colleges. My team lost both times, so maybe I'd better be a beachcomber, after all!

At Bainbridge, I was permanent personnel on a temporary field. Here I am temporary personnel on a permanent field, which is really less luxurious. The Club is on a very grand scale, but I don't feel at home in it, and being only temporarily on the field, can take part in only a few of its activities. Still, I'm having a pretty good time and am glad of the change. I fly about every other day for three or four hours, not as pilot, but as engineer, which will be very valuable experience. It's a big plane. I have had the fun of going through a B-29, which is even more impressive. I could hear your oh's and ah's if [you] saw it! We're busy between school and flying, but I like it.

Regards to all. Will write letter later.   As ever, Bill

October 5, 1944

Dear Mother:

I won't take time for much of a letter, because Roosevelt is going to speak in just a little while.

In the last few days, I've been able to get in some golf. We fly for four or five hours every second or third day, and on the days we do not fly, are supposed to just wait around on the flight line. But another fellow, a good natured, worldly wise, former New York cop and I have been ditching and going over to the golf course. The course is on the field and is one of the most beautiful I have ever seen. The first nine is especially so. It winds on and between some lovely hills near the Alabama river. My game is just as poor as ever, but I get a lot of fun out of playing.

In addition to the post Officer's Club, which is on a Grand Hotel standard (seriously), there is a post Golf Club, which is just what it should be. It is something like the clubhouse at Glencoe. There is, of course, a porch with suitable furniture, a lounge, a bar and bar room, a locker room, the inevitable slot machine and ping pong tables, etc. All very nice and informal.

Guess I won't have time for anymore tonight.

Oh, yes. I don't expect to be here more than two or three weeks more. Most of the B-24's have been moved out, and been replaced with B-29's, so it seems this is going to be a 29 school. When this engineering course is over, I will undoubtedly go up to Courtland, Alabama for the pilot course, in 24's, and may eventually come back here for the B-29's, but that is only what I would like to do and I have no real reason for thinking I will. I really don't much care one way or another. I am getting more and more excited about the prospect of flying one of these ships.

That's all for a while. Write and let me know how you and everyone else in Evanston is.

Much love to you, old girl.   As ever, Bill

October 9, 1944

Dear Dad:

Despite the Petrillo case, which you say illustrates the fact that Labor rules the country, I do not agree with you.[10] Of course, it is wrong for any faction, labor, agriculture, or business, to dominate the country, but if business were doing so, and in the past, it certainly has, I don't think you'd object so much. And if you were a laborer and a member of a union, you'd probably be pretty pleased to be getting an even break for a change, so that it seems to me you are seeing things from your position as a businessman looking out for his interests, and not as an impartial observer who sees where the most good, for the most people lies.

As you said, Alabama is notoriously pro-Roosevelt, but it is not Alabamians who boo Dewey in the post theaters. It is the soldiers.

No wonder the GOP made it difficult for soldiers to vote. I have already mailed in my ballot, however.

I have just finished reading a novel, *Revelry,* about the Harding administration, and to get the facts of those years, also read the sixth volume of *Our Times,* by Mark Sullivan, who I think is the recognized authority on the subject.[11] From now on whenever you mention "bungling and incompetence," I'll just say "Tea Pot Dome;" not that it is [an] excuse for bungling and incompetence, but it at least ought to remind you that the GOP has, as least once, (ha) made a few mistakes.

Please read the enclosed editorials and let me know what you think of them. You may have read Hillman's statement about his support of Dewey for D.A.[12] He said, "sure I supported him, and would again—for D.A." I have respect for Dewey, but from what I know of his record, and from his speeches, I am not at all convinced that he would make a good President and am sure he would not be as good at this time as Roosevelt. It looks to me like a landslide, Pop. Seriously, how would you like to raise the ante on that bet we have?

We have to fly tonight, and I have got to go and get some supper. I've got quite a bit of time in the B-24, but most of it as Engineer. It is really a truck and I definitely prefer single engine, but I've got a lot of respect for it and the damage it can do.

. . . Write again soon, Pop. Best of everything to you, and good luck.

As ever, Bill

October 15, 1944

Dear Mom:

As far as ease of living is concerned, there is no comparison between Bainbridge and Maxwell. There I was secure in a rather comprehensive understanding of the BT-13 and in the certainty that I knew more than my students. But here, wow! You should see this engineering course. It seems the pilot of a B-24 has to be more than a pilot; he has to be an aeronautical engineer. In fact, I wonder if he has to be a pilot at all. The Liberator certainly does not fly like an airplane. It is a big, heavy, unwieldy TRUCK. The difference between it and an airplane is the difference between a convertible Ford coupe and a moving van. I would much prefer single engine to this, but I have a lot of respect for the B-24 and the damage it can do, and I'm very glad to be out of the training command.

We have three hours of classes every day, taking up the electrical system, the hydraulic system, miscellaneous systems, the engines, the procedures, the instruments, in fact everything about the Consolidated Liberator. You know what my background is in this sort of work, so you have a pretty good idea of how I have to work. We have a daily quiz, and at the end of the course will have an exam on the whole works.

May not go up to Courtland [Field] after all, as I understand the runways are cracking up and the field has been condemned.[13] There are rumors (there always are) about going up to Shaw Field, South Carolina, and to a field in Arkansas. Personally, I'd like to stay here, near a sizable town, and where I can make good connections north.

The barracks are of permanent construction, so if you want to send some cookies and stuff down, I don't think we'll need to worry about ants . . . We're up in the air for five hours at a time, so I usually get hungry before time to come down . . .

Been having some cool weather lately, so I'm back in my pinks and greens. By the way, I don't think I've ever told you about the weather briefings we get every day. In the ready room, the weather station has set up a bulletin board on which they post the latest synoptic maps. Before each flying period, one of the meteorologists briefs us on the weather we are likely to encounter and points out on the map the movements of fronts and airmasses all over the country. So, lots of time I know what the weather in Chicago is, or will be, before you do! If I see any blizzards en route, I'll warn you . . .

Got a letter from my old pal Don Dalton, who is now a Sergeant radioman flying out of Italy.[14]

. . . So long for now. Much love, as always, Mom.   As ever, Bill

---

October 16, 1944

Dear Pop:

Your letter is far better than 9/10ths of the editorials you have sent, but I think there are answers to the points you made, and I'll try to hit them.

You said that the Republicans are not to be blamed for voting against certain defense measures offered by the Democrats, by saying that:

1. It is the function of the opposition party to oppose.
2. A majority vote in Congress makes a law and since 1933 the Dems. have had a small or a great majority.

"But," you say, "because the opposition was against certain legislation does not mean that they were against the principle." OK, fine. But your opposition must have known that if it was possible, with the aid of a few discontented Democrats, to block preparedness measures offered by the majority party, that it would be impossible for the minority party, still with the aid of the discontents, to pass their own measures. Since, as you say, they agree with the legislation in principle, and since they had no hope of passing their own bill wouldn't the wise thing have been to say "well, that's not quite what we wanted, but it's a darn site better than nothing," and go ahead and vote with the majority? To that extent, I think it is true that the Republicans are responsible for our lack of preparedness. But it is undoubtedly true that had the Democrats been the minority party, much the same thing would have happened. One of the great failings of our two-party system is that office holders are often forced to think of party before country.

Now to some other points. Dewey and Bricker and the other golden-haired boys have been yelling that Roosevelt is all tied up with the Communists and if he is elected will be greatly indebted to Earl Browder, etc., etc. I read a very interesting speech by that notorious Red Hillman, which answers that pretty well. He says it is absurd to accuse Roosevelt of being tied up with Communists just because they want him to be elected, because (and this is very generous of him) Ham Fish, Col. M'Cosmic, Gerald L.K. Smith and many others of similar stench are backing Dewey, and that is no sign little Tommy [Dewey] is a Fascist.[15]

Incidentally, the Communist vote last election was about 40,000 (correct me if I'm wrong), which hardly seems decisive.

Here is something else. Republicans have been shouting that Roosevelt has centered too much authority around himself. They even hint "dictatorship." Then they turn around and say Roosevelt does not have the support of Congress. Now which Dewey are you going to vote for: the Dewey who says Roosevelt is a dictator, or the Dewey who says Roosevelt cannot control Congress? And on top of all that, it has been the GOP which throughout its lifetime has been for a centralization of power in Washington, and the Democrats who want the power left to the individual states.

To tell you the truth, I am neither Republican nor Democrat, but since right now I can't do anything but vote, I'll vote for the party which comes closest to what I think is right, and that party in 1944 is the Democratic party. Under our systems, I doubt if it will ever be possible to provide well-paying jobs for all our citizens, and I don't think we shall ever have peace as long as we live in a world in which it is necessary to fight to earn a living. Therefore, I'm in favor of changing the system.

As far as the $25 bet is concerned, you called my bluff. I'm certain that FDR will be reelected, but the House is a little different and the Repubs. *might* gain a majority there. I'll take the matter up with my financial advisors and let you know. Meantime, we'll leave it so that I'll only take $5 of your money.

Have written mother a letter about things down here, and I presume she will send it to you. Have been to a couple more football games and am really surprised at what a big kick I get out of going. I yell for whatever team holds the ball, so I can't lose . . .

Write when you can and let me know how you feel about the above. Not much good political news in the paper. Very best regards and best of luck to you, old boy.

As ever, Bill

October 21, 1944

Dear Dad:

I have your two letters and have read the articles in the *Sat. Eve. Post* [Saturday Evening Post] and the *Reader's Digest*.

It is true our Army, Navy, and Air Force were in a dangerously weak condition when the war broke out, and if the blame must be put on one individual, that individual is naturally the President. But is he really at fault?

We've already talked about the bills for preparation and defense, which the Democrats did put up, and the fact that many of them were defeated by the Republicans and reactionary Democrats. But it is probably true that, even if all of those bills had been passed, our state of preparedness would still have been inadequate. In other words, Roosevelt did not attempt sufficient preparation and much of what he did attempt was beaten.

Why was it beaten, and why didn't he attempt more? It was beaten because the predominating school of thought in those days was that any step toward building up our defense was a step toward war. Republican Congressmen weren't the only ones who felt this way, either. I remember how we used to call the Lend-Lease Bill the "Dictator Bill," and how certain we were that it was the sort of entanglement that would lead to our going to war; and I think our attitude was typical of most Americans of the time. How many times did we call Roosevelt a "warmonger"? The truth of the matter is that even so much preparation as Roosevelt advocated was greatly opposed by a large percentage of the population, he could scarcely have asked for more without raising a real fight among the people.

Some people might think that, if Roosevelt saw the war coming, he should have prepared us for it regardless of public opinion. They say he should have sacrificed his political career, if necessary, to build up our defense. (He certainly would not have been elected in 1940 if he had done this.) But I think it is a very good thing for the country that he did *not* disregard public opinion and on his own go ahead and build an Army and Navy, because if he had done this, *the war which was sure to follow would be considered "Roosevelt's war,"* and we wouldn't have been able to get the unity upon which our war record is based. That is a very important point, but I'm afraid I haven't expressed it well.

When I quit my job that summer and the same day bought a car, you knew it wasn't a wise thing to do and you could foresee that I wouldn't be able to keep it up long. But you also knew it was useless to argue with me, because I had my mind made up and nothing but the experience itself would change it. If you had kept me from buying the car, I would have blamed you for keeping me from having a good time. OK, it all worked out as you expected . . . If you foresaw it, why didn't you stop it?

Nope, Roosevelt isn't to blame. Neither are the Republicans alone. Every one of us is to blame. We had to learn a lesson the hard way. But we're making up for it now, so let's not soil our record by trying to put the responsibility on one man.

. . . My experience with fellow soldiers is that they are unconcerned about domestic and economic issues involved in the election and think only of how the war may be brought to as quick an end as possible. Since almost everyone is satisfied with the way the war is shaping up, why change Commanders-in-Chief? Soldiers are interested in preventing another war, and I think most of them trust Roosevelt over Dewey in matters of relation with other countries. Think of the background and experience (don't say this isn't important) Roosevelt has had in dealing with Stalin and Churchill and the heads of other United Nations. Would you put in a rookie pinch hitter in a crucial game in a World Series?

You seem to be quite concerned over the fact that Earl Browder is supporting Roosevelt and seem to think he and Sidney Hillman are attempting to gain control of the country and are acting under the direction of Moscow. I don't see how you can believe this. It has been one of Hitler's aims to make the allies distrustful of each other, and he seems to be having some success.

There are lots of Americans (and I am not one) who would welcome a Democracy in Russia, and so it is reasonable to think that there are lots of Russians [who] would like to see a Communistic America. But this is no reason to say that they are plotting to overthrow our government. Before the war Communistic activities in America got a whole lot more attention than did the Fascist activities, and even now that is true. That is because our big boys stand to lose their shirts from Communism. The big industrialists and financiers profit from Fascism and even run little "Fascist" regimes of their own. The classic example of this is the Standard Oil Co., which has a fine record for shoving the little independent companies ("Backbone of the nation") out of the way. The system of private enterprise has not seemed to be a success, because as it has worked out, the companies compete fiercely between themselves and so become fewer and fewer and bigger and bigger, and this is a sort of Fascism, or at least it is something we do not want. The other alternative is to have restrictions put on these big boys, so the little ones have a chance. You may call this Communistic; I call it Democratic.

Browder may be supporting Roosevelt, but don't forget he has only a half million (at the very most) votes to give. As far as the PAC is concerned, I'd be more than pleased to give a dollar and join myself. You raise a big fuss over laborers giving one dollar a piece, but Pew and the others can give thousands and it's perfectly OK. I'd rather have Browder supporting me than G.L.K. Smith, Nye, McCormick, etc.[16]

[Continued from October 21, 1944 letter.]

October 23, 1944

So much for politics. I started the above a couple of days ago and was going to mail it to you at your new job. Your card telling me you were to be in Chicago arrived today. Swell that you can be home for a while. Hope it'll be a long job and that you can get in your usual 75 hours a week.

I learned today that we move up to Courtland, Ala. on Wed. [October 25] Courtland is a hundred miles north and a little west of Birmingham, and I understand [it] is rather a desolate spot. I understand there is only one runway in use there now, and it may even be that we won't stay there for long. There was a delicious rumor circulating that we were going up to Detroit, and so none of us Yankees are any too happy about Courtland.

We finished Ground School today. My daily average for the course was 92, and I don't think I could have gotten under 90 in the final exam, though the grades have not been posted yet. There were higher marks certainly, but I'm not at all ashamed considering the background I have had in this sort of work. Now if I can only have as good success in the piloting end! In many ways, my 720 hours will help me (most of the others have only 200 plus), but I am slightly handicapped by not having had any twin-engine work. I still can't get over my preference for single engine and become very nostalgic when I pass the BT's and AT's parked on the line. I'd love to take one up and wring it out again.

By the way, when the hurricane was approaching Florida, all the planes were evacuated and over 1750 were sent here.[17] They were all tactical ships, B-26's, 25's, 17's, P-47's, 51's and many other ships.

It was a very impressive sight to see all of them parked together on the grass.

So long for now . . . Dewey hasn't a chance.   As ever, Bill

New address
LT----------
Class 44-4H Air Base
Courtland, Ala

Correspondence From
COURTLAND ARMY AIR FIELD

October 29, 1944

Dear Mom:

No word from home for several days but presume letters will catch up with me soon.

Chaos rains [reigns] here! This is a new field, as far as B-24's are concerned, and all is greatly disorganized! Courtland is 4 miles away, has pop. of 600! Field is similar to Bainbridge, though takes up a great deal more space and has fewer buildings. One thing I like about it is the great number of big old trees around the barracks. Leaves are changing color and it's all very beautiful. Barracks are tarpaper, and very poorly constructed.

Did dad go to hear Dewey or FDR? I wish I could have gone. I listened to the radio both times. Love to all and write when you can.   As ever, Bill

November 1, 1944

Dear Mother and Dad:

Many thanks for this very handsome stationary and your letters, which I received yesterday. I feel quite important with this letterhead!

... I was very glad to be able to get a chance to drive through the country and was very surprised to discover that Alabama has some very pretty scenery. We drove up through the foothills of the Appalachians and past the various artificial lakes of the TVA [Tennessee Valley Authority] project. The leaves were in bright color and the day was one of the first cool ones we have had in some time. So, you can see that I thoroughly enjoyed the ride.

This place, as I wrote you in my card, is much like Bainbridge. It used to be a Basic school [for BT-13s], but the runways are very good ones, long and wide, and so they must have intended to use it for a Transition school.

We are living in the old Cadet barracks, and I am with a bunch of boys all of whom have just graduated and gotten their wings. Somehow, I got separated from the Bainbridge bunch. I've got more than three times as many flying hours as these guys and often put in a bit of sage advice in the eternal bunk-flying sessions.

We have done practically nothing since we arrived. There has been PT and a lecture whenever anyone could think of something to say. We do not start flying until next Sunday. If there had been any planning at all, we could have had a week at home, because everything important that we have done, could have been done in one or two days. Anyway, I've gotten a lot of sack time and finished Wese's *Presidential Agent*.[18]

I wish I had been there with you when you heard the President. I stayed home especially to hear him, and wondered if any of you had gone. I'm getting a big kick out of this campaign and read all the speeches I can't hear. I don't like this Stilwell-Chiang business at all.[19]

I am reading the Flynn article about Pearl Harbor, Dad, and will send it back to you when I finish it. I don't think we ought to draw any conclusions until we get all the evidence and there may be something very important in those Secret and Top-Secret documents, and they may *not* implicate FDR . . .

By the way, four of the boys who used to be in B Flight are in my barracks. Three were formerly [Phil] Labor's students and I have taken two of them up on a formation ride . . .

I'll write again later. Hope all are well. Much love, as usual.

As ever, Bill

[on back side]

Wese, thanks for sending Willkie's pamphlet. I'll write you a letter about what I think of it soon. Thanks for your letter! WLW [Wendell L. Willkie] was certainly a *great* man.[20]

November 1, 1944

Dear Dad:

I have finished Flynn's article about Pearl Harbor. He seems to have a case, but let's not form any definite opinion till we learn what evidence the Army and Navy Boards have uncovered. It now seems the Robert's report was incomplete, and perhaps biased. I know you will not deny that the Flynn report is also incomplete and biased. The truth of the whole affair probably lies somewhere between both reports.

It is probably true that months before Pearl Harbor, Roosevelt had probably decided that war with Japan was inevitable. If this world war is truly a war against Fascism, it would of course be true, because we could hardly "liberate" the people of half the world and let the people in the other half be enslaved. But Flynn's article makes it seem as though FDR was looking forward to the war, confident that our Navy would defeat the Japanese in "a few months" and that the Japs would oblige by attacking only in those parts of the Far East which could reasonably expect attack. Flynn creates the impression that Roosevelt provoked the Japanese government to the point that the only alternative the Nips had was to go to war, and that having done as much, Roosevelt happily went off to Warm Springs on a vacation to wait until the blow came.

This puts the President in the role of some sort of a fiend, scheming to involve the nation in a disastrous war, presumably with an eye to the third and fourth and fifth term. I resent this, Pop, and don't think even the most ardent Roosevelt hater should believe it with the evidence at hand.

What Flynn has done, Dad, is to take the facts and arrange them and interpret them so that his case seems indisputable. A lawyer defending a guilty client does the same thing. Perhaps Roberts did, too.

I will be very interested to learn why Roosevelt didn't accept Konoe's [Konoye's] proposal to meet him at Pearl Harbor.

Incidentally, here is a point which occurs to me. Flynn excuses Short and Kimmel on the grounds that they could take little action on their own because their orders come directly from Washington and the President. Therefore, says Flynn, the President, and not his commanders, is responsible. If Roosevelt is responsible for the defeat, because he, as Commander-in-Chief, did not recognize the danger to Pearl Harbor and seek means to prevent it, then Roosevelt, as Commander-in-Chief, is responsible for the victories of our Army and Navy all over the world. Why on earth do you want to get rid of such a successful commander, and do you still pooh-pooh that issue?[21]

I don't have any clippings for you this time, because I don't get a chance to buy a paper of my own. Keep on sending the ones you think especially good, however, and I'll do the same.

Very best regards and lots of luck. Write again soon.   As ever, Bill

---

November 13, 1944

Dear Mom:

. . . Shot 13 landings in the B-24 this morning. You'd be surprised at the amount of physical work involved. You feel as though you are holding all 36,000 lbs. of the plane in your left hand!

I fly for five hours, seven days a week, have three hours of ground school a day, and six hours of PT a week. I get up in the air only every second or third day, but on the off days have Link [Link Trainer], engineering, and cockpit time to get in. It's quite a schedule, but well worth the work it will take.[22]

In January, if my work is satisfactory, I will get my own plane and crew.

Goodbye for now, Mother. Love.   As ever, Bill

Thanks again for the packages and thoughts.

November 20, 1944

Dear Dad:

... As soon as I can get a picture of the B-24 I will send it to you. The wingspan is 110 feet. The fuselage is 67 feet and some inches long. If I remember correctly, the wingspan of the C-47, the plane you fly in which is known as the DC-3, is 95 feet. The B-24 has four Pratt-Whitney twin row radial, fourteen-cylinder engines, which can develop 1250 H.P. each at takeoff. It cruises at about 170, but in a war emergency could go "much faster." The normal combat crew consists of pilot, co-pilot, navigator, bombardier, engineer, radioman, ball turret gunner, waist gunner, and tail gunner. The engineer and radioman also man guns (also, bombardier [in B-24J nose turret]).

As I told you, the pilot's cockpit is very bewildering until you know something about it. The instruments extend the full width of the plane, three radios are on the ceiling, and a column containing throttles, superchargers, mixture controls, light, prop, cowl flap, and many other toggle switches is between the pilot and co-pilot.

Yesterday, I completed a blindfold cockpit check, touching everything as it was asked for. It's really not hard once you have the idea what everything is used for, and now the cockpit does not look so difficult.

We student officers fly in the left seat, the pilot's, and the instructor is on the right in the co-pilot's position. After we fly this way for a week or ten days longer, I will be checked out. That is, another student will go up instead of the instructor. A bomber is not like a single-engine ship, where the pilot can do all the work. It takes two men to start these engines, and while it would be possible for one man to fly the plane, it would not be safe and is never done, except in emergencies.

My instructor has not as many hours as I have, but his time is in the big ship. He is a fine fellow and is more patient than I was as an instructor.

There is so much procedure to flying one of these things that nothing is left to the imagination. There is a checklist for before starting the engines, after starting the engines, before takeoff, after takeoff, before landing, final approach to the field, and of the landing roll, before stopping engines, and after stopping engines. The checklists are read out to the pilot by the co-pilot and everything is done exactly in sequence so nothing will be forgotten.

The plane lands at 120 mph. Instead of having the third wheel underneath the tail, as in most planes, the third wheel is beneath the nose. When you come in for a landing, you hold this wheel up until you slow down, then the weight of the engines makes the plane settle forward.

I will be finished here sometime in January and then will get my own ship and crew and fly around with them for two or three months and then go overseas. The chances are that I will fly myself to China or wherever.[23] That would be a trip to look forward to! But in the last few classes, pilot replacements have been needed, and so the pilots have been flown over and get the ships on the other side.

Flying the big plane is nothing like flying in an AT-6, or even in a BT.

The plane is very heavy (34,000 lbs. empty - without anything, including crew and turrets) and when you kick the rudders you feel all the weight is resting on top of them. The elevators (the forward and backward motion on the wheel which control a climb or dive) are also stiff, and all of the controls are sluggish, so that when you make a movement you have to come in with a counteracting application of the controls, before the effect of the first has even been noticed!

A while ago you asked about the altimeter, how a landing could be made on instruments, if it was only accurate within 75 feet. That's a good question. Instrument landings are still in the experimental stage. There are several systems out. These make use of runway localizers, radio altimeters (not pressure altimeters) and one or two others. I have tried the runway localizer system in a Link trainer but would bail out a thousand times before I'd attempt it in an airplane. The day I worked the problem, the Link instructor, who is a Sergeant and not a pilot and is trained in Link trainer flying only, told me there was "nothing to be afraid of. Do it just like in a Link. I'm not a pilot, but I wouldn't be afraid to try it in an airplane right now." This guy is absolutely nuts. What he doesn't realize is that there is more to an airplane than to a Link trainer, and more to flying a plane than reading instruments. If you ever hear of anyone talking about an instrument landing, tell them they're crazy, unless they happen to be pilots and actually made one.

Sometime in December, probably toward the last of the month, I will take an overnight trip with my instructor and two others of his students. They all want to go to New York instead of Chicago, so I will bow to the majority, as the son of a Republican must do, and tag along up there. One leg of the trip must be at least eight hours long, and because we can get to N.Y.C. in much less than eight hours, we will fly up by way of Chicago! As soon as I learn the exact date, I will let mother and the others know, so they can be on the look-out. I'll fly over the house, but not at a low altitude. I can also give them a pretty good idea of the time I'll get there and will dip my wings a few times so they can be sure it's me.

Hear from Leila frequently. You will probably be surprised to hear that she "was very pleased at the result of the election." Remember when the doctors told her she would have to stop hating Roosevelt, for her health's sake? I think you, too, will see the light someday, Fat; instead of vice versa, as you said in your last letter.

Did you go to any Republican rallies? I remember when we heard Green, Brooks, and Church in the North Shore Hotel.[24]

I would have gone again this year. I may be a Democrat, but don't think I have become as fanatical as some. I suppose there are three Democrats as bad as the three above Republicans, but I can't think of any off hand. Seriously, I'm neither a Democrat or a Republican or a Socialist or a Communist. I'm just feeling my way around, with the majority of my sentiments presently between the Democrats and the Socialists.

Mrs. Burckhardt has sent me to read a book I know you would like. It is *World in Trance*, by Leopold Schwarzchild, and is one of the best thought of books to be written on the rise of Germany.[25] I have new respect for your theory that Germany could have been suppressed. But I also feel that we must do more than *suppress* evil when we see it.

Let me hear from you soon. Very best regards and good luck to you with your job.

As ever, Bill

November 21, 1944

Dear Mom:

Sunday night I saw *For Whom the Bell Tolls*, which is by far the finest movie I have ever seen.[26] And I have never seen one so loyal to the book it was taken from, both in tone and story. There was a lot more Hemingway than Hollywood in the movie. The audience here was unappreciative and actually disappointed. You'd be surprised at the low level of intelligence of Army audiences. They want nothing but to be amused, and so they laugh at anything, funny or not, and because they are either insensitive or embarrassed, they make fun of all love scenes . . .

No one is ever sorry to see a very low ceiling, or heavy rain, because then we don't have to fly. There are a number of BT's out on the line. For the fun of it, I sat in one the other day. I would love to take one up but won't be able to.

While I was writing the above sentence, the Major stomped through, seeing if we had made our beds or something. Two of us have to keep all our clothes in one locker about two feet wide. There would not be room enough for one comfortably. Our flying clothes, big sheep lined pants, boots, and jackets, take up far too much room, so we hang them on the door of the locker. The Major says they will have to go inside. He says he doesn't care how we do it. He knows damn well we can't do it. We have a word for guys like the Major. He has succeeded in making himself very unpopular with everyone . . .

Must grab some lunch, Mom. Send lots of love to you and to Wese and all the others.

As ever, Bill

November 29, 1944

Dear Pop:

Your swell letter arrived today. Golf picture is really a beaut, and I'm as glad as you to have it . . . Had the morning off today and was much surprised when I woke up to see that it was snowing hard. Pulled on fur-lined boots, flying suit, and heavy jacket, and walked down to the field. Very beautiful, and so unusual for Alabama . . .

Trip to NYC has been called off, due to maintenance difficulties there, but we are going to Fort Worth, Tex., via Chicago, probably on Dec. 16. Won't be as much fun as NYC, but there's nothing we can do about it. Trust letter about Jack and Marian will be forwarded to you. Afraid there's little chance of getting home the 25th, but a fair one for the middle of January.

Am due to fly tonight, weather permitting. I report to the flight line for five hours every day of the week but get up in the air only every third or fourth day.

Best regards, old boy, and let me hear from you again soon.

As ever, Bill

December 7, 1944

Dear Pop:

Thanks for your letter . . . Since writing last I have continued my flying and have gotten in more time during the last week than in the three previous ones. Two nights ago, I did nothing but shoot landings for five hours, from 8:30 till 1:30. In that time the other student and I made 14 landings a piece, so you can see that it takes quite a bit of time to get the big ship around the pattern and on the ground. When we shoot continuous landings like that, we make "running takeoffs," which means that we get the plane landed and before it has stopped rolling give it the throttle and takeoff on the run. By the time we get the nose wheel on the runway, the speed has fallen off to about 90-100 mph and so it does not take much more of a roll to get the plane off the ground. The runways here, by the way, are 5,000 feet, which is the minimum length for a B-24. The runways at Bainbridge were also 5,000 feet, but as you remarked, the BT's used only a little of them. Not so in a bomber. One time Tuesday night we were going to make a full stop landing, change seats, and then taxi back to takeoff again. Our approach to land was high, so instead of landing at the beginning of the runway, we landed almost in the middle, and I tell you we had a hard time stopping before the end of the runway. As a matter of fact, we couldn't have gone three feet more without going onto the grass! There's nothing dangerous about that, of course, but it's just not good planning.

Part of our training is learning how the plane handles on two and three engines. You can imagine that when the engines on one side are cut out and feathered, the plane will want to turn sharply to that side. It is so hard to hold that dead wing up and keep the plane going straight, that it is necessary to put both feet on the "live" rudder and hold all the pressure you possibly can. Even then, I usually have to call to the co-pilot to get on the rudder and help me.

If it's hard to hold the plane straight ahead, you can imagine how difficult it is to turn in the direction of the good engines. (It would be extremely dangerous, and probably fatal, to turn in the direction of the engines out, because that dead wing would drop and the plane would whip over out of control.) Anyway, the other day I was practicing a two-engine approach and could not get the plane to turn into the field. In this case, the procedure is to throttle back on one of the two good engines, to help the plane turn. Instead, I made the mistake of throttling back on both good engines, so in effect I didn't have any engines at all. That is the single-engine pilot in me, because you can turn nicely without any power in a single-engine ship. Well, I learned it doesn't work that way in a bomber! My instructor let me lose several hundred feet before he said, "This beats me," and took over. We ended up only a couple of hundred feet above the ground. I assure you I won't make that mistake again.

I am enclosing a couple of clippings. I think the one on Pearl Harbor is unusually good, and you will have to admit it is unbiased, as the clippings you send from the *Trib* seldom are.

. . . I know you're not fond of "batching" it and want to lead a more normal life as soon as you can. I sure hope you will make every effort to hasten that time.

I know I want nothing more than to be able to live at home and study, and your feelings on the subject must be something like mine.

Three years ago today, I was playing in a football game at Black Mountain; the students against the faculty, and the next day AA and I listened to OUR GREATEST PRESIDENT ask Congress for a declaration of war.

We can be satisfied with the way the war has gone since that time, but recent diplomatic relations have been awful. I am reminded of that poem of Robert Frost's, which said that the world would end in fire or ice, or desire and hate. Hitler messed things up out of hate, and the Allies (Britain, especially) seem to be doing it out of desire. So now the British troops are fighting the Greek communists. I for one have no sympathy whatsoever with the governments in exile who come back to their country when the danger is over and try to reestablish themselves in power. I would favor the partisans, communistic or not. I don't fear communism nearly so much as Imperialism, and to hell with the British Empire. We're perfectly willing to fight a war and create a peace, so long as we don't have to give up anything to do it.

We have been fighting a negative war all along. We fight to beat the Nazis and sink the rising sun, but we have no working ideal to strive for, other than the preservation of the liberties which we of the Allies already possess. This may be due to a reaction set in from Wilson's aims, which because they failed, we are apt to consider impossible and too idealistic.

At the beginning of the war, it looked as though we might have a new sort of world altogether, and that was worth fighting and dying for, but now it seems we will have nothing but a continuation of the old world of power diplomacy and the delicate, distrusting balance of power, and I'm in doubt if that is worth fighting and dying for.

The ultimate solution is for all of the goods and good things of the world to belong to all of the people, and not to the big interests and big nations. If that amounts to international communism, I'm greatly in favor of it.

[Continued from December 7, 1944 letter.]

December 11, 1944

Am enclosing several clippings which I think will interest and amuse you. Also, will send the Air Force magazine, which has several articles you might like to see. I will send you a copy more often, if you are interested.

Another snowstorm today! It's really more of a blizzard, with snow flurries and a strong, cold wind. The weather office missed it completely. Said we might have light precipitation.

By the way, have been officially checked-out in the B-24! 'Twas almost as big a thrill as my first solo.

Let me hear from you soon. Very best of everything. So long for now.

As ever, Bill

December 7, 1944

Dear Mom:

. . . Tonight, Walt Curtis [a friend] and I are going to the Post Theater to see *Thirty Seconds Over Tokyo*. We are usually amused by the movies dealing with flying and pilots; they are so inaccurate, but this may be an exception.[27]

Several of the old instructors are taking B-29 training now. Most of them had several hundred more hours than I, however, and my chances are not especially good. I don't care, because I don't like the Wright engine anyway. B-24's have Pratt-Whitney's [engine], which is the most reliable engine built, and I'm in no mood to have engine failure anywhere.

I'm living with a swell bunch of fellows; several old students of Phil Labor and others in B flight.

Time for supper, so I'll sign off for tonight. Lots of love Mom . . .

As ever, Bill

December 18, 1944

Dear Mother:

. . . Enclosed is a newspaper picture of the B-24. I'm sure if you keep your eyes open you will see many more in the papers and magazines. I like the plane, but it is not nearly as much fun to fly as the BT or AT-6, in fact, as I've said before, it often is not *flying* at all. But there is a certain thrill in being the master of some 5,000 horses high above the ground.

The trip which I mentioned to Fort Worth has been canceled, due to the condition of these planes. It seems that whenever a ship goes on an overnight trip, something happens to it, accidentally or not, and it has to stay away for several days instead of one. And we need all the planes we can get. As it is, most of them are old wrecks which shouldn't be flying as much as they are, but the need for the good ones is overseas and we can't kick about that.

It looks as though we will have to fly Christmas morning, which means that I won't be able to get to Birmingham to spend the day with Jack and Marian. They have written asking me to come, and I really would like to very much. So, it is too bad.[28]

I went to the movie *Wilson* yesterday afternoon. It is excellent, but despite fine acting on the part of Alexander Knox, I don't think they managed to get the character of Wilson, which was rather chilly. He also had a temper, which the movie only hinted at. They also over-humanized him, but it was a good movie nevertheless. J. [Josephus] Daniels is one of the characters. I met him in Chapel Hill, N.C. three years ago, and as I passed by him to see Mrs. Roosevelt, I stepped on his wife's toe! I understand he has written a book on the "Wilson Era," which would be fun to read under different circumstances.

I'm buying an extra $100 war bond for Christmas, and from the looks of things in Europe tonight, the money can be well used. The

Germans have got a lot of fight left in them, and it will be a long, long time before they are beaten.[29] I am no more optimistic about the way things are shaping up in the liberated countries. To think that the British are now actually fighting the elements of the Greeks, who fought the Germans for so long! Don't tell me that this is a war of "Right vs. Wrong."

I hope this letter is not lost or delayed in the last-minute jam. It would be wonderful if I could be home the 25th, but my chances of getting home in Jan. are pretty good, and that's not too long to wait. I send all of you my love and hope that you will have a Merry Christmas.

By the way, if you don't think you can use the present I sent you, don't hesitate to tell me. You may already have plenty, for all I know.

Anyway, Mom, I send you special love for Christmas.   As ever, Bill

---

December 27, 1944

Dear Mother:

This is perfect pilot's weather. The ceiling varies between 300 and 700 feet, visibility is down to 1 mile, and there's no chance of it clearing up for another 24 hours! ...

Here's my Christmas. On the 23rd, we were told that all of us would have to stand by Christmas day for flying in the morning. We were all pretty bitter about this, because when you fly seven days a week, it seems you could get one day off a year. Anyway, I called up Marian and told her I couldn't get down.

Next day, the captain selected about half the flight for flying and told the rest of us we could take off. That was the afternoon of the

24th. At 1800 same day I was in Birmingham and, after a chop suey dinner at a crowded restaurant, called up Jack, who came downtown and picked me up.

Marian's mother is living with them and we four, together with a very nice, but talkative, neighbor, whose husband is a Colonel with the First Army, spent Christmas Eve sitting around talking. Marian and Jack opened their presents and there were two nicely wrapped presents of candy and cookies for me. I had sent them a subscription to *Time*.

Jack and I set up cots in the living room, while Millie and Marian used the bedroom. Jack and I had a good time bulling until we fell asleep, about 0200. Christmas Day, Jack and I went to another apartment in the same building and played with a boy's electric train. It was his father who is overseas, a Colonel. His mother is youngish and attractive, and wears slacks and smokes one cigarette after another. I liked her. Very free and easy to get along with, but she does most of the talking. Another argument with her, and the others, about Roosevelt and the Jews. She said, "Oh, I wish my husband could hear you talk like that." I said being a 2nd Lieutenant, I was just as glad he couldn't.

Well, nothing much went on all day. Guests came for a few minutes, we lazed around the living room and stuffed ourselves before dinner, much as I would have at home. The dinner was magnificent . . .

Jack and I spent Monday night on the cots again and stayed awake talking till early morning. He is a swell fellow and is doing good work at the modification plant at the air field. He is working on B-29's and we talked about some of the bugs that have developed in the Wright engine. He is working on a foolproof plane. He thinks that it will be possible for someone who has never flown to take it off. I disagreed and told him about some of the pilot errors which could not be taken care of mechanically. But there is no doubt that he has some swell ideas. He talked of getting a patent; "then we could make some money on all planes produced." I thought that would be great because then I could spend my life damning capitalists in comfort. He said he'd look around for a new partner.

It was obvious to me that Jack knew a lot about airplanes, but very little about flying. I'd love to take him up sometime . . .

It was a good Christmas for me, and getting to spend the day with Jack and Marian helped a lot. Golly, but it was good to get in a home again, and to be able to take off my tie and really relax . . .

Thank you for the fine presents, Mom. Every one is something I want and can use.

The news is far from good, but I take neither an optimistic nor pessimistic view of it. I would like, and am expecting a strong counterattack in the south, and it is possible that we will even get a breakthrough. 1946 ought to see victory and a year from now we will be saying "next year."[30] I am enclosing an extra bond, by the way . . .   As ever, Bill

---

December 31, 1944

Dear Dad:

. . . A week ago, Friday, Dec. 22nd, three of us flew up to St. Louis, down to Walnut Ridge, Ark., and back to Courtland. Each one of us was to fly a leg, navigate a leg, and sleep a leg of the trip. I navigated the first. We crossed the Ohio river about 10 miles east of Cairo, and I had a good bird's eye view of the confluence of the Miss. and Ohio [rivers]. I have now seen that from an auto, a river boat, and an airplane!

As we crossed the Ohio, I called up on the Interphone and told the pilot and co-pilot to take off their hats, they were crossing over the Illinois border! Shortly afterward, I noticed that we were going about 15 mph faster than usual, so I called up to find out why. The reply was: "So we can get out of Illinois as quickly as possible!"

The leg down to Walnut Ridge I sat up on the flight deck and read the paper. At Walnut Ridge I took over as pilot. I was flying at 5,000 feet and about halfway back to Courtland, ran over a solid cloud deck, so the navigator had to work with radio only. When we got close to CAAF [Courtland Army Air Field] I turned on our radio range and started a holding problem, while waiting for instructions from the tower for letting down through the overcast. There were other planes ahead of me, so I was flying back and forth on the north and south legs of the beam for over an hour.[31] In the meantime, three of the other planes had to let down, but when they reached the minimum altitude, pulled up again, because the [they] had not broken out of the clouds.

The minimum altitude is an indicated 1,200′ on the altimeter. The ground elevation is about 700′ and there is a mountain west of the field at 920′. I finally got my clearance, and began an instrument let down. I've told you, I think, that when you're flying in clouds, it's impossible to tell what the altitude of your ship is, except by looking at the instruments. You could be in a steep bank and think you were flying straight and level. We let down to 1,200 and still had not broken out. But I was right on the beam and safely away from the mountain, so decided to cheat a little and kept on going down. We finally broke out at 1,000′ and I came on in and landed. (1,000′=300′ above ground)

It was a very valuable experience, and the first time I have ever made an instrument let down under actual conditions.

The planes that did not get through, by the way, had to fly up to Memphis and were there for two days before they could get back here. And because they had on flying clothes, they couldn't even get off the post.

I don't have my maps here, and I don't remember all the towns we passed over in southern Illinois. I saw Carbondale and thought I made out Herrin, though that was farther off course. It's surprising what a clear picture you get from the air, and how much closer all those towns seem.

[Continued from December 31, 1944 letter.]

January 1, 1945

Spent a very mild, but enjoyable, New Year's Eve.

Have read the clippings you sent. The *Trib* [*Chicago Tribune*] seems to be dropping Dewey like a hot potato. Why didn't they tell us he wasn't capable to lead the Republican Party before the election?

I feel just as sorry as you and the Colonel [M'Cosmic] do about the Atlantic Charter. And I'm just as much opposed as I suppose you are, to the plan of giving East Prussia to Poland, and western Germany to France. That seems like asking for trouble. As far as Russia and East Poland is concerned, I think the Poles in that section, and don't forget many of them who are not actually Russian have Russian backgrounds, would welcome entry into the USSR. Russia has a much stronger historical claim to that territory than France does to what she is demanding, and both nations want the land for the same reason, for buffers.

I congratulate you on your new raise. I hope you get in a lot of 54-

hour weeks.

Will get this off in the afternoon mail and hope you will be in Iowa City when it gets there. As ever, Bill

---

January 6, 1945

Dear Pop:

Now that you mention it, I don't know anything about the E. Poland situation, either, except that it is certain Russia is going to get what she wants. Someday, if you run across an article telling the historical background to the territory, send it to me . . .

I'm reading Edgar Snow's *Red Star Over China*, which Wese sent me for Xmas.[32] It is excellent, and you should read it when you have the time. But as someone pointed out, we are hardly in a position to criticize the Chinese for fighting among themselves, when that's exactly what we are doing; the British in Greece, and we over here. Don't think I'm not as concerned and disappointed as you are over our lack of a policy in dealing with our allies as well as our enemies. The difference is that I have the utmost confidence in Roosevelt, and you do not. Russia is clearly playing her hand in the Baltics and in Poland. Britain is doing the same in the Mediterranean. In such a case, when two of three great allies commit themselves so definitely, it might be very wise for us, the third party, to remain more or less aloof, to take a long-range viewpoint and keep our ace in the hole. When the proper time comes, it is probably here now, our weight may be the deciding factor. Anyway, I'm looking forward to Roosevelt's message to Congress, which I think is to be broadcast tonight.

It is a cinch that Germany will not surrender until there is a lot more unity among the allies.

Thursday night I flew up to Nashville, left a passenger there, and came home via Little Rock. As in the other trip, I navigated one leg, and flew one. I flew the leg to Nashville, landing there about 2100. The runways there are the widest I have ever seen. I think it might be possible to take a BT off across the width! The runways are lighted by smudge pots at night, which form a border along the sides and at each end. They were so wide at Nashville, that they looked short, though they were well over a mile long.

Yesterday afternoon we were making hooded takeoffs, which means that the pilot takes off on instruments alone, and the co-pilot looks outside. When this is done, a green shield is put across the windows in front of the pilot, who wears red goggles. This makes it impossible to see out, as red and green make black. We made a few of these, and the tower called us in to take a passenger down to Montgomery. We flew directly over Birmingham, but the smoke was so thick I could not see the city at all from as low an altitude as 3,000′! Had about an hour at Maxwell Field. I went through a B-29 from stem to stern, and will tell you that I am very much satisfied with the B-24. The 29 is just too much airplane. It's just a flying munitions plant.[33]

A funny thing happened to me today, I should say a stupid thing. I hate to think I would have said to one of my students had they done such a thing. [I] was up flying instruments and when I landed (darn good landing, by the way) I discovered that I had not brought my parachute harness! There I was with a parachute and no way to put it on! We use a different type of chute than the one I gave mother. These are chest packs and are separate from the harness.

We flew this morning, and it [is] raining hard now. PT was called off and so I have free from this noon at 1230 to tomorrow night when I fly again. We fly every third night, every third morning, every third afternoon, so there's variety, at least.

About my leave. It is not absolutely certain that I will get one, though most of the fellows do when they leave here. It all depends on the demand in phase training units for B-24 pilots. Since our class will finish a couple of weeks late, due to bad weather, we might be needed right away. It's hard to say where I'll go, or for what. Some will probably be sent to the 4th Air Force in Nebraska for combat training, and others as co-pilots on B-29's, others may be assigned to the ATC [Air Transport Command] to fly the cargo version of the B-24, the C-87.

As ever, Bill

January 16, 1945

[Editor's note: On this day the U.S. First and Third Armies met in Houffalize, Belgium. Their meeting "unbent the bulge" in the Allied line, leading to the final offensive to defeat Nazi Germany.]

Dear Mom:

Have been flying a lot lately, five hours at a time in the air, and that's why I've been so long in writing.

Yesterday, I was at 25,000 feet above Birmingham, which looked like a pleasant little village; Whitehall size, no more [Whitehall refers to Whitehall, Michigan, the town near White Lake].

The temp. was -30 C, which is about -23 F, which isn't too much colder than Chicago weather, but the heaters in the plane weren't working, so it did get rather chilly. At this altitude we have to use oxygen masks of course, putting them on at 10,000. I have never been higher than 25,000 in an airplane, though I've been up to

38,000 in an oxygen chamber.

It's not much fun flying at high altitude. The controls are extremely sluggish and mushy and the heavy flying clothes, which we don't always wear at lower altitudes, make it hard to move. The oxygen mask isn't exactly comfortable either, and if you have to sneeze it's just too bad. The moisture from your breath collects inside and when you take the mask off you just pour it out.

There have been lots of rumors circulating about when we will leave and where [we will] go, but they're all *strictly* from the latrine, as the saying goes, so I won't bother to tell you them. I am reasonably sure of a leave, and it ought to come around the first of February. I want to see "Oklahoma," so when I know when I'll be home, would you please make reservations for me? —say about four of the best seats in the house.

Fran has also mentioned going to a puppet opera, which I would like to do. I can tell you that if I'm home for more than a couple of days, we're going to do a lot of "going."

I trust you have already made your list of calls for me. If so, you can tear it up any time between now and the 31st.

How's the watch? . . . By the way, get in the habit of winding it at the same time every day. I wind mine at noon, because I'm always up at that time . . .

We are being encouraged to get our personal affairs in order, something that gives strength to my favorite latrenogram [*sic*] that we will be going to a POE [Port of Embarkation] next month. The only thing I have to worry about is my checking account, which I will probably have to change into a joint account.

It's almost time for supper. Am flying tonight so will have to eat early. I usually land about 0130 and get back to the barracks about

0230, after a breakfast at the mess hall.

So long for now. Hope everything is OK with you and all the others. Lots of love, old lass.   As ever, Bill

---

January 16, 1945

Dear Dad:

Yesterday I saw Birmingham from 25,000! You can imagine how small it looked. We use oxygen from 10,000 up and the old mask gets mighty uncomfortable after a few hours. Have written mother about the "mission," and I presume you will read the letter.

I was surprised to hear you did not react favorably to Roosevelt's message to Congress. I did not get to hear the speech and only read comments about it, but most of them were favorable. And Leila even wrote enthusiastically about it! You certainly could not criticize it on the grounds of flippancy, which I believe is one of the Republican grievances.

How do you stand on "work or fight" proposals? I'm in favor but can understand labor's hesitancy in "giving up" to business interests the progress they have made in recent years. I think that is their main fear.

Nothing much new about when we will leave, though there are lots of rumors going around. It still seems very likely that I'll be home near the 1st of Feb., but as I've said before, I won't know definitely until just before I can go.

Thanks for your letter and be sure to let me hear from you whenever you can find time to write. I'd hate to fly 55 hours a week! Bill

January 20, 1945

Dear Mother and Wese:

Thank you both for your letters. Haven't anything special to do tonight, so will answer them.

No, I'm not too busy now. I finished my last ground school course about a week ago and now have nothing but a six-hour flying period, and a one-hour physical training class a day. And don't think that isn't a big treat.

We are still far behind schedule, due to the poor condition of these ships as much as to the weather . . . My leave, if I get one, won't come till I'm through, of course.

. . . I agree that we must have a peace without revenge, but victory, total, complete victory is the only way we can start over again. Germany and Japan must be absolutely defeated and their capacity to rebuild their war machines kept under our control.

Today I planned a trip I will take next Wed. It is from here to Jacksonville to Daytona Beach to Tampa to Tallahassee to Courtland. It will be a nonstop affair and will take close to eight hours. The leg from Tampa back will be flown at 25,000 ft. We plan to shoot a couple landings at the Tampa Army Air Field.

I was interested to hear of your course in aeronautics, Wese, but don't really expect to learn how to draw weather maps and forecast weather. That takes many months of concentrated study and is a highly technical subject. But it will be good to have one member of the family know what an aileron is. Will you get any study of the radio range and other navigational aids?

There are a number of things I want to do when I get home.

As ever, Bill

January 25, 1945

Dear Dad:

I have your letter and have read the clippings. They are of the usual *Tribune* low-caliber, and one in particular is downright dangerous. I'll quote from it: "There was relatively little reason to fear an invasion of this continent, even by a victorious Hitler, and events seem to have borne that out. . . . it seemed probable that our navy and our air force could prevent an invasion. We know it (to be true) now. We know now . . . that our safety is in no [way] dependent upon the support of the British fleet. In other words, neither Germany nor Japan, nor Germany and Japan in combination, presented a threat of invasion to us that was so grave as to require a preventive war."

I know that you will not support such an editorial. The *Tribune* seems to think that our oceans are protection enough and that it little matters what happens to the rest of the world. To print such rot at a time like this seems to me like the highest kind of treason. That's the kind of talk that will help to sabotage the peace.

I am surprised that you didn't enclose more articles about the Wallace-Jones affair.[34]

[Continued from January 25, 1945 letter.]

Saturday evening, January 27, 1945

Four of us, with an engineer and radioman, took off early this morning on a course of 95°. About fifty miles out the sun came up. Rather a beautiful sight, too. One of the fellows lived in Georgia, so we went to his hometown and buzzed his house for a few minutes. It was still early, so I imagine we got his family out of bed. They were expecting us. We then headed SE and went to Jacksonville and followed the beach line to Daytona Beach. It was a swell day down in Florida, and I looked for people in swimming, but didn't see any. From Daytona, we cut diagonally across the state to Tampa, passing over Orlando and Lakeland. This is all familiar country for me now. I was navigating this leg, so I had an easy job. We followed the west Fla. Beach line north from Tampa to Tallahassee and came back to CAAF via Bainbridge and Birmingham.

We circled Bainbridge a couple of times, and I got a good look at the old place. It has been closed, you know, and as far as I could tell was completely deserted. There were no planes on the line, no people to be seen, and no one answered my radio call. Had some pretty good times at BAAF. All that seems very peaceful and easy, just as this will sometime. I can still see you standing on the ramp watching mother and me fly over. Golly, it's tough I couldn't have taken you up. We'll go on a trip someday, though, in my five passenger Stinson you're going to give me (about $8,000). As a matter of fact, I don't think I'd be satisfied with anything less than that type of plane, though I wouldn't object to an AT-6 or even a BT-13, which probably will sell for less after the war.

I am nearly done with my flying time, needing only a few more hours formation and my instrument check. The latter is given by the Squadron Commander, who makes the ride as difficult as possible to see if you'll react properly to unexpected situations. He makes it very confusing, according to some who have already gone up with him. If I give him a satisfactory ride, and I expect to, I will be given a new instrument card. Mine was issued last February 8, and as they're only good for one year, I would have had to take a check anyway.

An instrument card is a very valuable thing to have. There are two types of clearances. (Clearances have to be filed before each flight.)

One is a contact clearance, the other an instrument clearance, depending entirely upon the weather conditions to be met on the flight. If the weather is going to be slightly tough, a clearance will not be granted to a pilot who has only a relatively few hours on his card. This new card I will get will have my total time on it and will be "worth" lots more than my old one. Pilots with several thousand hours usually do not have any trouble in getting a clearance through any type of weather at all, and some are even allowed to sign their own clearances.

I don't remember much about Springfield. I remember Lincoln's house and tomb, but did not recognize the picture you sent of the capitol building. But I imagine it's a pretty nice town to work in. I think it's about the right size; not small townish, and yet not as impersonal as a big city.

Well, old boy, have several other notes to dash off. Let me hear from you soon and enclose some more clippings. I enjoy getting mad at them. Best of everything, Pop.

As ever, Bill

February 3, 1945

Dear Mom:

Your illustrated letter was very enjoyable except for one sentence which I thoroughly resent. You ask about my mustache, "Is it really visible?" What a blow to my pride! However, it is no longer visible, because due to pressure which might have become physical, put upon me by the fellows, I shaved it off. And no pictures to prove to you it could be seen! Serves you right.

The second piece of important news is that I have finished my course and expect to get home toward the end of next week. I'm not sure of the date and it may even be the week after, but it looks very much as though I'll be home soon. The latest latrine rumor, (I'm putting some stock in this one because it comes from my squadron commander), is that my shipment will go to California for assignment with the 4th Air Force. I had hoped to go to the east coast and hence to Europe, but apparently that is not to be . . .

. . . The strain is off. I'm as carefree as all hell and wait till I get home! Don't know if I can or not.   As ever, Bill

Chapter 9

FLYING IN THE FOURTH AIR FORCE

In mid-February 1945, Bill headed to California by train for assignment to one of the four air forces responsible for aircrew training and air defense of the continental United States. Describing his journey west, he noted that he had seen enough of the windy desolation of Nevada that he did not care if he ever saw it again. His first stop in the Fourth Air Force was Lemoore Army Air Field in California's San Joaquin Valley where personnel were processed for assignment to air fields across the western states. Bill described springtime and loved the California farmland with its rich, black soil.

At Lemoore, as the letter below describes, a routine developed of standing morning formation and attending courses without examinations. Bill had time to read more Sinclair Lewis and other authors in the air field library. One of the books he read was Lewis' *It Can't Happen Here* about the rise of a fascist dictatorship in the United States. He wrote an essay called *Fourth of July Americans,* which reflected his growing understanding and frustration with the way minorities were treated.

Bill hoped that he would be assigned to Washington state or stay in California. Rather than assignment to either of those more desirable options, Bill was assigned as a B-24 first pilot of a combat crew in the 422nd Army Air Forces Base Unit (AAFBU) at Tonopah Army Air Field in Nevada's high desert. It was the same area that he had hoped to never see again.

In mid-March, Bill arrived at Tonopah Field with his crew. Crew 256, Squadron T-4 included pilot Lieutenant William Hanchett, co-pilot Lieutenant William "Bill" Mellinger, navigator Lieutenant Peter "Pete" L. Strbick [spelling of last name was later changed to Sterbick], bombardier Lieutenant Robert "Bob" Field, flight engineer/gunner Corporal Robert R. "Red" Thompson, radio operator Sergeant Dean "McGrew" Levie, waist gunner

Corporal Hugh Butts, tail gunner Corporal Cal Howarth, and armorer-gunner Staff Sergeant Albert "Frenchy" Rouillard. Bill's correspondence describes the problems he faced as a new airplane commander, but through constant flying and drills, the crew began to work well together. On one simulated night air raid, Bill's crew "bombed" the San Diego Naval base with a camera.

President Franklin D. Roosevelt, whom Bill admired so much and who had prompted so much spirited discussion in the Hanchett family, died of a cerebral hemorrhage at his home in Warm Springs, Georgia on April 12, 1945. The Tonopah official history for April 1945 noted the president's death by saying that his death "cast a pall over social activities" at the base and a memorial service was held at the Base Chapel on Sunday, April 15. As other correspondence shows, Bill admired Roosevelt, so it is surprising there was no mention of the President's death in his correspondence.

Tonopah Field did not have a good safety record. During the war, many aircrews were lost in aviation accidents. In December 1944, a new commanding officer, Colonel John A. Feagin, started to improve overall conditions; training, safety, and even added new recreational facilities on and off-base. To improve communication between the commander and the troops, a new column, started by Colonel Feagin titled, "If I Were CO" began in the Tonopah Field newspaper, *The Desert Bomber*. It was called the "... morale-building idea of the month ..." in February 1945. By April, Feagin's efforts to reduce the number of accidents paid off when Tonopah Field received recognition for flying safety. On May 1, less than a month after Tonopah was recognized for safety, Bill was flying formation with other Liberators, as a P-63 Kingcobra fighter made a simulated attack on the formation. B-24s and P-63 fighters practiced a variety of missions; flying escort and aerial gunnery, dueling each other with gun cameras. As he was preparing to land at about six p.m., a crewman notified Bill that number two engine was smoking. Number two engine was the in-board engine on the left-hand side of the airplane. By the time Bill landed, the engine had burst into flames. He immediately called the control tower—an ambulance, fire truck and a crash truck were dispatched to the runway. Following procedures, the flight engineer turned off the gas to the number two engine, and the crew extinguished the fire with no injuries.

On May 8, 1945, came Victory Europe (VE) day, with a victory parade on the flight line, and a caution from Colonel Feagin, "that we could not afford to under-rate Japan and the amount of time and blood it will take to beat her . . ." Bill wrote that he might be sent to a staging area in the Philippines. There were many uncertainties and rumors about what might happen next. One rumor was that the crews would be broken up and the pilots would be transferred to B-32 Dominators, "the new super bomber." Now that he was feeling at home in B-24s, Bill did not want to transition to another bomber. He also felt his crew was "fine, super fine." Perhaps reflecting back to the informality at Black Mountain College, he liked that they called him "Skipper" or "Bill," rather than "sir" or "Lieutenant," as other airplane commanders demanded.

Bill barely mentions the first atomic bomb in a brief note written two days afterward on August 8, 1945, and then only in relation to how it may affect being transferred. With the end of the war in the Pacific, in early September Bill and his crew transferred to Mountain Home Army Air Field near Boise, Idaho to begin the discharge process.

Bill's letters at the end of this chapter discuss his future plans and his relationship with Jean Forster. It is interesting that in the entire collection of correspondence to his parents, Jean was mentioned platonically in only four letters written before Bill arrived in Tonopah, Nevada in March 1945. In these letters, Bill wrote brief passages about Jean graduating from Swarthmore College, his visit with her in Philadelphia, the stationery she sent him, and gifts he wanted to send her. However, after Bill arrived in Tonopah, their relationship appears to become more romantic. Based on the available correspondence from Tonopah, wedding plans appeared suddenly. Thanks to Bill's mother's "LATH Notes" for the summer of 1945, Alice Hanchett filled in some of the blanks. Alice wrote that Bill, on leave from Tonopah Field, met his parents in Colorado, and returned with them to Evanston to see Jean. Though not recorded, wedding plans must have been made during their time together in Evanston.

Nine letters, not part of the original collection, which Bill wrote to my mother, Jean, surfaced during the final preparation of this manuscript. Included in this chapter's correspondence are three of these letters, which cast a different light on Bill's perspective about his military experience and his view of the future.

My parents were married on September 30 at the base chapel at Mountain Home Field, and less than two months later, Bill was discharged in

November 1945 at nearby Gowen Army Air Field. A new life was about to begin. Responding to his father's suggestions, Bill made it clear that he did not want to stay in the army or pursue a career as an airline pilot or airline executive. His father may have suggested that he stay in the Army Air Forces because it would offer the financial security that he himself had lost in the Depression, but Bill was adamant. He wanted to continue where he left off at Black Mountain College and finish his college education. Though he did not return to Black Mountain, Jean encouraged and supported him in his academic goals at Southern Methodist University and the University of California, Berkeley.

The following letter describes the routine at Lemoore Field for personnel awaiting assignment to Fourth Air Force bases across the west.

February 28, 1945

Dear Mother:

Since arriving here one week ago tonight, I've been so darn busy I've only been able to read four books; *The Prodigal Parents, Elmer Gantry,* & *Mantrap* by Sinclair Lewis, and *The Financier,* by Theodore Dreiser.[1] The latter baffles me, because I'm trying to find a moral reason for having written it, a condemnation of business (which is hinted at in the last two paragraphs), at least, from Dreiser.

But beginning today, I have a regular schedule to meet, and so will be able to spend only my evenings in the library. Even so, I'm having it pretty soft. Have classes from 0830 to 1130 and from 1330 to 1630, with an hour of physical training. Unlike the other classes I've had, these are just lectures and training films, sometimes even interesting ones, and there are no examinations. I am doing no flying at all, and won't until I go to the new field, which ought to be in about two weeks. Probably not before, because there are more air crews available than can be accommodated. We are merely waiting for our turn here, and when it comes my evenings of reading will become fewer if they don't disappear. One thing I've learned to do since being in the army is to read for three or four hours at a time without being conscious of hours. The most important thing seems to be a comfortable chair and comparative quiet. Last night I surprised myself by reading all of *Mantrap*, something I never could have done before.

The food here is excellent. We're getting the fruit juices you thought we'd get in Alabama, and plenty of fresh vegetables, spinach, peas, tomatoes, etc. You decide, are tomatoes a vegetable?

I will probably hear from you this week about the pictures. Let me know what you decide to get and tell me the price. I will stand by my rather hasty offer of paying $30 and want two pictures for myself. I don't care which two.

Ken Glessner [another officer awaiting assignment] and I are planning to go down to Los Angeles this weekend. We may not be able to go, and I really don't much care if we do or not, though it will be fun to see L.A. and try to dislike Hollywood, which probably won't be difficult. But the trip down will. It is nearly eight hours by slow train, so we won't have much time to spend.

Today Ken and I played catch during PT. It's the first time in many years I've had on a glove and reminded me of the many other times I've played; in our backyard on Sheridan Rd., where I threw a ball through the dining room window; on the golf course with Ted Long and Tom Hanchett; the baseball games when I was a sophomore at ETHS and second baseman on the third team, and once struck out as a pinch-hitter when dad was there watching.

I have written dad a letter about what I'm doing here, which is really nothing, as you can see, so will not repeat myself. He has forwarded your letter written the day before our meeting in St. Louis. That makes it sound like a Big Two Conference, but golly what a swell time, and what a steak!

I can't tell you how fine it is to think back over my leave and to realize that I'm pretty well reacquainted with all of you. I can think of nothing I would have liked to do which I did not do with all of you, but especially you.

Sack time. Goodnight.   As ever, Bill

Correspondence From
TONOPAH ARMY AIR FIELD

March 16, 1945

Dear Dad:

. . . Wednesday afternoon I left Lemoore with about 400 others, enlisted men and officers. Tonopah is such an out-of-the-way place that we had to go by troop train, but I had an upper berth and the trip was comfortable enough, but very slow. My co-pilot and I flipped for the lower berth, and guess who lost.

I haven't known the crew members very long, but I'll tell you what little I know about them. Here's Crew 256:

Co-Pilot—Bill Mellinger, 26, married, from Fort Wayne, Indiana. Bill is close to six feet, well-built, handsome. Definitely the college hero type. I think we will get along very well, and we are living together.

Navigator—Peter Strbick, 27, single, from Tacoma, Washington. Pete is also a big fellow. His parents were born in Yugoslavia, and he even talks with a slight accent and in the same fast, breathy fashion as Mr. Holloway [unknown]. He takes his work very seriously and I know will be a good navigator. His brother is on Crew 257 and is very much like him. They call each other "brother."

Bombardier—Robert Fields, 25(?) married, a father as of yesterday, from Hastings, Michigan. I have seen less of him than of Bill and Pete, but he is a quiet, thin fellow, once an instructor.

The enlisted men I have scarcely more than met. Two of them are married and have children, the others are younger, about my age. You can see that I've got a bunch of old men in my crew and will be interested to learn that it is by all odds the best on the field.

Our routine has not started, but as I understand it, it will be something like this. Ground school for six days, flying for six, and a day off. Ground school lasts all day, and the flight line work is from 0300 till 1200, and from 1500 to 2400, on alternate days.

I am really dreading the first few days of flying. An instructor will go up with Bill (co-pilot) and me and pull engines and do his best to confuse us. It is really quite an ordeal and the biggest part of it falls upon the pilot, because he is the one who teaches the co-pilot. Bill has had only 25 hours in a B-24 and cannot be expected to know a great deal. I will also have to pass another instrument check and some night work. This is done in three or four days, and from then on, I will be flying with my crew alone. Of our various missions, I will write you later when I know more about them.

Incidentally, the boys are beginning to call me "Chief," which, I confess, I like. But since most of them, and all of the officers, are older than I am, I am going to have to gain their respect by flying proficiency and by taking hold of the command of the ship. It will be quite a job. Sometimes I wish I were just a gunner who didn't have to do anything but sit back by his gun, and let the others worry about the flying.

Bill's [Mellinger] and my room is about fifteen feet long and about eight feet wide. Our beds are foot to foot against the long wall, beneath the windows. The door is in the middle of the opposite wall. We each had a desk on either side of the door, and next to the desks, a rather large wooden locker. Though the room is small, I think it's the best I've had in the army, including the one you saw at Bainbridge, which is the next best. We have privacy, which is unusual, and I have some books and maps, so it is quite livable. My desk is really just a large packing box, four feet long and a foot and a half across. It is standing on edge so I have knee room, and big enough so I can keep my typewriter, manuals, and pictures on it without being crowded. I will be here for four months.

You've never been in Nevada, but you know pretty well what it's like. We are over 200 miles from Reno, in the middle of the desert. The field is about 6,000 feet high and all around there are mountains which reach to 10-, 12-, and in one case, 14,000 feet. The mountains are covered with snow, and we had an inch on the ground this morning. It is cold as the very devil and, of course, there is a strong wind. They say it gets real hot in the summer and the wind picks up a lot of dust. There is no grass, there are no trees or bushes, no growth of any kind.[2]

Well, Pop, I see you got to Red Wing after all. I have read your editorials, except the ones by Stuart Chase from the *Sun*, which will take some studying. I see occasionally you read a paper which dares to print the Truth. Lauren Bacall seems to be a favorite of yours. And of mine, too. Remember your old favorite, Elizabeth Allan?[3]

Not long ago you sent me another clipping by George Sokolsky, which accused Roosevelt and the Democratic Party of taking advantage of every possible excuse to exercise more and stronger control over the American people.[4] He even thought it not impossible that Roosevelt would take over the Labor Unions, or do away with them completely. Can you imagine anything more ridiculous! What won't the malcontents think of next? Some of them say Roosevelt is courting the unions, others that he means to liquidate them. They don't care what they say, just so they can try to convince people that FDR is their enemy, that he has designs on them. But that is part of Democracy, so let them yell. Don't work so hard [handwritten]!

As ever, Bill

[Handwritten after closing.]

The one drugstore in Tonopah advertises itself as being the only drugstore in 90,000 square miles!

March 19, 1945

Dear Mother:

I have about half an hour to write you, before going to my two o'clock. No, I am not at college. As I've written dad, we have six days of ground school, six days of flying, a day off, and so on. I have also written him about my room and a little about my crew members and the field.

I'm very pleased with "the boys." However, as Airplane Commander [AC], I cannot fraternize with the enlisted men.[5] Often, they say, the Co-Pilot has to smooth things over with the men, after the pilot has given orders.

We are being impressed with the responsibility an A.C. must assume. I not only have to know how to fly, but must see that every crew member knows and does his job, that they meet all formations promptly, etc. Apparently, I'm to be a sort of mother to them, minus the affection, at least apparent affection.

I have rigged up some shelves out of discarded flooring and have them above my desk, with several pictures, four pocket books, pipes, knife, etc. It is really a very nice room and it seems good to be able to settle down to a state of permanence; four months being an eternity at TAAF. Actually, it is not so bad, and I'm becoming very fond of the mountains. Most of them are snow-capped and have a certain rugged beauty. However, I do not like them as well as the North Carolina mountains, or the Green and White mountains in the east.

By the way, there is a dog hanging around the area which is a dead ringer for Rainey, though slightly smaller. She has the same sort of mussy fur, the same happy face. And she likes to chase stones, there being no wood. I call her "Ragged." I will not adopt her, because there are too many other interests (for her) around here, and I wouldn't be able to feed her regularly. But she's fun to play with and frequently follows us to our classes and the flight line . . .

Best of everything and love to all.   As ever, Bill

March 30, 1945

Dear Mother:

For the past week I've been flying in the morning, which means getting up at the comfortable hour of 0330. Briefing is promptly at 0430 and there is no such thing as being late for it. After a lengthy briefing session, we go to the clothing depot to draw flying clothes, and I pick up a lunch for the whole crew. Then comes a pre-flight inspection, my own personal briefing of the crew at the plane, and takeoff about 0700. We land at between 1300 & 1400, and if you don't think that is a strenuous day, I invite you to go through one with me.

Am having ground school this week, and next we will fly in the late afternoon and at night, so there won't be any more 0330 business for a couple of weeks. Thank God.

We had some bombing missions last week (Sat-Thurs) and made a very good record on one of them. The targets are laid out on the desert and we make regular runs over them. The navigator stands in the bomb bay and takes pictures as the bombs hit. Bombing, as you probably do not know, is a very tricky business. The bombardier controls the ship on the bombing run by means of his bombsight, but it is up to the pilot to keep a constant altitude and airspeed. A difference of just a couple of miles an hour can mean the bomb will land hundreds of feet off. Anyway, after making this particular mission, and after the pictures had been developed, I was told to report to the captain, head of the bombing section. He said he wanted to compliment me on the splendid mission, to tell me I had an A1 Bombardier, and to say that the navigator had excellent pictures and a minimum of film. We are all very pleased about it.

Yesterday we had a formation flight, with a P-63 [P-63 Kingcobra fighter plane] making passes at us while the gunners shot it with their camera guns. I saw the movies today, and the gunnery instructor who showed them told me they were pretty good, but nothing sensational. So, it looks like I've got a damn nice crew all around.[6]

As I wrote before, all the officers are old men. Bill Mellinger, the co-pilot, is the only one I'm not crazy about. He is a good flyer and rather resents being a co-pilot, which is understandable. He should very definitely have a ship of his own ...

Peter Strbick, navigator, is about the most conscientious guy I have ever known. In the army the word for it is eager. He is unimaginatively intelligent and a devout Catholic . . . He is a grand fellow.

Bob Field, bombardier, is slight and quiet. He has the habit of breaking out in the middle of a conversation with a witty comment, such as once noticing a sign which said, "No dogs allowed," saying "No dogs or bombardiers allowed." He is a former instructor and knows the sight [bomb sight] backward and forward.

Levie, the radio operator, is very serious about his work and responsibilities and loves to talk about them. Every time I look behind, he is sitting at his desk sending or receiving code. He is an older man and has three children.

Thompson, the engineer, is about 20 and redheaded. He is a carefree fellow but is eager to make a good impression, and so far as I know, understands the ship pretty well.

The gunners are all good fellows, but since they are in the waist [middle-rear positions] all the time, I don't see much of them in the air. I'm chiefly concerned that they're good gunners, and I think they are.

I have to conduct daily, when we fly, bail-out, ditching, and oxygen drills, and the crew has been working together very well, and already there seems to be a definite spirit among them.[7]

The catch phrase aboard ship has turned out to be "Howdy Doody," and we all are agreed that we will name our ship that. I'm in favor of it, too. But of course, we may change our minds before the time comes.

I think I'm working out all right, too, though I lost my temper unjustly the other day. We were flying air to ground gunnery over a dry lake at an altitude of 150 feet, which is very low, especially in a B-24. Anyway, once, when I had gained altitude to come in on another approach, I heard the top turret gun chattering away. This is very dangerous, because other planes may be in the area, and we were not over the dry lake . . .

My landings have not been sensational. We are flying B-24J's, which, unlike the planes at Courtland, have a nose turret, which changes the landing characteristics. But I think I'll be getting them down soon without a jar.

I don't think I've ever been more tired at the end of a day, and this past week it has been wonderful to find a letter in my box every day, but one. I have heard from everyone, including AA, and I sure hope it keeps up. A couple of weeks ago I told Jo she was my favorite sister because she had written me, and that seems to have had a good effect on the others. This week Jane is my favorite sister, with Wese a close second. Spread the news.

Last night I borrowed the library's record player and Beethoven's concerto, some Wagner and Chopin and had a concert in my room. And even that was interrupted by some sensitive fellow next door who shouted to turn that damn thing down.

Had ground school today and ten hours sleep last night, and so am feeling swell. It's about sack time so will quit.

Hope you are well and that everything is going ok with all of you. Much love to all, and until I get a chance to write them, thank them for their swell letters. Also tell Wese I am reading the TVA [Tennessee Valley Authority] which she sent. At Courtland, we were right on the Tennessee River and I've flown over several of the TVA dams many times. So long for now.   Bill

[Handwritten after closing.]

Bill M. [co-pilot] and I live together and there are many times when I really like him. You know how it is. The other day I remarked that

Easter coming on April first might be symbolic and did Strbick hit the ceiling!

April 3, 1945

[Handwritten at top.]

Wish we were having some of your weather. It's down to freezing every day and that wind is really cold.

Dear Dad:

. . . I am enclosing an article by Westbrook Pegler, which I think is disgraceful, but you'll get a kick out of it.[8] Your rightest sister [Leila] sent it to me. I was surprised because her clippings are usually of a different nature.

I haven't had a chance to read all the clippings, because I just got your letter a couple of hours ago, but those that I have read have failed to shake my confidence in Roosevelt. There have been mistakes, a lot of them, but no one is perfect, and the overall picture is very fine, as even you will admit.

I continue to get my news from *Time* magazine. Newspapers aren't much good, because they have to take a three-line communique and write a whole column about it. I do read the editorials, including Drew Pearson and Walter Winchell, in the Reno paper, and follow the war news on my maps.[9] This Okinawa invasion is swell, isn't it? Looks like we're going to bypass Formosa completely. From Okinawa, I hear from Nimitz, we will drive north to one of the main Japanese islands, maybe Shikoku, and from the Philippines send a landing force to southern China. How does that plan of attack sound to you?[10]

I am working pretty hard flying and going to school. I often wish that I were spending the same amount of energy and time on something more interesting and less destructive. What would I know about American history if I had been studying it as hard?

About the only postwar plan which interests me is getting a small chicken farm. I know you've always wanted something like that, and maybe we can work out something together. Keep your eyes open for a likely location. The south, and also Texas, is out. Wisconsin appeals to me a lot. I want something hilly, with woods on it, and near a lake. Perhaps I haven't come so far from my old south sea island dreams after all. Nevertheless, that's the only kind of life that makes any sense to me.

There is so little to do around here, I should be able to save a lot of money. I haven't been in Tonopah once!

Well, Pop, let me hear from you soon and get plenty of sack time. I do whenever possible. Best of luck and everything.   As ever, Bill

---

April 10, 1945

Dear Pop:

. . . Our week of flying ended this morning at 0200 and starting tomorrow, I'll have ground school for a week. I dropped no bombs last week, but theoretically wiped out Boulder [Hoover] Dam and the San Diego Naval base, which we "bombed" with a camera attached to the bombsight.[11]

It was very interesting to see Boulder Dam from some 10,000 feet. Perhaps you have been much closer than that. When we got to San Diego, it was dark, and I could not see the ocean clearly, but anyway, I now have seen both oceans.

The crew is coming along nicely, though the nose gunner is rather inefficient, (he is also the Armorer Gunner), and the tail gunner gets sick. I have put in for Corporal ratings for the tail and waist gunners, and they will go through this week. Naturally, the boys are very pleased about it. My engineer and radio operator are Corporals, and before we leave here, I'll have Sergeant ratings for them. The nose gunner is also a Corporal, but he'll have to do a lot better work before he is promoted. He doesn't seem to like to ride in the nose turret, for which I do not blame him. But nevertheless, he's got to. On these five-hour missions, bombing, formation, instrument, navigation, etc., the gunners have nothing to do, and it is hard to keep them awake. I have to do it, though, and probably they think I'm the original First Sergeant.

We have corn on the cob regularly, pork often, of course, and roast beef once a week or so. When we have the beef, there are always three roasts on the cafeteria line, and a piece is cut off of the one we like best. Pretty nice. The Officer's club is larger than the one at Bainbridge, and even nicer. Being in Nevada, it is full of slot machines. One night not long ago, I got $3 in nickels and put them all in one. I was certainly disgusted. But to make it all the worse, another guy came up just after I had finished and put in five nickels and WON THE JACKPOT. I controlled myself very well, however, and only let out one scream. I have not been near a slot machine since, at least not with so many nickels.

I have been in Tonopah a couple of times, but there is nothing there except gambling houses, which I keep away from. Some of the boys have lost as much as $100 in a night.

By the way, in one of the most recent *SATEVEPOSTS* [*Saturday Evening Post*] is a very good short story called "Hey Charley," or something like that. It is in the form of letters and is one of the most clever stories I have read. I got a big kick out of it. But outside of *Time*, I do not do much reading.

Well, Fat, this'll be all for now. Have some fun and let me hear from you again soon.

Best of luck with the job.   As ever, Bill

[Handwritten after closing.]

Why is it that my flying experiences don't impress me as being "thrilling?" When I step back a few years they do seem so, but now I merely dread them. And flying one of these big birds takes a lot of you, physically and mentally, and I'm always worried that I won't react right in an emergency.

That's one reason I like a fighter plane better—you've only got one life to worry about. My hair will be gray before yours.

May 1, 1945

Dear Dad:

I was pleased to get your letter and clippings. Congratulations on doing such a fine piece of work for the insurance company . . . I'm interested in some way to make money without having to work for it.

I'm very much impressed with the way Truman has started out, and am sure you are, too. He has none of Roosevelt's brilliance and color, but he is a typical honest, unimaginative, hardworking American, and probably will be very good for the country. So far, he has been calling a spade a spade, but whether he will be able to continue to do so when he meets more complex problems, remains to be seen. Anyway, I'm solidly behind him.[12]

I have fun flying nights this week, and would be flying now if some weather hadn't moved in. I came down this afternoon about six to let off the instructor gunner who was flying with me to check up on my gunners who were firing at a P-63 which was making passes at our formation. On my final approach to land, one of the gunners called me up on the interphone to tell me that #2 engine was smoking. By the time I had landed, it had burst into flames. I immediately called the Tower, and an ambulance, fire wagon, and crash truck was out to the plane almost before I had stopped talking. I had the engineer turn off the gas, and we got the fire out ourselves, and nothing serious happened. Nevertheless, it was my first real, though minor, emergency.[13]

My crew is doing extremely well, and I'm proud of them all. The nose gunner was very indifferent to the whole business at first, so much so that I threatened to demote him, but he has whipped around nicely and is over conscientious in his efforts to keep his stripes and to stay with the crew. I have told the boys that I'll excuse a little incompetency, because we are all learning new jobs, but that I will not put up with anyone who didn't do his best at all times.

Had a day off Saturday last, so took a bus Friday night for Reno. Played golf with two civilian men I met at the golf club and did pretty well, much better than average in fact. My drives were even straight, for a change. However, one hole paralleled a fence and road on the right. Of course, with that terrific mental hazard, my drive went in a typical first hole in community arc. Otherwise, I did all right. I got 55-53 on a regulation course, which did something to strengthen my reputation as a golfer (golf picture of family on my wall) and surprised the hell out of me.

Carl Anderson [AAF friend] is at the Will Rogers Field [Oklahoma City]. If you stay there longer give him a ring for me. He might be able to take you around the field and into a B-24, or some other plane. Anyway, it would be something to do on a Sunday. Best of everything,   As ever, Bill

May 8, 1945, V/E Day

Dear Mother:

Rumors run amuck. Most of them I don't believe, but it is certain that the end of the war in Europe and the transfer of many bombardment crews to the Pacific is going to affect me a lot. We still do not have enough big bases in the Pacific to do very much with B-24's, and the ones we do have are out of range for planes in mass, except B-29's.

The bunch that was supposed to leave here last month is still hanging around. We hear that the Ports of Embarkation are overflowing with combat air crews, because there's no place to send them. And it seems fairly certain that I'll be hanging around here for some weeks after my final phase has been completed.

It seems to me there will be no use for us until we have captured bases in China, and that we will sit on our fannies until then.[14] It is possible that the crews will be broken up and the pilots sent to B-32's, a new very heavy bomber which is to the B-29's what the B-24's are to the B-17's, or in other words, as large, or slightly larger [B-32, four-engine bomber]. Anyway, it seems very unlikely that I'll be going overseas this summer, as planned.

That is not rumor. The rumors are about furloughs, discharges, etc., and I'm sure there is nothing to most of them. But I am in a peculiar position. For two years I've been trained for a certain job, and now that I'm ready to go to work, I am not needed. But I feel that is a temporary condition, and when we get the China bases, we'll be sending thousands of heavy bombers over Japan, and the Air Forces will be glad enough to have another broken down Liberator pilot.

In the meantime, we are being rushed through our training as if there really were a need for hurry. My crew is fine, super fine. We probably have less military formality on it than any other crew, and I have been criticized for it, but the boys understand that an order, good or bad, must be obeyed, and so far there has been no disobedience. I'll be very glad if it can keep up, because it sure is good for morale to be friendly with each other. Most of the pilots insist that their men call them "Sir" or "Lt.," but I'm tickled to death with "Skipper" and "Bill," and I can't see how it hurts efficiency. As far as completing missions and minimum requirements, Crew 256 is about in the middle of the flight, and that's a comfortable place to be.

I'm looking around for a bicycle and may be able to pick one up in Tonopah Thursday, my day off. On that day, the whole crew is going horseback riding. (such a thing is unheard of!)

My nose gunner, a boy from Boston, has been grounded permanently because of a nervous trouble which so far had escaped the Flight Surgeons. He has a fear of crowds and when excited his legs become paralyzed. The strain of flying hasn't helped him any, so he has become worse than before. He wanted terribly to stay with the crew and asked me to speak to the Flight Surgeon about it. I thought I might be able to swing the deal, until I talked to the Doc and heard the whole story. Then I sided with the other side, and poor Joe lost his flight. He is very disappointed about it now, and maybe a little bitter toward me, but someday he will know it's for the best.

The florists and greeting card manufacturers tell me to wish you a happy Mother's Day, which I will do, because after 31 months in the Army it has become instinctive to follow orders. But you know that it is unnecessary for me to set one day aside to think of you.

Never fear that your letters are boring . . . Hope dad will get home soon and let me hear from you and all the others very soon.

Special love to you. As ever, Bill

[Handwritten on back of letter.]

The reverse was written this noon. This afternoon the entire military personnel on the field had a victory parade on the flight line.

The Colonel [Feagin] spoke, emphasizing that we could not afford to underrate Japan and the amount of time and blood it will take to beat her. He said that the Air Force policy was going to be to send all men overseas who have not yet been over, and to do so as quickly as they were prepared to go.[15]

So, I suppose things are very much the way they were before.

They might send us to the staging area, the Philippines, but I doubt very much that there will be any tactical use for us before we have carved out a big chunk of China.

The Japanese and I are looking for landings west of Hong Kong, and we may not have long to wait.

May 18, 1945

Dear Mother:

. . . I took some swell trips last week. We went down to Phoenix three times, and I had a swell view of the whole valley and the mountains beyond Tucson from 20,000 feet. But the best trip of all was from here to San Francisco to Los Angeles to San Diego to Death Valley to Tonopah. I flew instruments most of the way, that is, I put some green glass on windows in front of me and wore red goggles, making it impossible to see outside the cockpit, but going from San Francisco, where we "bombed" the Golden Gate Bridge, saw many ships in the harbor, and did not see Molotov, to San Diego, I took the green glass down and flew directly along the beach, in order to save Pete a little navigation. It was a beautiful day, and the Pacific was a bright blue. It was so pacific, it was hard to realize a war was going on at the opposite coast. What surprised me was that the breakers, which were a brilliant white and easily seen, did not seem to move up on the beach, but appeared to be standing still.

I circled L.A. at 3,000 feet for half an hour, giving the boys a view of the city and many, many blue lined swimming pools. While I was flying around, a B-26 and a P-38 came up and flew formation with me. I envied both of them their ships, but it was fun to realize that both of them had a certain respect for a four-engine bomber and its pilot.

I am enclosing several letters and the clipping about Uncle Charley [Great-uncle Charles Granger Hanchett, who passed away April 24, 1945] which dad asked me to return to you. Uncle Harold did not want me to send the picture home, because he said he looked like a hundred years. Actually, he looks rather less. He is thin, but not elderly looking, and is another who thinks and admits that his picture was not flattering.

There are no bikes in Tonopah, so I'll just have to walk. The latest latrine rumor is that we will leave here by June 20, and that the pilots, or some of them, will be sent to B-32's, the new super bomber I mentioned in my last letter. I hope I don't get them. I don't want to split up an A1 crew, and I don't want to have to learn a new ship. I feel at home in a 24 now, and that's where I want to stay, at home . . .

Write again soon, Mom, and love to all.   Bill

May 21, 1945

Dear Pop:

I want to thank you for the fudge you sent a week ago. It was really swell, and I don't know when I've ever had any better, and that includes the stuff Wese used to make, which would never harden and had to be eaten with a spoon. Did you have some yourself? If you ever run into more of it, sure would like to have it.

Just mailed you some more smokes, but I'm afraid I won't be able to send any more. We are restricted to two packs a day, and beginning the first, I believe we will only be able to get one. Pall Malls aren't a very popular cigarette, so I've been able to talk the Officer's Club out of a carton now and then, but I'm afraid even that will stop. I hope you like PM's. At least they last a little longer than most. How are you fixed for smokes? Can you manage to get them?

I am enclosing some clippings and a weather briefing sheet which is given to us pilots every day before we fly. The daily briefing lasts about two hours. All the crews to fly during the period, meet in a large room divided in the middle by an aisle. The pilots sit on the aisle seats on both sides, and their crews next to them in order of rank, or co-pilot, navigator, bombardier, engineer, radio operator, and gunners. Altogether there are about 300 in the room and we are given intelligence, weather, navigational, and operational briefings as a group. Then the gunners, navigators, etc., go to another room for special briefings on their subjects, and the pilots and co-pilots meet with the squadron and flight commanders.

After the briefing sessions, we go to the Clothing Pool to draw heavy flying clothes, which are drawn and turned in daily. Briefing for the morning period begins at 0430, and I manage to takeoff between 0630 and 0700, and land about 1300.

I have written mother a letter about the trips I took last week, and I presume you will see the letter in a few days. It was swell to hear that you had such a good weekend. I wish you could have more of them. In fact, I wish you could have all of them.

I'm not a bit enthusiastic about the way things are working out in Europe. We are feeling the absence of Roosevelt very strongly and will more so in the future. And we can't lay all the blame to Russia, either. We would feel just as they do if some other power was threatening our influence in South America. Nevertheless, things look very bad. A future war between England, the U.S., and Russia would probably be more than the world could stand. I'll tell you now that if it ever comes to that, I will not support the war and will go to jail if necessary. I would rather be a traitor to my country than to my ideals.

There will certainly be a period for general catching of wind, but if our relations continue to be so strained, and they may become more so, after the reality of this war has faded, we're damn liable to plunge headfirst into another.

Well, Pop, let me hear from you again soon. I think of you often and wish you a lot of luck.   As ever, Bill

---

May 26, 1945

Dear Mother and all:

Thank you, Mom . . . for the three packages you sent. The cake arrived in fair condition, not whole, but not wholly in crumbs, and in any state it would have been delicious. The funny thing about it is that it broke in just about the size of individual servings. Lots of the boys came down last night and stood in the doorway, bulling and munching their cake. The latter went in a hurry, though I had some for lunch today.

In addition to what I received from all of you, I gave myself a bicycle. I had combed Tonopah and the base thoroughly, I thought, and unable to find one, decided I'd do without one. But I told the crew that I'd give $5.00 to anyone who could find one for me, and the very next day, my waist gunner, whom I have had reassigned to the nose turret, said, "Skipper, where's my fin?" [Yiddish slang for five-dollar bill] The bike is in excellent shape. It was bought, ordered and sent from Reno, by a civilian living on the base, one week before the poor fellow was drafted. I got it at a fair price, a bargain during wartime, but hardly an inexpensive bargain. Anyway, I have a bike, and it is swell to be able to ride down to the line every day. I just got it yesterday, by the way. When I leave here, I think I will send it home, or to my next base, if I am to be there any length of time.

I do not know what will follow Tonopah. Normally, of course, my crew and I would get a brand-new ship on the coast, and fly it overseas, but that seems unlikely now. The two main possibilities are these: 1. The crew will be broken up and I will go to the new B-32's, probably as co-pilot, and 2. The crew will be sent together to a radar school, perhaps Langley, Va., and after a few weeks of learning about the equipment, get a ship with radar installed. I much prefer the radar deal.

It was a pretty good birthday. Two years from yesterday I expect to be eating at Sally's [Jo's]. Her offer is accepted hereby. And two years does not seem too long. Two years ago, I was at Nashville, celebrating my majority [21st birthday]. My twenty-third birthday saw a little progress since then and was marked by the appearance of two gray hairs prominently located at the top of my forehead, but so far as even I can tell, by the disappearance of none anywhere, which to date, is probably my greatest accomplishment. At least I'm proudest of it. I always told dad my hair would be gray before his. Now it only lasts as long.

Charley has asked me to go into partnership with him after the war, raising chicks, and selling them in our own store, in the style of Val-lo-will.[16] I can think of nothing I'd rather do. Both he and Fran have written about it, and I'm really glad that it was Chas's idea. Because I have had such great experience, I will probably handle the production angle, and Chas the distribution, but of course we both will do both together.

The telegram was received and greatly appreciated from Mrs. Pomeroy [unidentified]. I will drop her a card. Also, a fine telegram from dad. Apparently, the restrictions have been raised.

Do you still have the little chain I wove for your watch? My watch is working perfectly, and I don't know what I'd do without it. Most of the planes do not have clocks, and many of the radio problems I have to work on instruments have to be timed to the second.

You asked a few weeks ago if the name of our ship was "Howdy Doody." We don't have our own ship as yet, and seldom fly the same one two days in a row. They are all B-24J's, though each has its individual characteristics.

I had my second, and I hope last, emergency check-ride this morning. I made three, two, and one engine landings, and the sweat was just pouring off me. But I did so much better than two months ago, that I can take a few aching muscles with pleasure.

This'll be all for now. Be sure to thank the girls for me, and thanks to you too, old lass, for all your letters and thoughts, and the birthday presents. Much love.

As ever, Bill

June 11, 1945

Dear Mother:

By this time, you have seen Ginny [cousin] and know what a swell break I had Saturday night. I won't tell you the details on how it happened, because I'm sure she will.

You will be glad to hear that Tarry looked wonderful. I don't remember a time when she looked better. She does not seem thin anymore, though of course she is slight. But her face is much fuller and her hair is almost as beautiful as yours. You, of course, saw her last summer, but I hadn't seen her, or Gin or Pete [cousins] since they left Evanston.

I introduced Tar and Gin to all the boys, and they have raved about both ever since. Tell Ginny that Frenchy kept talking about her all the way home, till I got sick of telling him about her, what a tennis player she was, etc., and that no, I didn't think she was engaged to Jim. Jim seems like a swell guy, by the way. It probably wasn't easy to be with so many army men, all of whom were making eyes at his girl.

I'm hoping to be able to land at Tucson when Wese and Joan [Opperman] are there, but my chances are not good, because I can't land on such a feeble excuse again. I was called into the Colonel's [Feagin] office this morning to explain myself, which I did without making myself seem too much a fool. But there was obviously no need to land, and I wouldn't have thought of it if the Groses hadn't been there.

The attitude being taken here by the section is that "oh, well, he has a good record, and everyone is entitled to goof off once in a while." But it might not be so easy if I tried to do it again.

The day before Tucson, I had my final instrument check, flying in an overcast for four hours straight, mostly in circles, and under the instrument hood for an hour and a half. In addition, I had beam problems to work, letdowns on the range and with the radio compass, aural null orientation etc. I did pretty well, because I've been working on my instruments a lot. I got a grade of excellent, and also was graded excellent as an Airplane Commander.

I know nothing more about what will happen when I finish here the middle of July. But if the latrine is to be trusted, chances of staying with B-24's are better. Yes, B-24's will be used a lot against Japan, though chiefly, I think, against the Japs in China, when we get bases in China that is. The reason I might be sent to B-32's is that it is a larger, new plane, and pilots with a four-engine rating have to be selected to fly them, even as co-pilot . . .

Regards to all and thank you for your last, all-inclusive letter. Keep up the good work, and don't pass the buck to anyone.

As ever, Bill

June 13, 1945

Dear Dad:

I haven't been able to write to you for some time, because you haven't remained in one place for long. I am always glad to get your letters and cards and am especially glad that you are to be in Denver for a few weeks and will be able to see the Weeds, [Fran and her family].

By this time, you may have heard that I spent last Saturday night with the Groses in Tucson. I was scheduled for a non-stop trip down there, but over the city, couldn't resist the temptation to land to "check my lights." I had to call Tonopah to report my actions, and was told to stay all night, as it'd be too late by the time I got home, and no one wanted to wait up for me. Naturally, this was a tough break.

I had on my flying clothes, and was restricted to the field, but I sneaked out in Tarry's car and had a fine time. It was way after midnight when we got to their house, and we had to get up at 0600 Sunday, so it was strictly a rushed affair. I've written mother about it, and you will see the letter in due time.

As I took off from Tucson Sunday morning at 0900, I buzzed the house twice, flying over at an altitude of 1,000′ and changing my prop pitch for added noise. I have not yet heard if they were watching me, but I presume they were.

Tomorrow night I am going to call mother. Each week, one of the 160 crews on the field is chosen as being the "Crew of the Week." The choice is made not only on his record of the week but is accumulative over all the weeks he has been at the field. As a reward, the whole crew receives a three-day pass to L.A. and a plane ride down there.

The second best crew of the week, or runner up, receives a free phone call home, and that's that. I've had my eyes on crew of the week ever since I've been here, and if I don't make it, at least I came pretty close.

Today the whole crew, except the bombardier, had its picture taken. I think I will be able to get only one print, which I will send to mother. Tar met the entire crew, by the way, and liked them a lot. I also had the fun of taking Gin and her through a B-24, and let Tar sit in the pilot's seat.

There is definitely a possibility that I'll be able to fly to Denver while you and mother are there. I've got one more month to go here, but have already completed my minimum requirements, so if the others get their work under control, so that planes could be spared, I'll be able to land at Lowry Field and stay overnight.

I'll work on this all I can and will tell the section leader you are to be there, but please don't count on it. If I can make it, great. If I can't, tough.

The candy you sent so long ago was sure swell, and thanks a lot. Any more where that came from?

Give my regards to my partners in Golden [Weeds in Colorado], and let me hear from you again soon.

Am so glad you can have your vacation out there. Remember last year?

Best of everything. Bill

June 22, 1945

Dear Dad:

Thanks for your two letters and the clippings. Your remark that you are "sure I'll be able to get to Denver" shows that you do not know the Army as well as you did back in 17, 18. [1917-18] There is no possibility at all of getting time off, as that would ground my whole crew and throw the Fourth Air Force schedule off balance. My only chance is to be able to talk the section into letting me take an overnight cross-country with the entire crew. Several weeks ago, we were promised such a trip, and I have asked about it this week. I was told that they didn't know if they "could spare the planes." Don't expect me to come. There is a possibility that I may, and I will work as hard as I can on the matter, but right now it seems doubtful to me.

A little more encouraging is the possibility of a leave late next month. The situation here is more trying than you can imagine. Already we have more than completed the requirements for combat duties, and normally would be well on the way toward our fiftieth combat mission. But we are very definitely surplus crews, and I think there will be no place for us for several months. The training I am getting here formerly lasted for three months, three phases, as it is called. I am in the *fourth* phase already and there is a rumor that there will be a total of *six.* But the section which finished the fourth phase two weeks ago has been given a leave before reporting back here for further duty, and I expect the same will happen to my section. So, I will probably be home for a week or ten days, and then come back to dear old Tonopah, the garden spot of the desert.

Here is another possibility which there is no sense in speaking of to any but the *immediate* family. Yesterday my flight commander had a talk with me and told me that he and the section commander were considering my crew as the "crew of the class."[17] That means the all-around outstanding crew, and does not mean my pilot ability only, and I can't tell you how proud I'd be to get the honor. But I will tell you very frankly and sincerely that I do not expect to. I'm not saying that out of modesty, because I am not modest. If I thought we were really the outstanding crew I'd say so, but I don't think we're any better than the best of the other crews, so if I get it, it will be as much a matter of luck as anything else. But it is certainly something of an honor to even be considered for it. The weak link, as far as the section is concerned, is my bombardier, who, formerly an instructor, knows his bombing backward and forward, but whose attitude is not especially "eager." Bob is having some private troubles, and I can't say I blame him very much, but I will be very sorry if he keeps us from the award.

I am enclosing a picture of the crew, except for the bombardier. It's a pretty good picture taken beside a B-24.

Tuesday, I took a trip which lasted over eight hours. We flew from here to San Francisco to a point 100 miles over the ocean, directly south to a point west of Los Angeles. Because of the eastward slope of California, this put us 200 miles from land. There is lots of anti-aircraft activity along the coast, and we had to cross at a specified time, altitude and position. It was a lot of fun, but the tough part about it is that not once did we even see the ocean. We were only 11,000 feet, but there was an undercast of solid stratus clouds extending several hundreds of miles out!

Well, Pop, give my love to mother and you two have a swell time. I'm tickled to death that you are having this vacation with Fran, and I'll never forget the one you had last year with me. Best of everything.   As ever, Bill

---

[Editor's note: the following letter was written to Jean Forster before they met in Evanston. "Blue" was a short version of the nickname, "Bluejean."]

June 23, 1945

Blue dearest:

Your letter arrived fifteen minutes after I had mailed my card, and this may seem unnecessary. As far as I can figure out, July 28 is probably a good time for you to be in Evanston, but I'll be very PO'd (I hope you don't know what that means, but you probably do) if I can't make it at the same time.

Your message of Bon Voyage was a trifle chafing. This training was supposed to last three months, and I'm already well into my fourth. The group that finished just ahead of mine, is returning here after their leaves to go through the whole damn thing again. There is obviously no place to send us. Air fields in the United States and Hawaii are overflowing with heavy bombardment crews for whom there is no use, and I wouldn't be surprised to mark time in Nevada for many months. I have no desire to kill Japs, I hope I never drop a bomb on a human target, but just the same, I am good and sick of being a Training Command Commando. Besides, Brian is making me feel like a slacker.[18] Wanting to go overseas is pure ego in my case. I would like to be able to say I had been over, to put an APO in my return address, and even a little to know what war is like and how I could take it.

A cabin in the Alps sounds swell, if it were properly furnished, but I have a theory, which I half believe, about people who seek happiness, "their kind of life" etc., in foreign countries. Actually, your kind of life, (and mine) does not anymore exist in Switzerland than it does in an apple grove on top of a hill in Wisconsin. As Brian wrote, a paradise is not found, it is built. The reason we look for a paradise elsewhere is because we know so many people who have failed to build one here, and we feel that because of this, one cannot be built here, that America is too commercial-minded, too standardized, etc., which is, of course, true. But my twenty-acres and a library would seem to be a solution.

Lots of times I have pictured myself drinking beer in a German beer garden, bicycling through southern France, watching the sunrise over an English countryside. Ach, pure romanticism. The beer would be just as good in my own garden, the bicycle trip just as good in Wisconsin, the sunrise just as beautiful and many. But I understand the certain grace of living most of us in America lack, though I'm not so certain that we would find it as often in Europe as we think we would. Beauty, love, life, are where you see them, and certainly Americans are a blind race.

Jean, I must see you. And I don't want to go to Philadelphia. I know a beach north of Winnetka [Illinois] where we can have a picnic supper and roast marshmallows and go swimming after dark. I am not at all interested in going to nightclubs in either Philly or Chicago. I am anti-social. At least yours is the only society I want, and we could do nothing together much more easily in Evanston.

Can you possibly leave the date of your vacation open till I learn the date of mine? It can't be vice versa.

I have more faith in your aunt's sun than in her God, but that also is a long story.

Yes, your cooking at 6124 has always been good; especially your waffles.

Bill

July 4, 1945

Dear Mother:

I have looked through the complete stock of both stores in Tonopah, in addition to the PX's on the field, and have found nothing I would care to send you as a birthday present. You have no idea what it's like out here, but I know you'll understand why I'm not giving you anything.

A leave toward the 23rd of July is as certain as anything is certain in the Army, and so we'll make a day of it in the loop [Chicago Loop], and I'll find something I'd be proud to give you, not to mention lunch at the Glorified Hamburger and a movie at the State-Lake! Is it a date?

I really feel embarrassed about this, though I know there is no need for me to. But it's just that I would like so much to repay you for all your letters, packages, thoughtfulness, and love. Not that I think I could do it with one birthday present.

I've thought many times of you and dad at Golden and have pulled all the strings I could to join you. I guess it was just not to be. But I'm hoping to be able to stop and see Fran for a while on my way home. Too bad you won't be there, so we could come home together.

I've finished all of my flying, except for one more 1,000-mile trip, which I'll get Friday. There will be more days of flying, and when I get back from my leave there will be still more. I suppose we can't get too much of it, but it all has the aroma of "made work" and that's not much fun any time.

Because we are so far along with the phases, we had three days off last week. My radio operator, Dean Levie (McGrew), his wife, and I went camping in a canyon about fifty miles from here. We camped along a mountain stream in a grove of tall cotton woods. McGrew fished most of the time, and I sat under a tree and read *Lust for Life*.[19] It was a wonderful rest and change, and I'll tell you about it when I see you. I slept both nights in the open, by the fire, and loved it. But what a sissy I am! I couldn't even clean the fish! I prefer my meat already prepared from the butchers, and as long as I feel this way, I wonder if it wouldn't be more honest to be a vegetarian. Now you know what kind of men we are, training to kill Japs. I hope I never have to drop a bomb on a living target or take the life of one fish or one chicken.

I've been getting up at 0330 for the last six days and am very tired. In addition, I've angered my engineer and, on his account, the other enlisted men on the crew, by not recommending him for a promotion to Sergeant, which in effect is the same as recommending that he not be promoted. The other pilots think I've been too hard too, and maybe I have. I feel depressed, but I don't give a damn, and I'm not going to be intimidated into anything. To make it slightly worse, Thompson, the engineer, thinks I don't like him and thinks he deserves the promotion. I promoted the other two on my crew who were eligible.[20]

Well, Mom, I wish you a terribly happy birthday, and send you more love than usual to make up for the lack of something else.

Regards to all,   As ever Bill

[Editor's note: After the above letter was written, Bill was allowed a leave in Golden, Colorado, and then returned to Evanston with his parents, "LATH Notes," 1945. The following letter was written to Jean after Bill's leave.]

August 4, 1945

. . . Blue, I am very happy. It's good to be back in my room. I have three pictures of you (not enough), and one of Rainey on the shelf in front of my desk, your letters stuck in the crack between the upright wall supports and the plaster board, and your Greek postal card beneath a thumb tack holding down one corner of a map of Japan. I am surrounded by you.

And though I am much more anxious to get out of uniform than I ever have been, I am also much more patient. You have made me realize that there is something really worthwhile in life, and you have given me a great desire to become a part of it. I am also beginning to realize that my part in this war belongs to the same pattern of seeking truth and justice with which I want to design my life, and that it is not wasted time at all, at least that it won't be wasted time unless we lose sight of our ideals and seek only pleasure and happiness for ourselves. I've heard that a thousand times, but I've never felt it before.

. . . I want to work and work hard, but I've got to feel that my work means something besides a monthly check. My work must have some importance in our fight to live. What exactly it will be, God only knows, if there is a God, and I'm afraid I'm not now qualified for anything important, but I have seen the light and you can be damn sure I'm going to make the most of my "leisure" time. I really have been for a long time, but without much enthusiasm and without any plan. It's been like walking slowly through a dark hallway, knowing that sometime before you come to the end and fall out the window, you would see the light from under some doorway, and then you could open the door and walk as if you weren't afraid, but you never knew how long you were going to have to grope for your way. *You* lighted the candle, and I'm beginning to run toward it!

Which reminds me that it's time to put out the light and hit the sack. I love you more than somewhat.   Bill

---

August 6, 1945

[Editor's Note: Atomic Bomb dropped on Hiroshima, Japan.]

Dear Mother:

. . . My eighteen months in grade is up on the eighth, and I have told the proper person about it. He smiled and said he'd see what he could do, and I really feel that the promotion will come through this month. Then I'll be back in the chips. One thing I am glad about; that all during this "financial crisis" I have not stopped buying my $100 war bonds.

There is still nothing definite about my future, my future in the army, I mean. It looks as though I'll be here all month, and then go to Ephrata, Wash. [Army Air Field] That is as reliable a rumor as any, but of course, there is no way to tell if a rumor is reliable. Flying goes on as usual.

I have just finished *The Jungle* and am plunging into socialism with more enthusiasm than I've felt for a long time. Now it's *The Big Bosses*, to be followed by *Cooperative Democracy*.[21] I've done lots of reading in the Army, but now I'm buckling down to work. I've got to keep that girl [Jean Forster] of mine.

All for now. Love to all.   As ever, Bill

August 8, 1945

Dear Dad:

... Flying goes on as ever, and there is nothing definite. If the atomic bomb doesn't drastically change our timetable, I will probably leave at the end of the month, but now anything can happen. I think of the swell times we had and hope you can find something to do in Bismarck.   Regards. As ever, Bill

---

August 18, 1945

Dear Fat:

There is nothing I can tell you re the Army's plans for me, though I very much fear that I will have to put in a tour in the occupation Air Force. Meanwhile, flying and ground school go on as usual.

I did not get to make the Denver trip. One crew in the ten in my flight can go every week, the crew being chosen by lots, so I will have a chance every week while I am here.

Do you know much about the cooperative movement? I am reading about it now and am very interested. In fact, I have never found anything else which might interest me for after the war. College is a possibility, but there are many drawbacks.

At any rate, I think it's impossible that I'll be out in less than a year, and it will more likely be 18 months.

It will take several weeks for my promotion to go through, so I am still a shavetail [Army slang for a second lieutenant].

Let me hear from you soon, old boy, and I hope you find something to do in Bismarck.   Best of everything. Bill

---

[No greeting—addressed to Hanchett in Evanston.]

August 19, 1945

I should have thanked you long ago for the package with the candy and tobacco pouches. The latter are the best I have ever had and manage to keep moisture in even in the desert.

Sometime I wish you would send me *Co-op* by Upton Sinclair, which I think is on the radiator in Wese's room.[22]

Tomorrow begins a week of flying in the morning, which means getting up at 0330. I really won't mind, because we've had very little to do this past week, and I'm getting rather bored with lying on my sack.

There is still nothing I can tell you, except that I feel more strongly than before that I won't be getting out of the Army for some time. It's a big disappointment, but the war has been disgracefully easy for me, and it's not hard to be philosophical. But I would like to know, and not have to wonder so much.

I think of all of you lots and am glad to get your letters. The flying is a laugh. We continue to bomb and fire our guns! All "made work" and I'm getting good and sick of it.   Bill

---

[Editor's note: another letter written to Jean Forster about his impending discharge.]

August 26, 1945

I don't know if my letter yesterday made any sense. But I've had twenty-four hours to digest my good news, and I want to write again even if I only repeat myself.

That I will be discharged soon, probably next month, is certain. Plans for after that are less so, except that above everything else in the world, I want to marry you. I want to marry you this fall.

We won't need to rush off to Black Mountain or to Ireland or to anywhere else, until we're sure where we want to go and what we hope to accomplish when we go there.

We could buy BH [unidentified] on my mustering out pay and drive down to North Carolina to check up on things. If we like it we could stay there.

We could go around to different cooperative societies and learn how they work and whether or not we want to plunge right in, or plunge in at all.

But whatever we do, we will have decided to do, and what is much more important, we will do it together.

Darling, I know that I'll never be able to do anything without you. There is a certain sort of life I want to lead. I have ideas and ideals, but you are my incentive to attain those ideals. I love you with all my capacity for love, and with you and your love, my capacities for realizing life are horizonless.

Write me, Blue, and please be there when I get back. By the way, I love you.

[No greeting—addressed to Hanchett in Evanston.]

August 30, 1945

No Labor Day golf game. My section is moving next week to Mountain Home, Idaho, and I have to go with it, and separation proceedings will have to start all over from there. Anyway, I'll be home sometime this fall, if late in the fall.

Will send you my new address when I get it, probably a week from today. Will go up by special train, and though it's only about 600 miles, I'm sure the trip will take two or three days.

Flying has stopped, but classes continue. No one pays much attention to them, and I have plenty of free time. Am keeping my mind occupied with thoughts other than what I'm going to do as a civilian, for a good 30% of the time. Not at all good, I know. Currently am reading one of Lewis' I somehow missed last winter, *Work of Art*.[23]

Golly, I'm sorry to hear about AA's back. Are you sure it's not just another attempt to win sympathy? Give her my love, keep letters coming and love to you, too.   Bill

Correspondence From
MOUNTAIN HOME ARMY AIR FIELD

[NO DATE or POSTMARK, addressed to his mother.]

Would write a letter if there were anything I could tell you. This AAF is also in the desert, but not as far from civilization as Tonopah, and seems a lot better. The sage brush even looks greener.

Have a larger room than at TAAF and am sharing it again with Bill Mellinger.

I would like to know something definite for a change! Note new address. Bill

LT Wm F Hanchett J 1-824622
Crew 203, AAF
Mountain Home, Idaho

[NO DATE or POSTMARK, addressed to his father.]

Out in the desert again, but closer to civilization. Spent last evening in Boise. Quite a place. I presume you've been there.

Can tell you nothing about what I'll be doing here or when I'll be discharged!

Hope everything's OK with you, and that you'll write soon. Note new address [as above]. Good luck. As ever, Bill

[No Addressee.]

September 10, 1945

I've received so many letters of congratulation [re: impending marriage to Jean Forster] during the last two days, as the mail dribbles in from

Tonopah, that I realize I've got to tell you the story about my discharge.

As I mentioned in my last letter, which must for a time remain unexplained, I am no longer considered "surplus personnel," and am not eligible for separation. I was not told at Tonopah that I was surplus, in fact, was told that proceedings would go through here with only a few days delay. But when I reported to the classification office, I was told, oh no, I haven't enough points to get out, it's too bad I didn't stay at Tonopah!

So that's how it is. I will have enough points in April, and unless the standard is lowered before that time, I can expect a discharge in the spring. I really don't expect to go overseas, because I am in a low classification, "D," which I think I have explained to you.

I arrived here last Wednesday after a miserable 48-hour trip in a dirty and ancient day coach. We have roll call at 0900 and another at 1400, and no other duties! It is a disgraceful waste of time, and you can imagine how fed up I am with it, especially since I missed being discharged by only a few weeks. I would have been, you realize, if I had stayed at Tonopah.

But I don't expect this to last much longer. They're bound to give us something to do, if only to avoid large scale desertion . . .

As ever, Bill

September 18, 1945

Dear Mother:

I have to ask you to make another deposit for me, and because I know you hate as much as I do to see the war bonds melt away, I will give you an explanation.

In the first place, I have bought a car, a 1935 Chevrolet in quite good shape. If you knew this spot you would realize that one is essential, and it is more so than ever since I am going to commute the ten miles between field and town.

I have paid cash for the car, to save myself $54. I would have been charged for interest, carrying, etc. and that is why I am in need of money.

Saturday, I have to buy a new tie and two rings, so will have to ask you to deposit another *$250* or *more* in my account. It may be I do not have enough bonds that can be cashed. If so, deposit *all you can* and wire me. It is important I know the amount Friday night, so I can make purchases on Saturday.

I hope you don't think I'm losing my mind. The car is an investment, which will be worth at least something, and beginning in October my monthly salary will be $328. Surely, we will be able to save on that, and we plan to do so, because I very definitely am going to college, and fully realize the need I'll have for cash at that time.

I'm giving you these financial details so you will not feel too badly about cashing the bonds. Believe me, I have not closed my eyes to the future.

I have not yet received a letter from you, though I have a telegram from Fran.

I have received a note of unlimited confidence from her, and a decisive victory in Evanston. I've been amusing myself by guessing the three who oppose this marriage are, and on what grounds they oppose it.

I won't bother to tell you how I feel. I am very happy. I hope you will plan to see Jean, and perhaps her father and sister. Jean will probably arrive in Evanston Sunday or Monday, and flies here Wednesday, arriving Thursday morning.

If I can get excused from classes, which begin next week, we'll be married that afternoon.

Have an appointment for a dental exam, so will quit.

Very much love to you, Mother.   As ever, Bill

This letter needn't go the rounds.

Don't forget to wire so I'll receive it Friday. Am so sorry to cause you all these trips. But believe me, I appreciate them and will not forget.

September 25, 1945

Lost dad's address, tell him so, please? I'm very glad you stopped in to see Ethne & Dr. F., and I suppose you may be seeing them while Jean is at home.[24]

Everything has been arranged for 8:00 Thurs. evening in the Post Chapel. I'm inviting no one but Bill Mellinger (my co-pilot) and a boy from Evanston, whom I think Jean knows.

Thanks for your letters & telegrams, and for doing all those errands for me.

Car is working very well, but I'm having difficulty in getting to sleep. Will write soon.

Much love, Bill

September 27, 1945

Jean was grounded in Chicago last night because of weather, but wired that she may arrive tomorrow. I'll expect her by Saturday, anyway.

You probably know that I have again been alerted for discharge, and this time I think it means something. My crew has been taken away from me, and I am now in the waiting squadron. Instead of going to Ft. Sheridan, I will be separated at Gowen Field, Boise, because I own a car. I suppose you know that, by the way. There I will be paid for the drive home at the rate of $.08 a mile, with the same for Jean, but whether we will come right home remains to be seen. Jean has not been west, and this would be a good chance to show her a little of it.

In your last letter urging me to consider staying in the Army, you used the following arguments: 1. Financial security 2. Pension and retirement benefits and 3. The difficulty of making a living in a world where workers were demanding 52 hours pay for 40 hours work. You realized that I did not like life in the Army, or the Army itself, but implied that it would be worth what it cost. That is, that it would be worth spending a lifetime, or the better part of one, doing work in which I had no interest, for the sake of making a little more money than I might otherwise be able to do, and to be able to retire at an earlier age. That is dollar worshiping if I have ever heard of it.

In the same letter you write of your employer, "Naturally a member of the chosen race is dollar conscious."

I will not stay in the Army for its financial security any more than you would work for Earl Browder for the same reason. And I am not going to become, as you seem to think is inevitable if I shed the uniform, an airline pilot, an aircraft executive, or an insurance salesman. I know perfectly what sort of life I am going to follow, but I cannot say exactly what work I will do till I have prepared myself more for it.

This includes at least a year at college, perhaps more, and if at the end of that time I still am as interested in cooperatives as I am now, some study at one of the Cooperative League schools, in which are taught the theory of cooperation, organization and management of cooperatives, and the training of field men.

I have not yet picked a college, but I want to study these courses: European History, Economics, Political Theory, and one or two others.

I cannot see that making money and gaining some elusive thing called "financial security" is the aim and purpose of life. I hope I will never work for a salary, for the sake of one, I mean, and if sometimes I am forced to, I will feel that the best possibilities of my life have been wasted. Don't misunderstand this. What I mean is that I will be a failure, no matter how much money I happen to make, by the way, (though if it turned out to [be] any comfortable amount, I probably would not have the courage to admit it, or the perspective to see it) if my life's work bears no relation to my life's beliefs, and of course, if it didn't, my beliefs would not live long.

I don't think I know it all. But I've gone too far for you to shrug this off as being more adolescent twaddle. I like sirloin steaks, comfortable beds, and cars. I like good clothes and good books; I like to travel in style and to have money in my pocket, but I'll be damned if I'm going to sell my soul to the devil (or the Republicans) to get them.

I have no duties at all, so when Jean comes, I'm going to take off for a few days.

Write again when you get the chance and tell me if this is a satisfactory answer to your letter. You better give me up as a hopeless case.

Take care, old boy.

Best regards and good luck.   Bill

[Editor's note: Bill and Jean were married on September 30, 1945. Based on Bill's service records, he was discharged on November 8, 1945, at the Separation Center, Gowen Field, near Boise, Idaho. The postwar correspondence consists of two letters as Bill and Jean prepared for Christmas and the future].

Epilogue

As previously noted, Bill told his father that his AAF experience had been "disgracefully easy" when compared to others. This shows that he was aware of and sensitive to the sacrifices others made during the war. For example, a review of the available records of Bill's Primary Flying School at Douglas Field reveals that out of the 211 cadets, twenty-one were killed in combat, seven were wounded in action, eight became prisoners of war, and five died in aviation accidents.[1]

There were others whom Bill knew, who went overseas to the war and did not return. Harriet Engelhardt, a Black Mountain College graduate, who with her family provided Bill some relief from the stress of preflight training, went to Europe with the American Red Cross Clubmobiles. The Clubmobiles supported the front-line troops across northern France and into Germany. Harriet wrote vivid descriptions of her experiences, however, just before she was to return home after the war, she tragically died in a jeep accident.[2]

Joseph John "Denny" Dennison, Jr., an ETHS classmate mentioned in Bill's August 15, 1943, correspondence, served as a U.S. Navy Hospital Corpsman during the invasion of North Africa in late 1942. While attached to the Fourth Marine Division during the Marianas Campaign in the Pacific, Dennison was killed on July 27, 1944, and was posthumously awarded the Bronze Star for heroism on Saipan and Tinian treating wounded Marines.[3]

Another one of Bill's good friends and a colleague in the history department at San Diego State University was Daniel L. Rader. As a B-17 bombardier, Dan flew over thirty missions in the European theater with the 509th Squadron of the 351st Bombardment Group (Heavy).[4]

Through his experiences, Bill's attitude changed from wanting to fly "hot ships" to disliking "made work" flying which seemed pointless to him. He was ready to move on. The idea of following his father into business had died with the bankruptcy of the company during the Depression. He now followed the example of his influential brother-in-law, Bob Babcock, and went into academics and teaching.[5] His service as an instructor-pilot and airplane commander provided him with practical teaching experience, something his correspondence showed he enjoyed.

Following his discharge, Bill planned to enroll again at Black Mountain College but did not, because of a lack of housing for married students. Instead, Bill attended Roosevelt College in Chicago for a year and a half and then moved to Dallas, Texas where his parents were living. While he completed a Bachelor of Arts in History from Southern Methodist University, Jean worked as a secretary at the university. It was there that Jean first saw a drinking fountain labeled "Colored." At first, she naively thought colored water came from that fountain.

Bill received the Master of Arts and Ph.D. degrees from the University of California, Berkeley. After working as an historian for the U.S. Air Force, Bill became an assistant professor of history at the Colorado State College of Agriculture and Mechanical Arts, Fort Collins, where my sister Emily was born. In 1956, he began his teaching career as an assistant professor of history at San Diego State University. Three years later, in January, 1959, seventeen years to the month that he had almost met Mrs. Eleanor Roosevelt in North Carolina, Bill was finally able to meet and speak with her when one of his nieces married Mrs. Roosevelt's grandson, Elliott.

Bill taught U.S. History, specializing in Abraham Lincoln and the Civil War for over thirty years at San Diego State University. In 1970, Bill published a biography of an influential Civil War era journalist, poet, and soldier, *Irish: Charles G. Halpine in Civil War America*. An expert on Lincoln's assassination, he wrote an acclaimed book, *The Lincoln Murder Conspiracies*, (1983), which examined the historiography of the assassination, and debunked various theories about the assassination. In relation to this book, another renowned Lincoln/Civil War historian, Gabor S. Boritt, gave Bill a nickname which I am sure he was proud of: "superior sleuth."[6] After retirement Bill wrote an introduction to the reprint of a classic 1940 study of the assassination, *The Great American Myth* by George S. Bryan, (1990). Four years later he published a short biography of Abraham Lincoln, *Out of the Wilderness: The Life of Abraham Lincoln* (1994), designed to introduce the sixteenth president to the general reader and to students. He also wrote video documentary scripts for *Out of the Wilderness* and *Black Easter*, about Lincoln's Assassination.

In addition, he published numerous articles in professional journals like *Civil War History and The Lincoln Herald*, where he served on the Editorial Board. Along with other Lincoln and Civil War scholars, Bill also contributed essays to several books on the sixteenth president and served as an expert defense witness in a court case concerning Lincoln's assassin.

In the late 1990s, at a Watchorn Lincoln Dinner at the Lincoln Memorial Shrine in Redlands, California, prefacing his remarks, the guest speaker spoke about military service and asked that veterans in the audience stand to be acknowledged. My father was among those who stood up, and I remember that one person at the banquet table was visibly impressed that Bill had been a B-24 pilot. Thinking back, that one incident at the Lincoln Dinner combined my father's youthful accomplishment—becoming a pilot—and his lifelong academic, serious study of Abraham Lincoln. Though flying and the AAF were far behind him, my father enjoyed touring B-24s when one would come to San Diego and, along with his air field booklets and flight manuals, he had several books on B-24s in his extensive library.

During one visit to a B-24 and B-17 tour in the San Diego area, Bill met an author sitting under the B-17 wing who was selling a memoir describing his experiences as a bombardier. I stayed back as the two men discussed their service. My father did not share the conversation, except to show me the memoir he had bought from the veteran bombardier. Doing research for this manuscript, I stumbled upon an interesting coincidence. Records of the 351st Bomb Group Association confirm that this man, Charles N. Stevens, served in the same bombardment group, in the same squadron, and during the same timeframe as my father's long-time friend, Dan Rader. I do not know if my father made the connection.[7]

There were times when he ruefully thought about flying fighter planes. One of the last times was on a Thanksgiving several years before he died, when I drove him by a static display of World War II Navy and Marine Corps fighters at Miramar Marine Corps Air Station. He told me that he wished he could have flown planes like those.

After the war, rather than continue to fly, Bill started sailing again just for fun. One of the things my father enjoyed most was sailing his sloop on San Diego Bay, which he had camera "bombed" so many years before. Out on the water with him, I wish I had known about his "bombing raid."

Years after he retired, Bill was interviewed about his experiences at Black Mountain College. During this interview he mentioned that BMC faculty member, Ted Dreier, had referred to him, though not by name, as the "poultry-mad" student. Some fellow students even called him "4H."

In the interview he laughed, denied that he was "poultry-mad," and said, "I was not crazy about chickens." Though he remembered the chickens, unlike fighter planes, he may not have remembered his youthful interest in chickens.[8] What Bill did remember, and what he wanted to be remembered for, was his career as a historian and Lincoln scholar.

After supporting Bill's education and raising two children, Jean received a Master of Arts degree in Political Science from San Diego State University. Later, she completed both a law degree and a paralegal specialist program. She told me she had almost finished requirements for a political science master's degree in the 1940s, but due to the time lapse, had to start the academic program from scratch. In the field of political science, her main interest was comparative government. She was also excellent with foreign languages: French, German, Russian, and Spanish. Her interest in comparative government and affinity with languages led to an adventure at the height of the Cold War in the early 1960s when, as part of an academic tour, she passed through Checkpoint Charlie into East Berlin on a trip that took her through East Germany and Poland to the USSR, now the Russian Federation. Much later, she received a Fulbright scholarship and studied a new political party in Great Britain. In receipt of another Fulbright, my mother spent a summer in Egypt. After retiring from teaching advanced placement courses in high school and community college courses, she worked as a paralegal for a law firm where she gained a reputation as an excellent legal researcher. A talented artist, she also enjoyed painting landscapes.

Bill and Jean, although divorced for many years and living separate lives, both passed away in 2016, Bill in July and Jean in October.

Acknowledgments

As the editor of this World War II correspondence, I gratefully acknowledge and thank those who helped make the book possible. First, to my father, Bill Hanchett, who wrote the letters and postal cards, and to my grandparents, William and Alice Hanchett, who saved them, and to my aunt Jo who passed them on to my father. The correspondence lay dormant for years until late July 2016, when it was discovered in his study around the time my father died.

The book would not have come about without the skills and patience of Sarah Conner Morgan, who transcribed all the original correspondence, enabling me to work with the material. I also thank Amanda Lanthorne at San Diego State University Library, Special Collections, who recommended Sarah to me.

Several historians provided me with guidance on this project. William C. "Jack" Davis, Virginia Tech emeritus faculty, read several drafts of the manuscript and gave me counsel that improved my writing. Jack wisely advised me to "let the letters tell the story." Gregory Daddis, San Diego State University history professor, referred me to Karl Zingheim, Historian, U.S.S. Midway Museum and San Diego State University history lecturer, and Brian Laslie, Command Historian at the U.S. Air Force Academy. Brian and Karl reviewed the manuscript, encouraged the project, and provided valuable suggestions. Peter Stekel, a writer who has investigated World War II aircraft accidents, saved me from mistakes early on in my work on this project. Paul Hoffman, Director, U.S. Air Force Air University Press, Air Education and Training Command, also read the manuscript and provided useful advice.

Archangelo Difante, Archivist, and Tammy Horton, Archives Technician of the U.S. Air Force Historical Research Agency at Maxwell Air Force Base, Alabama, patiently responded to my continuous requests for official records of the air fields where my father served during the war.

At the Central Nevada Museum, Tonopah, Nevada, Allen Metscher, Director and Arlene Melton, a researcher, provided information regarding

Tonopah Army Air Field, and access to photographs. Additionally, Melissa Culbertson, San Diego Air and Space Museum Librarian, helped with acquiring a photograph of an AT-6 Texan.

Susan Harrington of the 63rd Preservation Society and the WWII Flight Training Museum, Douglas, Georgia, provided documentation and photographs of the air field where my father completed Primary Flying School. The late Janet Fogg, author and historian of the 359th Fighter Group; Jennifer Thompson, Director of Education and Grace Lehner, Archivist at the Evanston (Illinois) History Center all cheerfully responded to requests for information.

Megan Atkinson, University Archivist, and Jennifer Dewar, Archives Assistant at the Angelo and Jennette Volpe Library at Tennessee Technological University, provided information about a faculty member mentioned in the correspondence.

Heather South, Lead Archivist, Western Regional Archives State of North Carolina and Mary Emma Harris, experts on Black Mountain College, shared their knowledge and documentation that shed light on the unique college that Bill Hanchett attended before entering the Army Air Forces.

Emily Hanchett provided several letters written to our mother not included in the main collection of correspondence. Wese's daughters, Amy Nachman and Linda Connelly, gave me our grandmother's valuable notebook of Hanchett family events covering 1910-1950, referred to as "LATH Notes," which provided additional perspective and corroboration of certain events.

I thank the Acorn Publishing staff, especially Holly Kammier, Jessica Hammett and editor Laura Taylor for their assistance and expertise in guiding me through the publishing process.

Finally, this book would not have been possible without the steadfast love, support, patience, editing and computer expertise of my wife, Connie Wilbur, who brought it all together. She learned more about World War II airplanes than she ever expected or wished to know.

Thanks to all.

—Tom Hanchett

Notes

INTRODUCTION NOTES

1. Mary Guernsey Lydecker, Elizabeth Hart Pennell, eds., *Twenty-Fifth Reunion Record Class of 1912: Wellesley College* (Wellesley: Wellesley College Press, 1937), Alice Trowbridge, page unnumbered. See also Wellesley College, *Wellesley College Record 1875-1912: A General Catalogue of Officers and Students* (Wellesley: Wellesley College Press, 1937), L. Alice Trowbridge 1908-1909, 266, https://books. google.com/books?id=z1lIAAAAYAAJ&pg=PA266&lpg=PA266&dq=wellesley+c ollege+student+Alice+Trowbridge&source=bl&ots=-Kefe6K0le&sig=ACfU3U0f 5oh83FpUu8rpib96WufwnsAdrw&hl=en&sa=X&ved=2ahUKEwjzyunT-YzkAhV KSq0KHeZRAu8Q6AEwAnoECAkQAQ#v=onepage&q&f=false. Alice's younger sisters were Jessie and Carolyn. Also, William Hanchett, "Biographical Sketch of Father and Grandfather," unpublished and undated, 1.

2. Hanchett, "Biographical Sketch of Father and Grandfather," 1. Personal family records, collection of letters upon Lucius Trowbridge's retirement in 1922, compiled in 1929, and reproduced by Clyde Louis Young, unpublished, July 2009. Lucie Alice Trowbridge Hanchett, "Personal Notes of Family Events 1910-1950," unpublished and identified hereinafter as "LATH Notes," also provides family background information.

3. Personal records of Leila A. Hanchett, American Red Cross Foreign Service Certificate and Keith Seymour, *The Descendants of Thomas Hanchett* (San Francisco, K.M. Seymour, 1985), 166.

4. Alice Hanchett recorded a visit to White Lake in 1912, and the first summer living there in 1926. In 1912 she noted that her first child, one-year-old daughter Jane, learned to walk at White Lake. Alice also recorded her daughters being sick during the 1918 flu pandemic. "LATH Notes," 1912, 1918, 1926.

5. Jane, Josephine, Frances, Alice Ann, William and Louise Hanchett, "We Are Six" (Evanston: unpublished writings, 1931).

6. "LATH Notes," 1937-1945. The Hanchett home of ten years was sold in 1937 and an unsettled lifestyle ensued throughout the war years. "LATH Notes" show that Alice and Will had ten different primary residences between 1937-1945.

7. Andrew Ferguson, *Land of Lincoln: Adventures in Abe's America* (New York: Atlantic Monthly Press, 2007), 77-81.

8. See "Christina Elizabeth Kammerer b. 2 June 1886, d. 14 January 1945," Vorwerk & Wilson Families, published July 13, 2012, https://www.woodvorwerk.com/vorwerk/ g1/p1632.htm.

CHAPTER 1 NOTES

1. No author noted, "Introducing Bill," *The Evanstonian* (ETHS Newspaper), unknown vol./no. (October 27, 1939): page unknown. Regarding Marion "Anne" Kappes, "LATH Notes," 1939, indicate that after dropping off Anne in Quebec, Bill hitch-hiked through Vermont and Massachusetts, visiting family and friends along the way. He saw the house where his father grew up in Westfield, Massachusetts. In later correspondence discussing this trip, Bill reminded his father that he visited the 1939 New York World's Fair which ran from April 30, 1939-October 27, 1940.

2. During the war, Bill Hubbell served in the Eighth Air Force in England as an assistant crew chief in the 369th Fighter Squadron of the 359th Fighter Group which first flew P-47 Thunderbolts and later, P-51 Mustangs. Information and photographs regarding Delmer F. "Bill" Hubbell's military service courtesy of the late Janet Fogg, author and historian of the 359th Fighter Group, received July 21, 2019.

3. Black Mountain College records of William F. Hanchett, Jr., 1941-1942, records held by the State of North Carolina Department of Natural and Cultural Resources. This archive includes documentation concerning Evanston Township High School. Courtesy of Heather South, Lead Archivist, Western Regional Archives, State of North Carolina Department of Archives and History, received on August 16, 2019.

4. BMC, see "Black Mountain College," Our State, accessed August 10, 2019, https://www.ourstate.com/mythic-mountain-college/. For an authoritative history of Black Mountain College, see Martin Duberman, *Black Mountain An Exploration in Community* (Garden City: Anchor Press/Doubleday, 1973).

5. At the time Bill speculated about joining the Army and serving in the cavalry, there were two cavalry divisions still on horseback. Bill's horseback riding may have served him well in the coming years as he became a pilot. Even after his first solo flights, when he was feeling more confident in the air, Bill told his mother he preferred the more personal touch when riding an animal. In his 1942 book *Bombs Away: The Story of a Bomber Team*, John Steinbeck describes an instructor explaining to his cadet student the similarities between riding a horse and flying an airplane. John Steinbeck, *Bombs Away: The Story of a Bomber Team* (New York: The Viking Press, First Published, 1942. New York: Penguin Classics, Second Edition, 2009), 94.

6. For brief background on Mary Gregory, see Duberman, *Black Mountain*, 156.

7. The conference subject was "Youth's Stake in War Aims and Peace Plans" and there were delegates from thirty-two colleges gathered at the University of North Carolina, Chapel Hill. From "A View to Hugh," University of North Carolina Libraries, accessed July 28, 2018, https://blogs.lib.unc.edu/morton/index.php/2012/01/eleanor-roosevelt-visits-chapel-hill/. During the First World War, Franklin D. Roosevelt served as Assistant Secretary of the Navy under Josephus Daniels, a North Carolina newspaper publisher, and Secretary of the Navy for President Woodrow Wilson. His wife, Addie Daniels, who accompanied him at the conference, was referred to as a "southern wit," by Jean Edward Smith, *FDR* (New York: Random House Trade Paperbacks, 2008), 117. In a subsequent letter, two years later, on December 18, 1944, (Chapter 8), Bill recalled that when he met former Secretary of the Navy Josephus Daniels at this conference, he stepped on Mrs. Daniels' toe and missed meeting Mrs. Roosevelt.

8. Records concerning Bob Babcock's civil service appointment in the Treasury Department are in his BMC file: Babcock, Robert BMC File in Western Regional Archives, State of North Carolina Department of Archives and History. Babcock's naval training at Wellesley College is in "LATH Notes," 1944.

9. For information about the departures of Babcock, Boyden, Evarts and his knowledge of the German language, see Duberman, *Black Mountain,* 45, 167.

CHAPTER 2 NOTES

1. The use of hotels in cities like Miami Beach was an innovation to meet the housing and training needs of the rapidly expanding Army Air Forces. Major General Walter R. Weaver, commander of the Army Air Forces Technical Training Command, whose responsibility included Miami Beach, came up with the idea. Weaver, a 1908 graduate of the United States Military Academy, served in the infantry before becoming a pilot in 1920. A 1942 Army Air Forces biographical sketch of Weaver described his coordination of relief operations in Alabama after the Mississippi River flood in 1929. In August 1941, as commanding general of the Southeast Air Corps Training Center, General Weaver inaugurated the air training program for African Americans at Tuskegee Institute. In early 1942, Weaver took command of the new AAF Technical Training Command. According to the official history, General Weaver decided that hotels would provide appropriate quarters for the massive housing required by the wartime expansion of training. Weaver's plan was approved, and hotels and other facilities in Atlantic City, Chicago, St. Petersburg, Miami Beach, and elsewhere were taken over for a variety of housing and training needs. According to the official history, Miami Beach was the largest training center, where approximately 82,000 personnel took over more than 300 hotels and apartment buildings for housing and training for the Army Air Forces Technical Training Command. For a biographical sketch of General Walter R. Weaver (1885-1944), see "War Changes High Commands," *Air Forces Newsletter*, Vol 25, February 1942, No.1, 6, accessed October 19, 2019, https://media.defense.gov/2011/Apr/20/2001330087/-1/-1/0/AFD-110420-016.pdf. Weaver's U. S. Air Force official biography is: "Major General Walter Reed Weaver," U.S. Air Force Biographies, accessed March 15, 2020, https://www.af.mil/About-Us/Biographies/Display/Article/2141849/major-general-walter-reed-weaver/.

For Weaver and Tuskegee, see Ulysses Lee, *The Employment of Negro Troops, USAWWII* (Washington, D.C.: Center of Military History, United States Army, 2000, First printed 1966), 120.

For General Weaver's use of hotels see the official history, Frank Futrell, "The Development of Base Facilities," *The Army Air Forces in World War II, Volume VI, Men and Planes, I. The Organizations and Responsibilities,* Wesley Frank Craven, James Lea Cate, eds. (Chicago: University of Chicago Press, 1955; New Imprint: Washington, D. C., United States Air Force, Office of Air Force History, 1983), 152-155, https://media.defense.gov/2010/Nov/05/2001329891/-1/-1/0/AFD-101105-019.pdf.

Miami Beach Basic Training Center official records: Air Force Historical Research Agency (AFHRA), Reel A2356, History of Basic Training Center #9, November 19, 1942-November 1, 1943, Frames 3-50. For a more recent article about the Miami Beach Training Center see: Editor, "Miami Beach Wartime Training Center, Flashback Miami column," *Miami Herald*, February 25, 2015, https://flashbackmiami.com/2015/02/25/miami-beach-wartime-training-center/.

2. The Coral Reef Hotel, 3601 Collins Avenue, Miami Beach, had 103 rooms with a capacity for 206 men, and the annual rental was $31,000. See the record of the U.S. Congress Senate Special Committee, *Investigation of the National Defense Program,* Exhibit 987, Miami Beach, FL Leased Hotels retained by Army Air Forces 1944 - Industrial mobilization, accessed December 17, 2019, https://books.google.com/books?id=P5kjAQAAMAAJ&pg=PA9114&lpg=PA9114&dq=Army+Air+Forces+Miami+Beach+Basic+Training+Center+February+11,+1943&source=bl&ots=W7FN_lV9Xc&sig=ACfU3U2TlJu9UxwzTP43jdLq4GEjtZzntA&hl=en&sa=X&ved=2ahUKEwjr-sOB373mAhWVPM0KHa93AJQQ6AEwEHoECAoQAQ#v=onepage&q=Army%20Air%20Forces%20Miami%20Beach%20Basic%20Training%20Center%20February%2011%2C%201943&f=false.

3. Regarding development of the Army Air Forces and the idea of an independent air arm, see Russell F. Weigley, *History of the United States Army* (New York and London: The Macmillan Company, Collier-Macmillan Ltd., 1967), 442-443, and 458. See also Edward M. Coffman, *The Regulars: The American Army 1898-1941* (Cambridge MA: Belknap Press of Harvard College, 2004), 381-384.

4. Regarding "huge parade for the Colonel," the colonel referred to in the correspondence may be Colonel Ralph M. Parker, identified as the Commanding Officer, Miami Air Base Command in a photograph dated March 3. 1943, in Editor, "MBWTC Flashback Miami Column." According to official U.S.A.F. records for Basic Training Center Number 9 Miami Beach (AFHRA Reel A2356 Miami BTC), there were several colonels stationed there, so it is difficult to be certain of the identity of the officer referred to here. As commanding officer, Colonel Parker wrote an open letter to the citizens of Miami regarding noise made at the base on 6 February 1943, (AFHRA Reel A2356, Frame 1897).

5. Lily Pons (April 12, 1898-February 13, 1976), was a popular French opera singer, performing from the late 1920s through the early 1970s. "Lily Pons," Britannica, accessed March 20, 2022, https://www.britannica.com/biography/Lily-Pons.

6. Walter Locke (1875-1957), journalist/columnist, was a friend of John Andrew Rice, founder and first rector of Black Mountain College. In November 1934 he wrote an article describing the new college. See "Walter Leonard Locke 1875-1957 [RG 1186.AM]," Nebraska State Historical Society, accessed May 16, 2021, https://history.nebraska.gov/collections/walter-leonard-locke-1875-1957-rg1186am. See also Duberman, *Black Mountain*, 469.

7. February 14, 1943, letter: regarding Lieutenant General Henry "Hap" Arnold (1886-1950) whereabouts: General Arnold's diary shows that he was flying from Karachi, India to Khartoum, Sudan on February 11, 1943. See Major General John W. Huston, U.S. Air Force Retired, ed., *American Airpower Comes of Age: General Henry H. "Hap" Arnold's World War II Diaries*, Volume 1 (Montgomery, Maxwell Air Force Base: Air University Press, 2002), 501, https://media.defense.gov/2017/Mar/31/2001725201/-1/-1/0/B_0084_HUSTON_AMERICAN_AIRPOWER_DIARIES.PDF. The two generals mentioned by Bill may have been Generals Weaver and Krogstad. General Weaver is identified in endnote 1 above. Brigadier General Arnold N. Krogstad, (U.S. Military Academy 1909) was the commander of the Fifth District, Army Air Forces Technical Training Command, headquartered in Miami. See also "Brigadier General Arnold N. Krogstad," U.S. Air Force Biographies, accessed November 27, 2020, https://www.af.mil/AboutUs/Biographies/Display/Article/108098/brigadier-general-arnold-n- krogstad/.

8. Fyodor Dostoevsky, *Crime and Punishment* (Moscow: *The Russian Messenger*, originally published as monthly submissions, 1866). *Moon over Miami* was a 1941 movie starring Don Ameche and Betty Grable. See "Moon over Miami," IMDB, accessed May 15, 2021, https://www.imdb.com/title/tt0033918/.

CHAPTER 3 NOTES

1. The Flying Training Command report on flying instruction in college training detachments is covered in the "Post History of the Bainbridge Army Air Field January 1, 1943- February 1944, under "Students," AFHRA Reel B2031, Frame 1274. For information about the origin and termination of the AAF College Training Detachments, see Thomas H. Greer, "Individual Training of Flying Personnel," *The Army Air Forces in World War II Volume 6 Men and Planes, II. Equipment and Services,* Wesley Frank Craven and James Lea Cate, eds. (Chicago: University of Chicago Press, 1955, New Imprint: Washington, D. C.: United States Air Force, Office of Air Force History, 1983), 562-564, https://media.defense.gov/2010/Nov/05/2001329891/-1/-1/0/AFD-101105-019.pdf.

See also A/C Albert J. Hamilton, "From Whence We Came," *44B Preflight U.S. Army Air Forces Corps of Aviation Cadets Pre-Flight School for Pilots* (Montgomery: Maxwell Field, The Aviation Cadet Social Fund, Paragon Press, Volume Three, Number Seven, July 1943), 8-9. There were more than 150 college training detachments around the country. Army Air Forces Aid Society, *The Official Guide to the Army Air Forces AAF* (New York: Pocket Books, 1944), 211. Tennessee Polytechnic Institute (TPI) hosted the 46th College Training Detachment. College President William Everett Derryberry said, ". . . If we can give up one little thing to further the training of a cadet, that one little thing will go in with many other little things to form a big contribution to the work in which we are all interested." Author unknown, "Greetings Cadets," identified as a college newspaper article/clipping by Bill Hanchett, unknown publication title and date, estimated March 1943.

2. For information about the May Company see "George S. May International Company - Company Profile, Information, Business Description, History, Background Information on George S. May International Company," Reference for Business, accessed March 20, 2022, https://www.referenceforbusiness.com/ history2/45/George-S-May-International-Company.html.

3. Donald Dalton, along with Gene Reilly, friends from TPI.

4. Fort Sheridan, where Bill was processed into the AAF. 500,000 men and women were processed into the military at Fort Sheridan during World War II. From "Fort Sheridan," Encyclopedia of Chicago, accessed September 1, 2019, http://www.encyclopedia.chicagohistory.org/pages/478.html.

5. Gene Reilly wrote the undated news story, "All Cadence Breaks Out When Four Aviation Students Risk Lives to Halt Runaway Wagon," *College Training Detachment Newspaper,* Tennessee Polytechnic Institute, clipping, unknown date, estimated May 1943.

6. Willkie's book, *One World,* published in April 1943, described his around the world trip made in 49 days, coincidently in a modified B-24. The book called for an end to colonialism, equality for all in the United States and promoted World Federalism, a movement that supported the creation of a United Nations organization. Wendell L. Willkie, *One World* (New York: Simon and Schuster, 1943).

7. Dr. Sidney Lamont McGee (1897-1976), taught at Tennessee Polytechnic Institute and its successor, Tennessee Technological University, from 1939-1968. He founded the foreign language department at the college, and also taught English. From "Sidney [Doc] McGee papersRG.0000.0008," Tennessee Technological University Library, Special Collections, accessed August 5, 2021, https://www.tntech.edu/ library/pdf/RG8-SidneyMcGeePapers.pdf.

CHAPTER 4 NOTES

1. For background information on life in Preflight, see articles by A/C Stanley Dennison, "They Also Serve," and A/C Karl E. Yohn, "Off . . . Into the Wild Blue Yonder," *44B Preflight U.S. Army Air Forces Corps of Aviation Cadets Pre-Flight School for Pilots* (Montgomery, Maxwell Field: The Aviation Cadet Social Fund, Paragon Press, Volume Three, Number Seven, July 1943), 5-7.

2. According to Bill, "rats" was a term for underclassmen in the Preflight program at Maxwell Field.

3. For Burma Road, "Burma Road," a two-mile cross-country course which the official AAF Preflight booklet said humorously, was ". . . exactly 77,098,675,233 miles in length." See article by A/C Charles G. Caffery, "Fun's Fun, But Must We Be So Physical," *44B Preflight U.S. Army Air Forces Corps of Aviation Cadets Pre-Flight School for Pilots* (Montgomery, Maxwell Field: The Aviation Cadet Social Fund, Paragon Press, Volume Three, Number Seven, July 1943), 10.

4. John L. Lewis (February 12, 1880-June 11, 1969) was a labor leader and president of the United Mine Workers from 1920-1960. From "John L. Lewis," Britannica, accessed March 28, 2022, https://www.britannica.com/biography/John-L-Lewis.

5. For Morse Code: Thomas H. Greer, "Individual Training of Flying Personnel," *The Army Air Forces in World War II Volume 6 Men and Planes, II. Equipment and Services,* Wesley Frank Craven and James Lea Cate, eds. (Chicago: University of Chicago Press, 1955, New Imprint: Washington, D. C.: United States Air Force, Office of Air Force History, 1983), 560, accessed August 2, 2019, https://www.ibiblio.org/hyperwar/AAF/VI/AAF-VI-6.html.

6. Harriet Pinkston Engelhardt's experiences with American Red Cross Clubmobiles in Europe during the war were documented throughout a thesis by Julia A. Ramsey, "'Girls' In Name Only, A Study of American Red Cross Volunteers on the Frontlines of World War II," (Master's thesis, Auburn University, 2011), https:// etd.auburn.edu/bitstream/handle/10415/2616/ramsey_julia_ma_thesis_history_po st_defense_and_AUETD_check_5.9.11.pdf?sequence=3.

7. Don Dalton washed out for medical reasons and later served as a radio operator, flying combat missions in a B-24 heavy bomber group. See endnote 22 below.

8. Regarding Joe McWilliams: In several pieces of correspondence, (July 25 and 28, 1943 postal cards and August 8, 1943 letter) Bill mentions Joseph Elsberry "Joe" McWilliams (1904-1996) working at the George S. May Company in the summer of 1943 at the same time his father, William Sr., worked there. Apparently, William Hanchett, Sr. and McWilliams knew each other. In the August 8 letter Bill says that according to columnist Walter Winchell, ". . . the May Company had wakened up to Joe McWilliams. I hope his association with [the] company is over by now and that it will have no bad effects on the business." McWilliams was a notorious American Nazi sympathizer, who was indicted for sedition in 1943. See Henry Hoke, *It's A Secret* (New York: Reynal & Hitchcock, Inc., 1946), 48, 206, 220-21, https://ia801206.us.archive.org/27/items/ItsASecret/ItsASecret.pdf.

9. Jack Hanchett and Tom Hanchett were brothers, two of Bill's first cousins.

10. An autobiographical novel, William Bradford Huie, *Mud on the Stars: A Novel* (New York: L. B. Fischer, 1942).

11. Re: Larry Kocher: A. Lawrence Kocher, Architect (1885-1969), designed the Studies Building at BMC. See Duberman, *Black Mountain*, 155.

12. At Douglas Field Bill's instructor was a civilian. Bill did not name Dillard in his correspondence from Douglas Field but did use Dillard's name after he had moved on to Basic Flying School. For information on civilian instructor, William B. Dillard (1919-1982), see "Civilian Personnel—Flight Instructors," World War II Flight Training Museum and the 63rd Army Air Forces Flying Training Detachment, accessed November 13, 2020, https://wwiiflighttraining.org/?page_id=949. Major Thomas W. Bonner, Douglas Field commanding officer, stayed in the Army, transitioned to the U.S. Air Force when it was established in 1947 and retired from the Air Force Reserve as a Lieutenant Colonel. See "Army Air Forces Officers," World War II Flight Training Museum and the 63rd Army Air Forces Flying Training Detachment, accessed November 13, 2020, https://wwiiflighttraining.org/?page_id=986. In civilian life Bonner was a teacher and school principal in South Carolina. From "Lt. Col. Thomas Wilton Bonner," Eggers Funeral Home, accessed September 3, 2024, https://www.eggersfuneralhome.com/obituary/lt-col-thomas-wilton-bonner.

13. Re: World War I biplane: Bill was referring to the PT-17, a bi-plane primary trainer.

14. Walter Winchell (April 7, 1897-February 20, 1972) was a newspaper columnist and radio commentator. From "Walter Winchell," Britannica, accessed March 28, 2022, https://www.britannica.com/biography/Walter-Winchell.

15. Robert Frost (March 26, 1874-January 29, 1963) was an American poet. See "Robert Frost," Britannica, accessed March 28, 2022, https://www.britannica.com/biography/Robert-Frost.

16. Jim Hoel: Jim Hoel graduated from Evanston Township High School in 1939, entered Colgate University and after Pearl Harbor, left college and entered the Army Air Forces and served as a Second Lieutenant and bombardier/navigator in a B-26 Marauder, a twin-engine medium bomber. On May 17, 1943, Hoel's plane was shot down over Holland on his first bombing mission. Hoel was captured and spent the next two years as a German prisoner of war. From "James R. 'Jim' Hoel," *Chicago Tribune* Obituaries by Legacy, published August 7, 2014, https://www.legacy.com/obituaries/chicagotribune/obituary.aspx?n=james-r-hoel-jim&pid=172006289.

17. Bill was confusing his ETHS classmate Joseph J. "Denny" Dennison with John Virgil "Danny" Deaver, a BMC friend who served as a navigator flying numerous missions over Europe and was awarded the Distinguished Flying Cross. After the war, he had a long career as an Economist. From "John V. Deaver," *Detroit Free Press*, Obituaries, published March 24, 2020, https://www.freep.com/obituaries/det086422. Regarding the B-25 Mitchell Bomber: according to the AAF official history, the B-25 was "ranked consistently as a favorite among AAF pilots . . ." Alfred Goldberg, "AAF Aircraft of World War II," *The Army Air Forces in World War II Volume 6 Men and Planes, II. Equipment and Services,* Wesley Frank Craven and James Lea Cate, eds. (Chicago: University of Chicago Press, 1955, New Imprint: Washington, D. C.: United States Air Force, Office of Air Force History, 1983), 200, accessed August 2, 2019, https://www.ibiblio.org/hyperwar/AAF/VI/AAF-VI-6.html.

18. Link Trainer, a flight simulator roughly shaped like an airplane fuselage, had a cockpit with an instrument panel and controls for a cadet or pilot to practice instrument flying under various conditions. It was fastened to a swivel mount. The cadet/pilot would communicate by radio with an instructor seated nearby who recorded the actions of the simulator. The Link trainer was first used during Primary flying school (September 1, 1943 letter) and afterward. See Army Air Forces Aid Society, *The Official Guide to the AAF*, 105.

19. After the initial invasion of Sicily, July 9-10, 1943, the surrender of Italy took place September 8, 1943. See Lt. Col. Albert N. Garland and Howard McGaw Smyth, assisted by Martin Blumenson, *Sicily and the Surrender of Italy*, USAWWII (Washington D.C.: Office of the Chief of Military History, Department of the Army, 1965), 115-120 and 510-521.

20. Mabel M. Dodd (July 25, 1884-July 31, 1943) was an English teacher and the dining room supervisor at ETHS. Bill worked under her direction in the dining room. Miss Dodd wrote a letter of recommendation for Bill's admission to Black Mountain College. See "Mabel Dodd," Find A Grave, accessed August 30, 2023, https://www.findagrave.com/memorial/233552717/mabel-dodd.

21. *USA* was a trilogy of novels that tell the story of early twentieth century America. One of the innovative techniques used in the books was "the Newsreels" which describe historical events taking place. John Dos Passos, *USA*, comprising the novel *The 42nd Parallel* (1930), *1919* (1932), and *The Big Money* (1936), (New York: Modern Library, first complete edition, 1937).

22. Danny Deaver, see endnote 17 above. Don Dalton, Bill's friend from TPI, washed out of the aviation cadet program for medical reasons, and at the time of this letter, was in AAF radio operator school at Scott Field, Illinois.

23. There was also an Army Air Field at Douglas, Arizona.

CHAPTER 5 NOTES

1. Bainbridge Army Air Field (BAAF) in southwest Georgia was developed from "... pine forests, swamps and farm land ... into one of the largest and most beautiful flying schools ..." The field, activated on June 15, 1942, was a Basic Flying School, part of the Army Air Forces Southeast Training Center. During the time Bill was assigned to Bainbridge Field, the commanding officer was Colonel Mills S. Savage, rated as a Command Pilot, a graduate of the Air Corps tactical school, who had been flying in the Army since the late 1920s. Before taking command at Bainbridge, Colonel Savage served as Executive Officer of Hendricks Army Air Field, Florida, a B-17 combat crew school. After commanding at Bainbridge, Savage served overseas as deputy chief of staff for operations, in the Mediterranean Allied Air Forces (MAAF). After the war, Colonel Savage served as Chief of Staff for the Civil Air Patrol and as commander of Maxwell Air Force Base. From: Army Air Forces, *Bainbridge Army Air Field Basic Flying School* (Montgomery: E.M. Berry, circa 1943). Colonel Mills S. Savage information is from Bainbridge Field historical records in AFHRA Reel B2031, Frames 1416-1417 and an official U.S.A.F. biography, circa 1957, courtesy of Air Force Historical Research Agency, Maxwell Air Force Base.

2. Mabel M. Dodd: throughout October, Bill made inquiries about the passing of Miss Dodd, a favorite teacher.

3. "Top" refers to when, during the First World War, Will Hanchett served as a First Sergeant in the First Infantry Regiment of the Illinois Reserve Militia. "Topkick" or "Top" is a common nickname for the First Sergeant of an Army company. William F. Hanchett. Sr. personal records: discharge papers, April 27, 1920.

4. Philip H. Dodd (December 17, 1921-September 19, 2012) was Bill's high school friend, class of 1939; Phil was Mabel M. Dodd's nephew. Phil served in World War II as a First Lieutenant. After the war he completed his education and worked as a geologist for the federal government. From "Phillip H. Dodd," *The Daily Sentinel* Obituaries by Legacy, published September 25, 2012, https://www.legacy.com/obituaries/gjsentinel/obituary.aspx?n=philip-h-dodd&pid=160102935.

5. An aileron is the small, hinged surface in the trailing edge of an airplane wing, used to control the aircraft. From Army Air Forces Headquarters, Training Command, Central Instructors School and Headquarters, AAF Office of Flying Safety, *BT-13A Basic Trainer Students' Manual* (Los Angeles: Periscope Film LLC, 2011 reprint), 20-21.

6. Re: National College of Education, Bill's younger sister Wese attended and graduated from the National College of Education, a private teacher's college in Evanston, Illinois.

7. In reference to correspondence dated November 13, November 17, and November 21, 1943, the P-47 Thunderbolt had a ceiling of 40,000 feet and the P-51 Mustang had a ceiling of 43,000 feet. From Historical Office of the Army Air Forces, *The Official Pictorial History of the AAF* (New York: Duell, Sloan and Pearce, 1947), 192.

8. Regarding the accident with the parachute, when flying solo, cadets were cautioned to check the rear cockpit of their BT-13, according to Army Air Forces Headquarters, Training Command, *BT-13A Basic Trainer Students' Manual*, 12.

9. Bill requested these books for Christmas presents: Nathaniel Hawthorne, *House of Seven Gables* (originally published 1851); Charlotte Bronte, *Jane Eyre* (originally published 1847); and George Eliot (pen name of Mary Ann Evans), *Adam Bede* (originally published 1859).

10. Class 44-B Report in *History of Bainbridge Army Air Field*, January 1, 1943-February 1, 1944, in AFHRA Reel B2031, Frame 1274 and Frames 1346-1347. The official AAF report for Bill's 44-B class indicated that there were 372 aviation cadets from eight Primary schools throughout the southeastern United States, including 184 students from Douglas Field, Bill's alma mater. Bill was one of the eighty-five per cent of the class who had gone through college training detachments. Thirteen from the original class were dropped for flying deficiency, four were dropped for physical deficiency and three dropped out on their own. The report stated that there were nineteen holdovers. In all, 333 cadets graduated from Basic Flying School and 114, including Bill, were selected for the Advanced-Single Engine Flying School at Marianna Field in northern Florida's panhandle.

CHAPTER 6 NOTES

1. For AT-6 see "Transition to AT-6C Airplane," Chapter 1, *Instructor's Manual AAFAFS* [Army Air Field Advanced Flying School] *Marianna, Florida,* in *A History of the AAF PILOT SCHOOL (ADVANCED-SINGLE ENGINE),* Marianna Army Air Field, Marianna, Florida, March 10, 1944, in AFHRA Reel B2385, Frames 194-203. This manual focuses on the AT-6C airplane. For general background on Marianna Air Field, see Army Air Forces, *Marianna Field A.A.F. Pilot School (Advanced Single Engine)* (Montgomery: E. M. Berry Publisher, circa 1943).

2. Colonel Robert Lee Scott (1908-2006), P-40 Warhawk pilot and author, was a career U.S. Air Force officer. Col. Scott wrote *God is My Co-Pilot* in 1943.

   The War Room, or Intelligence Library was established in January 1943, by the Director of the Ground School at Marianna Field. Several of these were set up to provide classified reading material, war information and maps. Yarn was used on the maps to show changes on the battle fronts, and the locations of new invasions and naval operations were marked by cards. The room also contained models of airplanes, tanks and ships. From *A History of the AAF PILOT SCHOOL (ADVANCED-SINGLE ENGINE),* AFHRA Reel B2385, Frames 45-46.

3. Regarding procedures for flying the beam, see Army Air Forces Headquarters, *Pilot's Information File, AAF Regulation No. 62-15* (Washington, D.C.: Army Air Forces Headquarters, 1944), PIF 7-5-2, 7-5-3. See also Chapter 8, endnote 31.

4. For a description of the aviation training program at Tuskegee, see Lee, *The Employment of Negro Troops,* numerous page references.

5. For altitude ceilings of subject aircraft, see Historical Office of the Army Air Forces, *The Official Pictorial History of the AAF,* 177 (AT-6), 192 (P-38, P-40, P-47, P-51), and 199 (B-24). The advanced fighter airplanes Bill wanted to fly had ceilings of around 40,000 feet and more. The A-36 Apache, the attack version of the P-51, had a ceiling of 27,000 feet, 205.

6. For French pilot training, see Clément Thiery, "When the Free French Forces Trained in the U.S.," *France-Amerique Magazine,* September 26, 2019, https://france-amerique.com/en/when-the-free-french-forces-trained-in-the-u-s/. One of Bill's classmates at Douglas Field became an instructor of French aviation cadets. "Class 1944-B," World War II Flight Training Museum and the 63rd Army Air Forces Flying Training Detachment, accessed November 4, 2022, https://wwiiflighttraining.org/Cadets/Class-1944-B.php.

7. 287 graduates in Class 44B, in Chapter 2 "Training Programs," Advanced Single-Engine Pilot Training, *A History of the AAF PILOT SCHOOL (ADVANCED-SINGLE ENGINE),* AFHRA Reel B2385, Frame 19.

8. Regarding Major General Persons (1899-1972), see "Major General John W. Persons," U.S. Air Force Biographies, accessed October 6, 2019, http://www.af.mil/About-Us/Biographies/Display/Article/105948/major-general-john-w-persons/. Re: "Major in charge of flight training," it is unclear which major was in charge. According to official Army Air Forces records, Major Clifford B. Olson was Director of Training at Marianna Field, and Major Leslie W. Seppala was listed as Director of Flying in the Preface of *A History of the AAF PILOT SCHOOL (ADVANCED-SINGLE ENGINE)*, AFHRA Reel B2385, Frame 8. The "Major in charge of flight training" in Bill's letter was probably either Major Seppala or Major Olson.

CHAPTER 7 NOTES

1. Peter Grose told the editor the story of his ride with his older cousin Fran when they heard the news on the car radio about the D-Day invasion. Peter Grose, telephone call with editor, September 25, 2017.

2. Bruce A. Ashcroft, *We Wanted Wings: A History of the Aviation Cadet Program* (San Antonio: Headquarters, Air Education Training Command, U.S. Air Force, 2005), 23, https://media.defense.gov/2015/Sep/11/2001329827/-1/-1/.../AFD-150911-028.pdf. *See also* Historical Office of the Army Air Forces, *The Official Pictorial History of the AAF*, 76-77.

   For instructor training see: Linda Garza, "Memory Lane: Pilot Training Comes to Randolph," *Joint Base San Antonio News* (October 31, 2013): no page number, https://www.jbsa.mil/News/News/Article/599330/memory-lane-pilot-training-comes-to-randolph/. Re: Newell McCartney, a friend from ETHS, no further information located. *Evanston Township High School Alumni Directory 2009* (Evanston: Evanston Township High School, Harris Connect LLC, 2009), 617.

3. Nathaniel Hawthorne, *House of the Seven Gables* (Boston: Ticknor and Fields, 1851).

4. Ernest Hemingway, *For Whom the Bell Tolls* (New York: Charles Scribner's Sons, 1940). The novel *Between Two Worlds* was published in 1941 and was a volume in Sinclair's Lanny Budd series of stories, which Bill enjoyed. From "Lanny Budd," A Fan's Guide to Spy Series! accessed October 15, 2022, https://spyguysandgals.com/sgShowChar.aspx?id=1638.

5. Most likely the "colonel" was Colonel Mills S. Savage, commanding officer of Bainbridge Field during 1943-1944. See Army Air Forces, *Bainbridge Army Air Field Basic Flying School* (Montgomery: E.M. Berry, circa 1943), 2. See also Chapter 5, endnote 1, and U.S. Air Force Biography of Colonel Mills S. Savage, dated around 1957, courtesy of AFHRA, Maxwell AFB. Colonel Savage transferred from Bainbridge to Buckingham Army Air Field, Florida in October 1944, so at the time Bill met with the "colonel," Savage was still in command at Bainbridge, per AFHRA Reel B2032, Frame 1040.

6. Ernest J. Gyurits: Gyurits became a B-17 pilot and served in the 305th Bombardment Group (Heavy) in England. From World War II Flight Training Museum and the 63rd Army Air Forces Flying Training Detachment, "Class 1944-B."

7. Refers to First Lieutenant Robert D. Conary, *History of Bainbridge Army Air Field*, AFHRA Reel B2032, Frames 489-490 and Frame 767.

8. Bill's first group of aviation cadets were: Charles Jocot, Jr., William E. Jackson, Milosav V. Jajich, Ralph E. Ingram, George E. Ingham, and Iverson (first name unknown). See *History of Bainbridge Army Air Field*, Class 44-G Aviation Cadets, AFHRA Reel B2032, Frames 755-758. Iverson was not on the list of cadets, presumably because he washed out of flight training in early April 1944.

9. Re: *Hull House*, this book was published in 1910 as *Twenty Years At Hull House*. Jane Addams was a Progressive, a social worker, an advocate for women's suffrage and a co-founder of Hull House in Chicago. In 1920 she was one of the founders of the American Civil Liberties Union. From "About Jane Addams Hull-House Museum," Jane Addams Hull-House Museum, accessed September 13, 2021, https://www.hullhousemuseum.org/about-jane-addams.

10. Re: Instructor-Pilot Physical Training, see Army Air Forces, *Instructor's Guide, AAF Advanced Flying School, Marianna Army Air Field*, July 22, 1943. This guide references AAF Regulation #50-14 which established the requirement for "compulsory physical athletics" for all flying instructors and supervisory personnel, in AFHRA Reel B2385, Frame 200. For Link Trainer description, see Chapter 4, endnote 18. The Link Trainer, first used during Primary flying school (September 1, 1943 letter), was used throughout Bill's flight training.

11. Sinclair Lewis, *Dodsworth* (New York: Harcourt Brace, & Co., 1929).

12. May refer to Major James A. Gibson, Squadron II, *History of Bainbridge Army Air Field*, AFHRA Reel B2032, Frame 408.

13. Tonette: a simple fipple flute with a range somewhat larger than an octave that is often used in elementary music education. From "Tonette," Merriam Webster Online Dictionary, accessed July 31, 2018, https://www.merriam-webster.com/dictionary/tonette.

14. Re: "Rat races," the BT-13 student manual listed flying too close to other airplanes as an error pilots should not make, just as Bill observed in his letter. Army Air Forces Headquarters, Training Command, et. al., *BT-13A Basic Trainer Students' Manual*, 22-23. In the correspondence the first names of officers listed were not always noted. Complete names of officers were derived from official records in *History of Bainbridge Army Air Field*, AFHRA Reel B2032, Frames 766-768.

15. *The Little Prince* written by Antoine de Saint-Exupery, was published in the United States in 1943. Saint-Exupery was a journalist, poet and a Free French pilot who disappeared in 1944 while on a reconnaissance flight off the coast of southern France. From "Antoine de Saint-Exupery," Britannica, accessed September 13, 2022, https://www.britannica.com/biography/Antoine-de-Saint-Exupery.

16. Thomas E. Dewey (March 21, 1902-March 16, 1971), Governor of New York, was the Republican candidate for President in both 1944 versus Franklin D. Roosevelt, and in 1948 against Democratic President Harry S. Truman. Refer to "Gov. Thomas Edmund Dewey," National Governors Association, accessed September 13, 2022, https://www.nga.org/governor/thomas-edmund-dewey/.

17. Instrument Training: *History of Bainbridge Army Air Field, Department of Training*, February-June 30, 1944, *Instrument Training,* AFHRA Reel B2032, Frames 419-421. For BT-13A formation, Army Air Forces Headquarters, Training Command, *BT-13A Basic Trainer Students' Manual*, 111.

18. For June 1944 bivouac, see *History of Bainbridge Army Air Field, Troop Training*, February 1944-July 1944. Based on his June 4 letter and the bivouac dates listed in the Bainbridge Field official history, Bill took part in the bivouac exercise on June 1. Other service members participated in bivouacs throughout June to orient AAF personnel to ground operations. AFHRA Reel B2032, Frames 560-564. The dates of the June 1944 bivouac are specified on Frame 562.

19. Dorr Army Air Field, a Primary Flying School, was in the process of shutting down. It was formally de-activated on October 16, 1944. From: "Dorr Field," American Air Museum in Britain, accessed September 13, 2022, https://www.americanair museum.com/place/159482.

20. Referring to John W. Bricker (1893-1986), Ohio Governor, unsuccessful Presidential candidate and Republican Vice-Presidential nominee in 1944. See Smith, *FDR*, 455, 617.

21. Jean Forster worked at the National War Labor Board created to mediate labor issues and regulate wages after the United States entered the war. The War Labor Board also promoted equal pay and treatment of African American workers. There were regional offices throughout the country, including one in Philadelphia where my mother Jean worked. Linda Willard is shown as an ETHS graduate, class of 1940, so Bill was mistaken or made a typo about when Linda left Evanston. *Evanston Township High School Alumni Directory 2009*, 617.

22. Ken Allen, ETHS class of 1940, was a lifelong friend of Bill and Jean. *Evanston Township High School Alumni Directory 2009*, 616.

23. Second Lieutenant James A. Gould, a weather officer who reported to the Base Weather Station at Bainbridge Field in June, along with Second Lieutenant William E. Recktenwald, another weather officer (see August 6, 1944 letter) and two other new weather officers. These four weather officers were new meteorologists. Gould trained at Chanute Field, Il, and Recktenwald received training at the University of Chicago. See *History of Bainbridge Army Air Field*, Feb 1, 1944-July 1, 1944, AFHRA Reel B2032, Frame 471.

24. The Upton Sinclair novel, *Oil!* was published in 1927 and was loosely based on the Teapot Dome oil scandals during the Harding Administration. This is the first novel Bill read about these scandals. See "Upton Sinclair," Britannica, accessed October 15, 2022, https://www.britannica.com/biography/Upton-Sinclair. Also see notations about the book *Revelry,* also on the Harding Oil scandals, in Chapter 8. *Autobiography of Lincoln Steffens* was an autobiography of the muckraking Progressive journalist published in 1931, five years before his death. From "Lincoln Steffens Papers, 1863-1936," Columbia University Libraries, accessed September 13, 2022, http://www.columbia.edu/cu/lweb/archival/collections/ldpd_4079365/.

25. *Days of Our Years*: in this book, Pierre Van Paassen, a Dutch journalist, covered events in Europe and the Middle East in the early twentieth century leading up to World War II. From "Days of Our Years," BIBLIO, accessed October 16, 2022, https://www.biblio.com/book/days-our-years-paassen-pierre-van/d/148900018? gclid=Cj0KCQjw166aBhDEARIsAMEyZh5roUGuo5YHgiXDqHv_7QZ8ARBQ F-OjoA-pRKE0qz4cGOf7ZY5a9_saAoh6EALw_wcB. *PM* was a liberal-leaning daily newspaper published in New York City by Ralph Ingersoll from June 1940 to June 1948 and financed by Chicago millionaire Marshall Field III. See *"Pm* (New York) 1940-1948," Library of Congress, accessed September 13, 2022, https://www.loc.gov/item/sn83030640.

26. Bill's correspondence is full of observations, but one that did not appear in his correspondence, later described to the editor, was his first-hand observation of the treatment African American soldiers received in the Jim Crow Army. He saw that German prisoners of war received better accommodations on trains in the south than African American soldiers. He may have seen this at Bainbridge Field, because there was a prisoner of war camp at Bainbridge. See Dr. Kathryn Roe Coker and Jason Wetzel, *Georgia POW Camps in World War II* (Charleston: The History Press, 2019), 107-110, https://www.google.com/books/ edition/Georgia_POW_Camps_in_World_War_II/pvLGwQEACAAJ?hl=en&gb pv=1&printsec=frontcover. The problems faced by African American soldiers travelling by train in the south are examined by Lee, *The Employment of Negro Troops,* 316-321.

27. The Very Reverend Hewlett Johnson, Dean of Canterbury, the author of *The Soviet Power* published in 1940, introduces himself to the reader as a "Friend of the Soviet Union," a "progressive," a champion of "essential truth," "morality" and "science." He worships the "scientific mind"; enjoys only the company of men to whom "truth (is) sacred and whose assertions are capable of concrete verification." From "John G. Wright, The Dean of Canterbury's *Soviet Power,* (February 1941)," Encyclopedia of Trotskyism Online, accessed June 28, 2021, https://www.marxists.org/history/ etol/writers/wright/1941/02/dean.htm.

CHAPTER 8 NOTES

1. In his 1942 book written to publicize Army Air Forces training, John Steinbeck thought that the B-24 looked like an "Anopheles mosquito." See Steinbeck, *Bombs Away,* 7, 130.

   While Bill was still in high school, the first experimental B-24 flown by Consolidated Aircraft test pilot William B. Wheatley took off on December 29, 1939 for a test flight over San Diego. Mr. Wheatley later died in a B-24 crash. Consolidated Aircraft built B-24s in San Diego, Fort Worth and Tulsa. Ford also built B-24s, turning out one airplane each hour! More than 18,000 B-24s were built during the war. Bill would fly two models of the B-24: the D and J. For the William Wheatley test flight see Larry Davis, *B-24 Liberator in Action* (Carrollton, TX: Squadron/Signal Publications Inc., 1987), 5 and 12. For the Wheatley B-24 test flight, and B-24 production see Steve Birdsall, *The B-24 Liberator* (New York: Arco Publishing Company Inc., 1968), 21, 24. For B-24s built at Willow Run, see Smith, *FDR,* 572.

2. The commanding general was Major General William Ormond Butler. Army Air Forces, Eastern Flying Training Command Headquarters, Army Air Forces Pre-Flight School (Pilot) . . . Liberator Pilot Transition School, *Maxwell Field, Alabama* (Montgomery: Army Air Forces, no date, circa 1944), 2, and "William Ormond Butler," Find A Grave, accessed July 2, 2020, https://www.findagrave.com/memorial/11274657/william-ormond-butler. For command of the 11th Air Force see "On to Tokyo, The Fighters Pour It On," *Air Force: The Official Service Journal of the U.S. Army Air Forces*, October 1943, 21, https://media.defense.gov/2011/Apr/25/2001330208/-1/-1/0/AFD-110425-057.pdf. Also see Army Air Forces Aid Society, *Official Guide to the AAF*, 297.

3. *Moment in Peking* by Lin Yutang was a novel covering the history of China from 1900 to 1938. From "Moment in Peking, by Yutang, Lin," BIBLIO, accessed October 16, 2022, https://www.biblio.com/moment-in-peking-by-yutang-lin/work/36145.

4. *Maisie Goes To Reno* was a 1944 movie starring Ann Sothern and Ava Gardner. The movie was one of a series of movies featuring Ann Sothern's character, "Maisie" and her adventures.

5. Clara Burckhardt (Mrs. Enrico, January 3, 1866-July 6, 1951) was a long-time friend of Bill's aunt, Leila Hanchett, in Syracuse, New York. In the early 1900s, she was Treasurer of the Shelter for Unprotected Girls in Syracuse.

6. Thomas E. Dewey, see Chapter 7, endnote 16.

7. Regarding the Prohibition ticket, Ida B. Wise Smith (July 3, 1871-February 16, 1952) promoted women's suffrage and was an active member of the Women's Christian Temperance Union (WCTU). President Herbert Hoover appointed her to the White House Conference on Child Health and Protection, and she served on the White House Conference on Children in Democracy under President Roosevelt. See "Smith, Ida B. Wise," University of Iowa, The Biographical Dictionary of Iowa, accessed September 5, 2024, https://uipress.lib.uiowa.edu/bdi/DetailsPage.aspx?id=348.

8. *Revelry* was a 1926 novel about the scandals in the administration of President Warren G. Harding. Samuel H. Adams was a muckraking journalist known for his investigation of public health problems. From "Revelry by Adams, Samuel Hopkins," BIBLIO, accessed October 16, 2022, https://www.biblio.com/book/revelry-adams-samuel-hopkins/d/1111111891. This book is the second novel Bill read about the scandals of the Harding Administration. See notation about Upton Sinclair's book *Oil!,* which is listed in Chapter 7, endnote 24.

9. The "Fala Affair" refers to the time when Republicans falsely accused Roosevelt of sending a Navy destroyer to pick up his pet Scottish terrier Fala, who had supposedly been left on one of the Aleutian Islands. See Smith, *FDR*, 788, note 120.

10. Jimmy Petrillo (March 16, 1892-October 23, 1984) was the President of the American Federation of Musicians (AFM), which had been on strike against American recording companies over royalty payments since 1942. At the time of the October 9 letter, President Roosevelt had just appealed to Petrillo to comply with a National Labor Relations Board and War Labor Board directive that the AFM rescind its ban on musicians recording for several record companies. From "James C. Petrillo American labor leader," Britannica, accessed October 16, 2022, https://www.britannica.com/biography/James-C-Petrillo.

11. Re: *Our Times,* Bill wrote that he was reading Volume VI, titled *The Twenties*, of this six-volume history of the early twentieth century. Bill used the book as a companion to *Revelry*. From "The Twenties (Our Times, Volume 6) by Mark Sullivan," BIBLIO, accessed October 16, 2022, https://www.biblio.com/book/twenties-our-times-volume-6-mark/d/1398964437.

12. Sidney Hillman (March 23, 1887-July 10, 1946) was one of the founders of the Congress of Industrial Organizations. From "Sidney Hillman," AFL-CIO America's Unions, accessed October 16, 2022, https://aflcio.org/about/history/labor-history-people/sidney-hillman.

13. Billy Singleton, *Alabama Aviation* (Mount Pleasant, South Carolina: Arcadia Publishing, 2018), 78, https://www.google.com/books/edition/Alabama_Aviation/Z-ZDDwAAQBAJ?hl=en&gbpv=0.

14. Don Dalton, Bill's friend from the College Training Detachment in Cookeville, Tennessee, served as a radio operator on a B-24 with the 465th Bombardment Group (Heavy) of the Fifteenth Air Force based in Pantanella, Italy. Dalton was a radio operator in the Richard L. Crutcher, Jr. crew. He kept a diary, which is quoted throughout the squadron history. Dalton received the Air Medal with two bronze oak leaf clusters. For Dalton, see Harry S. Carl, ed., *781st Bombardment Squadron (H) AAF 465th Bombardment Group (H),14 August 1943-31 July 1945* (Atherton, CA: 781st Bomb Squadron Association, 1989), 57-58, 61, 64, 72, 128, 184, http://465th.org/History/PDFs/781st%20History.pdf.

15. Biographical information for the politicians mentioned in the October 16, 1944 letter: For John W. Bricker see Chapter 7, endnote 20. Earl Browder was active in American politics and was General Secretary of the Communist Party of the United States of America in the 1930s and early 1940s. See Smith, *FDR*, 624.
Hamilton Fish III was a New York Congressman and critic of President Roosevelt. See Smith, *FDR*, 476.
Colonel M'Cosmic was a caricature of *The Chicago Tribune* publisher Robert McCormick, an officer in the First World War who was an opponent of President Roosevelt, and the New Deal. Before the attack on Pearl Harbor, McCormick, known as "The Colonel," was a prominent America First leader opposed to involvement in the war in Europe. In his letters, Bill referred to him as Colonel McCosmic, but the correct name of the cartoon strip character was M'Cosmic.
Colonel Robert McCormick: from: "Robert R. McCormick," New World Encyclopedia, accessed October 17, 2022, https://www.newworldencyclopedia.org/entry/Robert_R._McCormick. For McCormick as a "Roosevelt hater" and the America First movement see David J. Bercuson and Holger Herwig, *One Christmas in Washington* (Woodstock & New York: The Overlook Press, 2005), 44, 57-58.
Colonel M'Cosmic: *The Adventures of Colonel M'Cosmic*, was a cartoon strip drawn by Cecil Jensen, appearing in the *Chicago Daily News*. From: "Cecil Jensen, Elmo, and Colonel M'Cosmic: An Editoonist who also Drew a Comic Strip," The Comics Journal, accessed October 17, 2022, https://www.tcj.com/cecil-jensen-elmo-and-colonel-mcosmic-the-first-editoonist-to-simultaneously-draw-a-comic-strip/.
Gerald Lyman Kenneth Smith (February 27, 1898-April 15, 1976), an American clergyman, populist political organizer and Nazi sympathizer, became a leader of the Share Our Wealth movement during the Great Depression, and he later founded the Christian Nationalist Crusade. Smith founded the America First Party in 1943, for which he was a presidential candidate in 1944. From "Gerald Lyman Kenneth Smith 1898-1976," Encyclopedia of Arkansas, accessed October 16, 2022, https://encyclopediaofarkansas.net/entries/gerald-lyman-kenneth-smith-1767/.

16. Re: Republican politicians McCormick, Nye, and Pew mentioned in October 21, 1944 letter:
Ruth Hanna McCormick (March 29, 1880-December 31, 1944) was a Republican member of Congress from Illinois who supported Thomas E. Dewey. She was married to Joseph Medill McCormick, the older brother of the *Chicago Tribune* publisher. From "McCormick, Ruth Hanna," Biographical Directory of the United States Congress, accessed October 16, 2022, https://bioguide.congress.gov/search/bio/M000372.
Gerald Prentice Nye (December 19, 1892-July 17, 1971) was a Republican United States Senator and an America First member, who represented North Dakota from 1925 to 1945. From "Nye, Gerald Prentice," Biographical Directory of the United States Congress, accessed October 16, 2022, https://bioguide.congress.gov/search/bio/N000176.
Joseph Newton Pew Jr. (November 12, 1886-April 9, 1963) was in the oil and shipping business and an influential member of the Republican Party. From "Joseph N. Pew, Jr. American Industrialist," Britannica, accessed October 17, 2022, https://www.britannica.com/biography/Joseph-N-Pew-Jr.

17. The 1944 Great Atlantic Hurricane was a Category Four storm that caused widespread damage across the western Caribbean and Southeastern United States in October. This hurricane caused $100 million in damage and 46 U.S. deaths. Five ships, including two U. S. Navy ships, two U. S. Coast Guard cutters, and a light vessel, sank in the storm. From "Hurricanes in History," National Hurricane Center and Central Pacific Hurricane Center, National Oceanic and Atmospheric Administration, accessed October 17, 2022, https://www.nhc.noaa.gov/outreach/history/#great.

18. *Presidential Agent* was written by one of Bill's favorite authors, Upton Sinclair. It was published in 1944 as part of the Lanny Budd series. From A Fan's Guide to Spy Series! "Lanny Budd."

19. There are no details provided, but based on the date of this correspondence, Bill may be referring to the recall of General Joseph W. Stilwell in late October 1944 from the China-Burma-India Theater at the request of Chinese Generalissimo Chiang Kai-shek. The problems and issues between Stilwell and Chiang, leading to Stilwell's recall, are covered in detail in Charles F. Romanus and Riley Sunderland, *Stilwell's Command Problems*, *USAWWII* (Washington, D.C.: Center of Military History, 1956, 1987), 468-471, https://history.army.mil/html/books/009/9-2/index.html.

20. Wendell L. Willkie (February 18, 1892-October 8, 1944) was a Republican politician and presidential candidate in 1940. After that election, in a bipartisan spirit he served as President Roosevelt's emissary to British Prime Minister Winston Churchill. See Smith, *FDR*, 452-455, 488-489.

21. John T. Flynn (October 25, 1882-April 13, 1964), a journalist opposed to Roosevelt and U.S. entry into World War II, one of the founders of the America First Committee in 1940. He was first to promote the Pearl Harbor conspiracy theory that Roosevelt had advance knowledge of the attack and let it happen. From "John T. Flynn," Spartacus Educational, accessed October 17, 2022, https://spartacus-educational.com/USAflynnJT.htm. *The Roberts Commission Report* was issued by the Roberts Commission, a presidential commission chaired by Supreme Court Justice Owen Josephus Roberts to investigate the Japanese attack on Pearl Harbor. Re: Short and Kimmel—The commission found that General Walter Short and Admiral Husband Kimmel, respectively the Army and Navy commanders at the time of the attack, were guilty of "dereliction of duty." See Smith. *FDR*, 550. Prince Fumimaro Konoye was Japanese Prime Minister at the time of the attack on Pearl Harbor on December 7, 1941. Smith, *FDR*, 519.

22. On the difficulty of flying the B-24, see Betty McNarney, *Pilot Transition to Combat Aircraft*, Army Air Forces Historical Studies No. 18 (Washington, D.C.: Assistant Chief of Air Staff Intelligence Historical Division, September 1944), 147-149, https://www.afhra.af.mil/Portals/16/documents/Studies/1-50/AFD-090602-044.pdf. This document states that it was recognized during a B-24 Program of Instruction conference in March 1943 that "the actual flying of a B-24 airplane, by a young pilot, was thirty percent more difficult than the flying of a B-17 airplane, as the B-17 was more conventional in design and operation and more what the young pilot had been accustomed to . . ." This study goes on to review the different iterations that B-24 transition training went through. Other authors describe similar difficulties flying the B-24 that Bill Hanchett experienced, but they were writing about flying B-24s under combat conditions. For instance, see Thomas Childers, *Wings of Morning: The Story of the Last American Bomber Shot Down Over Germany in World War II* (Reading, MA: Addison-Wesley Publishing Company, 1995), 20-21.

23. Re: "fly myself to China or wherever," November 20, 1944 letter. Since 1943, B-24s had been flying combat missions over China, Burma, and India from air fields in China. For information see Edward M. Young, *B-24 Liberator Units of the CBI* (Oxford: UK Osprey Publishing Ltd., 2011) and Edward M. Young, *B-24 Liberator vs Ki-43 Oscar China and Burma 1943* (Oxford: Osprey Publishing Ltd., 2012).

24. Dwight H. Green (January 9, 1897-February 20, 1958) was Governor of Illinois from 1941-1949. From "Governor Dwight Herbert Green," National Governors Association, accessed October 17, 2022, https://www.nga.org/governor/dwight-herbert-green/. Charles W. Brooks (March 8, 1897-January 14, 1957) was U.S. Senator for Illinois from 1940-1948. From "Brooks, Charles Wayland," Biographical Directory of the United States Congress, accessed October 16, 2022, https://bioguide.congress.gov/search/bio/B000874. Ralph E. Church (May 5, 1883-March 21, 1950) was U.S. Representative for Illinois, for the northern suburbs of Chicago, including Evanston, from 1935-1941 and 1943-1950. From "Church, Ralph Edwin," Biographical Directory of the United States Congress, accessed October 16, 2022, https://bioguide.congress.gov/search/bio/c000390.

25. In 1942 Leopold Schwarzschild wrote *World in Trance: From Versailles to Pearl Harbor*. It was translated by Norbert Guteman. From "World in Trance; From Versailles to Pearl Harbor," WorldCat, accessed August 9, 2021, https://www.worldcat.org/title/world-in-trance-from-versailles-to-pearl-harbor/oclc/1493294.

26. *For Whom the Bell Tolls* was a 1943 movie about the Spanish Civil War with Gary Cooper and Ingrid Bergman.

27. The 1944 movie *Thirty Seconds Over Tokyo* was about the April 1942 Tokyo raid, starring Spencer Tracy and Van Johnson.

28. For information on John "Jack" C. Hanchett, Jr., see Seymour, *Descendants of Thomas Hanchett*, 281. The air field at Courtland was north of Birmingham where Bill's older cousin Jack Hanchett worked as an Administrative Assistant with Bechtel-McCone Parsons, a company with a U.S. Government contract to modify Army Air Forces aircraft and prepare newly produced aircraft, including B-24s and B-29s, for active service. Jack was one of thousands of workers who supported the B-29 Superfortress program. See Thomas West, Jr., "Remembering Bechtel-McCone World War II in Birmingham," *JCHA Newsletter* (April 2012), http://www.jeffcohistory.com/newsletter_apr_12_pg4.html. For B-29 production see Rick Atkinson, *The Guns At Last Light The War in Western Europe 1944-1945, Volume Three of The Liberation Trilogy* (New York: Henry Holt and Company, 2013), 408.

29. Battle of the Bulge: on December 16, 1944 the Germans launched a massive counterattack in the Belgian Ardennes Forest, commonly referred to as the Battle of the Bulge. For an authoritative, detailed account of the battle, see Charles B. MacDonald, *A Time for Trumpets: The Untold Story of the Battle of the Bulge* (New York: William Morrow and Company Inc., 1985).

30. The strong counterattack in the south that Bill mentioned in his letter was already underway. In fact, the day before, on December 26, units of General George Patton's Third Army had broken through to the surrounded American airborne and armored units in Bastogne, Belgium. See MacDonald, *A Time for Trumpets,* 531-32. The husband of the unidentified "talkative" neighbor was a colonel in the First Army. Since the First Army bore the brunt of the German attack, he must have been in the middle of the Battle of the Bulge.

31. The phrase "... the north and south legs of the beam ..." refers to using radio beacons as a navigation tool. By following radio beacons, a pilot/navigator could plan and revise flight plans from the point of departure to the destination of the flight. Radio beacons would serve as landmarks along the way. Army Air Forces, Headquarters, Office of Flying Safety, *Pilot Training Manual B-24 The Liberator* (Washington, D.C.: Headquarters Army Air Forces, Office of the Assistant Chief of Air Staff Training, Training Aids Division, February 1945), 244. See also Peter Stekel, *Beneath Haunted Waters: The Tragic Tale of Two B-24s Lost in the Sierra Nevada Mountains During World War II* (Guilford, CT: Lyons Press, 2017), 234.

32. *Red Star Over China,* originally published in 1937, was written by Edgar Snow, an American journalist who spent many years in China. From Edgar Snow, *Red Star Over China* (New York: Grove Press, 1968), https://www.google.com/books/edition/Red_Star_Over_China/amXicbM6BCkC?hl=en.

33. Regarding B-29 tours: touring a B-29 "stem to stern" meant crawling through a pressurized forty-foot tunnel connecting the forward crew compartments to the aft crew section. The tunnel is described in Larry Davis, *B-29 Superfortress in Action* (Carrollton, TX: Squadron/Signal Publications, Inc., 1997), 5.

34. Henry Wallace was a government official and U.S. Vice President during Roosevelt's third term. Jesse H. Jones was Secretary of Commerce from 1940-1945. After Roosevelt was re-elected in 1944, he asked Jones to resign from his position. Wallace was not Roosevelt's vice-presidential running mate in the election, but instead was nominated to be Secretary of Commerce. Jones criticized this nomination based on Wallace's lack of business experience. From "The Fight Against Wallace," *TIME Magazine*, February 5, 1945, https://content.time.com/time/subscriber/article/0,33009,797029-1,00.html.

CHAPTER 9 NOTES

1. Sinclair Lewis novels: *The Prodigal Parents*, 1938, *Elmer Gantry*, 1927 and *Mantrap*, 1926. From "Sinclair Lewis-Biographical," The Nobel Prize-1930 Literature Prize, accessed October 19, 2022, https://www.nobelprize.org/prizes/literature/1930/lewis/biographical/.

   The Financier, written by Theodore Dreiser and published in 1912, was the first of a trilogy based on a Chicago businessman. *The Financier* refers to events in American history like the Civil War and local events like the Great Chicago fire of 1871, which would have been of interest to Bill, a developing historian who grew up in the Chicago area. From "Theodore Dreiser," Britannica, accessed October 19, 2022, https://www.britannica.com/biography/Theodore-Dreiser.

2. Tonopah Field opened in the summer of 1942 in the high desert of Nevada. Two small towns, Tonopah and Goldfield, were nearby. Initially there were several Bell P-39 Airacobra fighter squadrons at Tonopah. In 1944, B-24 Liberator combat crew training commenced at Tonopah Field and by the end of the war 742 crews had been trained. See Frederick A. Johnsen, *Consolidated B-24 Liberator Volume I*, (North Branch, MN: Specialty Press Publishers and Wholesalers, 1996), 72-80. The aviation accident record at Tonopah was very poor. Between 1943-1944, 115 aircrewmen were killed in eighteen B-24 crashes. A U.S. Air Force history of Tonopah Field in World War II noted that pilot error and mechanical problems were primary reasons for the poor record. See Tracy Henderson-Elder and Keith Myhrer, *The History of the World War II Tonopah Army Air Field, Nevada*, (Las Vegas: Nellis Air Force Base, Asset Management Flight/Civil Engineer Squadron, 2010, Revision of 2009 edition), 74. According to Bill Hanchett, B-24 crews used the phrase, "bomb 'em, strafe 'em, fall on 'em," Bill Hanchett to editor, February 25, 1998. Bill was glad that he did not do any of those things.

3. Elizabeth Allan (April 9, 1910-July 27, 1990) was a British theater and movie actress.

4. George Sokolsky (September 5, 1893-December 12, 1962), journalist and radio broadcaster. Sokolsky was a frequent critic of Roosevelt and his policies. From "George E. Sokolsky Papers, 1916-1962," ARCHIVEGRID, accessed September 4, 2023, https://researchworks.oclc.org/archivegrid/archiveComponent/754868998.

5. For pilot's responsibilities see Army Air Forces, Headquarters, *Pilot's Information File,* PIF 1-1-1, 1-1-2. See also Army Air Forces, Headquarters, *The Airplane Commander, Air Forces Manual No. 65* (Washington, D.C.: Headquarters, Army Air Forces, Office of the Assistant Chief of Air Staff Training, Training Aids Division, 1945), 1-32.

6. For AAF bomber and fighter combat training in the Fourth Air Force, see Thomas H. Greer, "Combat Crew and Unit Training," in *The Army Air Forces in World War II Volume 6 Men and Planes, III. Recruitment and Training,* Wesley Frank Craven and James Lea Cate, eds. (Chicago: University of Chicago Press, 1955, New Imprint: Washington, D. C., United States Air Force, Office of Air Force History, 1983), 610, https://media.defense.gov/2010/Nov/05/2001329891/-1/-1/0/AFD-101105-019.pdf.

7. For ditching training at Tonopah, see Henderson-Elder and Myhrer, *History of Tonopah Air Field,* 25, 66. For general B-24 ditching training see also Army Air Forces Headquarters, Office of Flying Safety, *Pilot Training Manual B-24 The Liberator,* 137-141.

8. James Westbrook Pegler (August 2, 1894-June 24, 1969) was a journalist and writer whose articles criticized Roosevelt, the New Deal and labor unions. From "Westbrook Pegler," Britannica, accessed October 19, 2022, https://www.britannica .com/biography/Westbrook-Pegler.

9. Andrew "Drew" Russell Pearson (December 13, 1897-September 1, 1969) was a journalist and syndicated columnist. From "Drew Pearson Biography," American University Library Archives, accessed October 19, 2022, https://www.american.edu/ library/archives/pearson/drewpearson_bio.cfm.

10. April 3, 1945 letter: On April 1, 1945 the Japanese home island of Okinawa was invaded by the U.S. Tenth Army commanded by Lieutenant General Simon B. Buckner, Jr. See Roy E. Appleman, James M. Burns, Russell A. Gugeler and John Stevens, *Okinawa: The Last Battle, USAWWII* (Washington, D.C.: Center of Military History, 1947, 1993), 68, https://history.army.mil/html/books/005/5-11-1/CMH_Pub_5-11-1.pdf. Admiral Chester W. Nimitz (February 24, 1885-February 20, 1966) graduated from the U.S. Naval Academy, Annapolis in 1905 and throughout World War II served as Commander-in-Chief, U.S. Pacific fleet and Pacific Ocean Areas. From "Chester William Nimitz," Naval History and Heritage Command, Histories, Naval Profiles, accessed July 28, 2021, https://www.history .navy.mil/research/histories/biographies-list/bios-n/nimitz-chester-w.html.

11. Fourth Air Force responsibilities included Washington State. An agreement was made for air force fighters to share space with naval fighter squadrons to improve air defense. After the Pearl Harbor attack, San Diego with its naval bases and defense industry, was considered a potential Japanese target, however the type of agreement with the U.S. Navy in Washington State was not made for San Diego. For AAF and Navy defense agreement: see Futrell, "The Development of Base Facilities," *The Army Air Forces in World War II Volume VI Men and Planes,* 166, 167.

12. Harry S. Truman (May 8, 1884-December 26, 1972), President of the United States. From "Harry S. Truman Library and Museum," National Archives, accessed October 18, 2022, https://www.trumanlibrary.gov/. President Franklin D. Roosevelt's death: *History of Tonopah Army Air Field,* Chapter IV, Life and Morale, April 1, 1945-April 30, 1945, in AFHRA Reel B2617, Frame 759.

13. For engine fire extinguishing procedures see, Army Air Forces Headquarters, Office of Flying Safety, *Pilot Training Manual B-24 The Liberator,* 142-144. The fire occurred just after Tonopah Field was recognized for safety, per "Tonopah Breaks Safety Records," *Mineral County Independent News* (Hawthorne, Nevada), April 18, 1945, 6, accessed January 1, 2020, http://mci.stparchive.com/Archive/MCI/ MCI04181945p06.php. Also, *History of Tonopah Army Air Field,* Chapter II Operations and Training April 1, 1945-April 30, 1945, AFHRA Reel B2617, Frame 753, and Commendation for Safety Record letter, dated 29 May 1945, signed by Brigadier General Edward M. Morris, commanding general of Fourth Air Force, AFHRA Reel B2617, Frame 1039.

14. Re: letters dated May 8, 1945 and June 11, 1945: there were B-24s operating in China against the Japanese in China, Burma, India, and Indochina (Vietnam). See Young, *B-24 Liberator vs Ki-43 Oscar China and Burma 1943*, 36. Re: May 8, 1945, V.E. Day speech by Colonel, Tonopah Field commanding officer, Colonel John A. Feagin spoke to the command regarding the German surrender and end of the war in Europe. See *History of Tonopah Army Air Field,* 1 May 1945-31 May 1945, Chapter IV Life and Morale, AFHRA Reel B2617, Frame 881.

15. The colonel referred to was probably Colonel John A. Feagin, Tonopah Field commanding officer. Colonel Feagin of Evergreen, Alabama, graduated from the U. S. Military Academy, West Point, class of 1931. Feagin received his pilot's wings in late 1932. As part of the Army's involvement with President Franklin Roosevelt's New Deal Civilian Conservation Corps (CCC), Feagin organized a CCC unit in Texas. Assigned to the Second Bombardment Group at Langley Army Air Field, Virginia in 1937, Feagin flew the B-17 Flying Fortress and served as wing operations officer. He commanded four stations of the Air Transport Command, flying missions over "the Hump" in the China, Burma, India (CBI) theater of operations supporting General Claire Chennault's Fourteenth Air Force. Before taking command at Tonopah on December 5, 1944, he served as commanding officer of Lemoore Field for several months. According to his biography, Feagin was married with two children when he took command at Tonopah, and he was one of the youngest command pilots in the Army Air Forces. In tribute to their commanding officer, pilots at Tonopah affectionately said that they were flying for "Colonel Feagin Airlines." For USMA class of 1931, see Charles N. Branham. ed*., Register of Graduates, United States Military Academy, West Point 1802-1967* (West Point, New York: The West Point Alumni Foundation, Inc., 1967), 420. See also Colonel Feagin biography in *The Desert Bomber* issue dated 8 December 1944, in *History of Tonopah Army Air Field*, AFHRA Reel B2617, Frame 601. "Colonel Feagin Airlines" is mentioned in *The Desert Bomber*, undated clipping.

16. For Val-Lo-Will: William C. Grunow (April 30, 1893-July 6, 1951) founded General Household Utilities in 1933, which also produced radios and refrigerators. When that business failed, Grunow sold a Phoenix, Arizona estate to finance a poultry-raising venture, Val-Lo-Will Farms, Inc., of Lake Geneva, Wisconsin. The farm was named for his three children: Valerie, Lois, and William. Eventually, Grunow owned twenty-four Val-Lo-Will Farms stores in Illinois. From "Grunow, William C.," Franzo Senbusch Heritage Project, published November 24, 2002, http://www.fhproject.org/Histories/ForestPark_Harlem/William%20C%20Grunow.htm.

17. Crew #256 was listed as the runner-up for "crew of the week" in the June 16, 1945 edition of *The Desert Bomber*, AFHRA Reel B2617, Frame 1103. In the August 11, 1945 edition of *The Desert Bomber*, the crew was recognized for "air discipline," AFHRA Reel B2617, Frames 1278, and 1282.

18. At this time, Jean's younger brother, Brian, was in the Pacific with the U.S. Navy.

19. Irving Stone, *Lust for Life* (New York: Grosset & Dunlap, 1934) was a novel about Dutch painter Vincent Van Gogh.

20. Engineer Robert R. Thompson is identified as a Sergeant, AFHRA Reel B2617, Frame 1282. He was promoted Sergeant (Temp) 13 July 1945, AFHRA Reel B2617, Frame 1185.

21. *The Jungle* by Upton Sinclair was published in 1906. See Britannica, "Upton Sinclair." There are several books with similar titles to *The Big Bosses* and *Co-operative Democracy*. The books referred to in the letter of August 6, 1945 are most likely *The Big Bosses* by Charles W. Van Devander, 1944, and *Co-operative Democracy: Attained Through Voluntary Association of the People as Consumers* by James Peter Warbasse, 1923. For information regarding these books see "The Big Bosses," WorldCat, accessed August 4, 2021, https://www.worldcat.org/title/big-bosses/oclc/290649, and "Co-operative Democracy: Attained Through Voluntary Association of the People as Consumers," WorldCat, accessed August 4, 2021, https://www.worldcat.org/title/co-operative-democracy-attained-through-voluntary-association-of-the-people-as-consumers-a-discussion-of-the-co-operative-movement-its-philosophy-methods-accomplishments-and-possibilities-and-its-relation-to-the-state-to-science-art-and-commerce-and-to-other-systems-of-economic-organization/oclc/1442427.

22. Upton Sinclair, *CO-OP: A Novel of Living Together* (New York: Farrar & Rinehart, 1936).

23. *Work of Art* by Sinclair Lewis was published in 1934. See The Nobel Prize-1930 Literature Prize, "Sinclair Lewis-Biographical."

24. Re: Ethne and Dr. F: Refers to Jean's sister, Ethne, and their father, Dr. Arthur Haire-Forster. Jean's mother Christina, who had knitted a sweater for Bill to wear while flying, died of cancer in January 1945.

EPILOGUE NOTES

1. World War II Flight Training Museum and 63rd AAF Flying Training Detachment, "Class 1944-B."

2. Re: Harriet P. Engelhardt, see Ramsey, "'Girls' In Name Only," 134, and Chapter 4, Preflight correspondence.

3. Re: Joseph J. Dennison: military record in *The History of the Medical Department of the United States Navy in World War II: A Compilation of the Killed Wounded and Decorated Personnel*, Navmed P-5021 Vol. II, Fleet Marine Force Reference Publication (FMFRP) 12-12-Il, Department of the Navy, Headquarters United States Marine Corps (Washington D.C.: Government Printing Office, 1953; reissued November 1989), 25, 51, and 162, https://www.marines.mil/portals/1/Publications/FMFRP%2012-12-II%20History%20of%20Medical%20Dept%20of%20U.S.%20Navy%20in%20WW%20II-Vol%20II.pdf?ver=2012-10-11-164059-387. Also, Dennison corresponded with *The Evanston Review* about his wartime experiences, specifically in articles dated December 10, 1942, April 6, 1944, and May 11, 1944. His death and Bronze Star medal were reported by *The Evanston Review*, newspaper articles dated August 31, 1944 and May 10, 1945. Provided by the Evanston History Center Record Archives.

4. "Rader, Daniel Crew Member Search," 351st Bomb Group Association 1943-1945, accessed January 12, 2023, http://www.351st.org/loadlist/search.php.

5. William Hanchett Interview, San Diego, CA on February 15, 1998, with Mary Emma Harris, Black Mountain Project, Inc., 13.

6. Boritt, Gabor S., "*The Lincoln Murder Conspiracies* Book Review," *The American Historical Review* 89, Issue 5 (December 1984):1395, https://doi.org/10.1086/ahr/89.5.1395.

7. "Stevens, Charles N. Crew Member Search," 351st Bomb Group Association 1943-1945, accessed January 12, 2023, http://www.351st.org/loadlist/search.php.

8. Duberman, *Black Mountain*, 165. William Hanchett Interview, Harris, Black Mountain Project, Inc., 6.

Bibliography

BOOKS

Appleman, Roy E., James M. Burns, Russell A. Gugeler and John Stevens.
Okinawa: The Last Battle. United States Army in World War II. Washington, D.C.:
Center of Military History, 1947, 1993. https://history.army.mil/html/books/005/
5-11-1/CMH_Pub_5-11-1.pdf.

Army Air Forces.
Bainbridge Army Air Field Basic Flying School. Montgomery: E.M. Berry, circa 1943.

Marianna Field A.A.F. Pilot School (Advanced Single Engine). Montgomery: E. M.
Berry, circa 1943.

Army Air Forces Aid Society.
The Official Guide to the Army Air Forces AAF. New York: Pocket Books, 1944.

Army Air Forces, Eastern Flying Training Command Headquarters . . . Army Air Forces
Pre-Flight School (Pilot) . . . Liberator Pilot Transition School.
Maxwell Field, Alabama. Montgomery: Army Air Forces, no date, circa 1944.

Army Air Forces Headquarters.
The Airplane Commander, Air Forces Manual No. 65. Washington, D.C.: Army Air
Forces Headquarters, Office of the Assistant Chief of Air Staff Training, Training
Aids Division, 1945.

Pilot's Information File, AAF Regulation No. 62-15. Washington, D.C.: Army Air
Forces Headquarters, 1944.

Office of Flying Safety. *Pilot Training Manual B-24 The Liberator*. Washington,
D.C.: Headquarters Army Air Forces, Office of the Assistant Chief of Air Staff
Training, Training Aids Division, February 1945.

Training Command, Central Instructors School and Headquarters, AAF Office of
Flying Safety. *BT-13A Basic Trainer Students' Manual*. Los Angeles: Periscope Film
LLC, 2011 reprint.

Ashcroft Bruce A.
We Wanted Wings: A History of the Aviation Cadet Program. San Antonio:
Headquarters, Air Education Training Command, U.S. Air Force, 2005.
https://media.defense.gov/2015/Sep/11/2001329827/-1/-1/.../AFD-150911-
028.pdf.

Atkinson, Rick.
*The Guns At Last Light The War in Western Europe 1944-1945, Volume Three of The
Liberation Trilogy*. New York: Henry Holt and Company, 2013.

Bercuson. David J. and Holger Herwig.
One Christmas in Washington. Woodstock & New York: The Overlook Press, 2005.

Birdsall, Steve.
The B-24 Liberator. New York: Arco Publishing Company Inc., 1968.

Branham, Charles N. ed.
Register of Graduates, United States Military Academy, West Point 1802-1967. West Point, New York: The West Point Alumni Foundation, Inc., 1967.

Caffery, A/C Charles G.
"Fun's Fun, But Must We Be So Physical." *44B Preflight U.S. Army Air Forces Corps of Aviation Cadets Pre-Flight School for Pilots.* Montgomery, Maxwell Field: The Aviation Cadet Social Fund, Paragon Press, Volume Three, Number Seven, July 1943.

Carl, Harry S. ed.
781st Bombardment Squadron (H) AAF 465th Bombardment Group (H),14 August 1943-31 July 1945. Atherton, CA: 781st Bomb Squadron Association, 1989. http://465th.org/History/PDFs/781st%20History.pdf.

Childers, Thomas.
Wings of Morning: The Story of the Last American Bomber Shot Down Over Germany in World War II. Reading, MA: Addison-Wesley Publishing Company, 1995.

Coffman, Edward M.
The Regulars: The American Army 1898-1941. Cambridge MA: Belknap Press of Harvard College, 2004.

Coker, Dr. Kathryn Roe and Jason Wetzel.
Georgia POW Camps in World War II. Charleston: The History Press, 2019. https://www.google.com/books/edition/Georgia_POW_Camps_in_World_War_II/pvLGwQEACAAJ?hl=en&gbpv=1&printsec=frontcover.

Davis, Larry.
B-24 Liberator in Action. Carrollton, TX: Squadron/Signal Publications, Inc., 1987.

B-29 Superfortress in Action. Carrollton, TX: Squadron/Signal Publications, Inc., 1997.

Dennison, A/C Stanley.
"They Also Serve." *44B Preflight U.S. Army Air Forces Corps of Aviation Cadets Pre-Flight School for Pilots.* Montgomery, Maxwell Field: The Aviation Cadet Social Fund, Paragon Press, Volume Three, Number Seven, July 1943.

Department of the Navy, Headquarters United States Marine Corps.
The History of the Medical Department of the United States Navy in World War II: A Compilation of the Killed Wounded and Decorated Personnel, Navmed P-5021 Vol. II, Fleet Marine Force Reference Publication (FMFRP) 12-12-II. Washington D.C.: Government Printing Office, 1953; reissued November 1989. https://www.marines.mil/portals/1/Publications/FMFRP%2012-12-II%20History%20of%20Medical%20Dept%20of%20U.S.%20Navy%20in%20WW%20II-Vol%20II.pdf?ver=2012-10-11-164059-387.

Duberman, Martin.
Black Mountain An Exploration in Community. Garden City: Anchor Press/Doubleday, 1973.

Evanston Township High School Alumni Directory 2009.
Evanston: Evanston Township High School, Harris Connect LLC, 2009.

Ferguson, Andrew.
Land of Lincoln: Adventures in Abe's America. New York: Atlantic Monthly Press, 2007.

Futrell, Frank.
"The Development of Base Facilities." *The Army Air Forces in World War II, Volume VI, Men and Planes, I. The Organizations and Responsibilities,* Wesley Frank Craven, James Lea Cate, eds. Chicago: University of Chicago Press, 1955, New Imprint: Washington, D. C.: United States Air Force, Office of Air Force History, 1983. https://media.defense.gov/2010/Nov/05/2001329891/-1/-1/0/AFD-101105-019.pdf.

Garland, Lieutenant Colonel Albert N. and Howard McGaw Smyth, Assisted by Martin Blumenson.
Sicily and the Surrender of Italy. United States Army in World War II. Washington, D.C.: Office of the Chief of Military History, Department of the Army, 1965.

Goldberg, Alfred.
"AAF Aircraft of World War II." *The Army Air Forces in World War II Volume 6 Men and Planes, II. Equipment and Services.* Wesley Frank Craven and James Lea Cate, eds. Chicago: University of Chicago Press, 1955, New Imprint: Washington, D. C.: United States Air Force, Office of Air Force History, 1983. https://www.ibiblio.org/hyperwar/AAF/VI/AAF-VI-6.html.

Greer, Thomas H.
"Combat Crew and Unit Training." *The Army Air Forces in World War II Volume 6 Men and Planes, III. Recruitment and Training.* Wesley Frank Craven and James Lea Cate, eds. Chicago: University of Chicago Press, 1955, New Imprint: Washington, D. C., United States Air Force, Office of Air Force History, 1983. https://media.defense.gov/2010/Nov/05/2001329891/-1/-1/0/AFD-101105-019.pdf.

"Individual Training of Flying Personnel." *The Army Air Forces in World War II Volume 6 Men and Planes, II. Equipment and Services.* Wesley Frank Craven and James Lea Cate, eds. Chicago: University of Chicago Press, 1955, New Imprint: Washington, D. C.: United States Air Force, Office of Air Force History, 1983. https://media.defense.gov/2010/Nov/05/2001329891/-1/-1/0/AFD-101105-019.pdf.

Hamilton, A/C Albert J.
"From Whence We Came." *44B Preflight U.S. Army Air Forces Corps of Aviation Cadets Pre-Flight School for Pilots.* Montgomery: Maxwell Field, The Aviation Cadet Social Fund, Paragon Press, Volume Three, Number Seven, July 1943.

Henderson-Elder, Tracy and Keith Myhrer.
The History of the World War II Tonopah Army Air Field, Nevada. Las Vegas: Nellis Air Force Base, Asset Management Flight/Civil Engineer Squadron, 2010, Revision of 2009 edition.

Historical Office of the Army Air Forces.
The Official Pictorial History of the AAF. New York: Duell, Sloan and Pearce, 1947.

Hoke, Henry.
It's A Secret. New York: Reynal & Hitchcock, Inc., 1946. https://ia801206.us.archive.org/27/items/ItsASecret/ItsASecret.pdf.

Huston, Major General John W. U.S. Air Force Retired, ed.
American Airpower Comes of Age: General Henry H. "Hap" Arnold's World War II Diaries, Volume 1. Montgomery, Maxwell Air Force Base: Air University Press, 2002. https://media.defense.gov/2017/Mar/31/2001725201/-1/-1/0/B_0084_ HUSTON_AMERICAN_AIRPOWER_DIARIES.PDF.

Johnsen, Frederick A.
Consolidated B-24 Liberator Volume I. North Branch, MN: Specialty Press Publishers and Wholesalers, 1996.

Lee, Ulysses.
The Employment of Negro Troops. United States Army in World War II. Washington, D.C.: Center of Military History, United States Army, 2000, First printed 1966.

Lydecker, Mary Guernsey, and Elizabeth Hart Pennell, eds.
Twenty-Fifth Reunion Record Class of 1912: Wellesley College. Wellesley: Wellesley College Press, 1937.

MacDonald, Charles B.
A Time for Trumpets: The Untold Story of the Battle of the Bulge. New York: William Morrow and Company, Inc., 1985.

McNarney, Betty.
Pilot Transition to Combat Aircraft, Army Air Forces Historical Studies No. 18. Washington, D.C.: Assistant Chief of Air Staff Intelligence Historical Division, September 1944. https://www.afhra.af.mil/Portals/16/documents/Studies/1-50/AFD-090602-044.pdf.

Romanus, Charles F. and Riley Sunderland.
Stilwell's Command Problems. United States Army in World War II. Washington, D.C.: Center of Military History, 1956/1987. https://history.army.mil/html/books/009/9-2/index.html.

Seymour, Keith.
The Descendants of Thomas Hanchett. San Francisco: K.M. Seymour, 1985.

Singleton, Billy.
Alabama Aviation. Mount Pleasant, South Carolina: Arcadia Publishing, 2018. https://www.google.com/books/edition/Alabama_Aviation/Z-ZDDwAAQBAJ? hl=en&gbpv=0.

Smith, Jean Edward.
FDR. New York: Random House Trade Paperbacks, 2008.

Snow, Edgar.
Red Star Over China. New York: Grove Press, 1968. https://www.google.com/books/edition/Red_Star_Over_China/amXicbM6BCkC?hl=en.

Steinbeck, John.
Bombs Away: The Story of a Bomber Team. New York: The Viking Press, First Published, 1942. New York: Penguin Classics, Second Edition, 2009.

Stekel, Peter.
Beneath Haunted Waters: The Tragic Tale of Two B-24s Lost in the Sierra Nevada Mountains During World War II. Guilford, CT: Lyons Press, 2017.

U.S. Congress Senate Special Committee.
Investigation of the National Defense Program, Exhibit 987, Miami Beach, FL Leased Hotels retained by Army Air Forces 1944 - Industrial mobilization. https://books .google.com/books?id=P5kjAQAAMAAJ&pg=PA9114&lpg=PA9114&dq=Army +Air+Forces+Miami+Beach+Basic+Training+Center+February+11,+1943&sourc e=bl&ots=W7FN_lV9Xc&sig=ACfU3U2TlJu9UxwzTP43jdLq4GEjtZzntA&hl= en&sa=X&ved=2ahUKEwjr-sOB373mAhWVPM0KHa93AJQQ6AEwEHoECAo QAQ#v=onepage&q=Army%20Air%20Forces%20Miami%20Beach%20Basic%20 Training%20Center%20February%2011%2C%201943&f=false.

Weigley, Russell F.
History of the United States Army. New York and London: The Macmillan Company, Collier-Macmillan Ltd., 1967.

Wellesley College.
Wellesley College Record 1875-1912: A General Catalogue of Officers and Students. Wellesley: Wellesley College Press, 1937. https://books.google.com/books ?id=z1lIAAAAYAAJ&pg=PA266&lpg=PA266&dq=wellesley+college+student+A lice+Trowbridge&source=bl&ots=-Kefe6K0le&sig=A.CfU3U0f5oh83FpUu8rpib 96WufwnsAdrw&hl=en&sa=X&ved=2ahUKEwjzyunT-YzkAhVKSq0KHeZRAu 8Q6AEwAnoECAkQAQ#v=onepage&q&f=false.

Yohn, A/C Karl E.
"Off . . . Into the Wild Blue Yonder." *44B Preflight U.S. Army Air Forces Corps of Aviation Cadets Pre-Flight School for Pilots.* Montgomery, Maxwell Field: The Aviation Cadet Social Fund, Paragon Press, Volume Three, Number Seven, July 1943.

Young, Edward M.
B-24 Liberator Units of the CBI. Oxford: UK Osprey Publishing Ltd., 2011.

B-24 Liberator vs Ki-43 Oscar China and Burma 1943. Oxford: UK Osprey Publishing Ltd., 2012.

NEWSPAPER AND PERIODICAL ARTICLES

Air Force: The Official Service Journal of the U.S. Army Air Forces.
"On to Tokyo, The Fighters Pour It On." October 1943. https://media.defense.gov/ 2011/Apr/25/2001330208/-1/-1/0/AFD-110425-057.pdf.

Air Forces Newsletter.
"War Changes High Commands." Vol 25, February 1942, No.1. https://media .defense.gov/2011/Apr/20/2001330087/-1/-1/0/AFD-110420-016.pdf.

Boritt, Gabor S.
"*Lincoln Murder Conspiracies* Book Review." *The American Historical Review,* Volume 89, Issue 5 (December 1984): 1395. https://doi.org/10.1086/ahr/89.5.1395.

The Evanston Review.
Joseph J. Dennison article clippings dated December 10, 1942, April 6, 1944, and May 11, 1944, August 31, 1944, and May 10, 1945. Courtesy of the Evanston History Center Record Archives. Grace Lehner, Archivist.

The Evanstonian (Evanston Township High School newspaper).
"Introducing Bill." unknown vol./no. October 27, 1939. page unknown.

"The Fight Against Wallace."
    TIME Magazine. February 5, 1945. https://content.time.com/time/subscriber/
    article/0,33009,797029-1,00.html.

Garza, Linda.
    "Memory Lane: Pilot Training Comes to Randolph." *Joint Base San Antonio News.*
    October 31, 2013. no page number. https://www.jbsa.mil/News/News/Article/
    599330/memory-lane-pilot-training-comes-to-randolph/.

Miami Herald.
    "Miami Beach Wartime Training Center, Flashback Miami column." Editorial.
    February 25, 2015. https://flashbackmiami.com/2015/02/25/miami-beach-
    wartime-training-center/.

Mineral County Independent News (Hawthorne, Nevada).
    "Tonopah Breaks Safety Records." April 18, 1945. http://mci.stparchive.com/
    Archive/MCI/MCI04181945p06.php.

Reilly, Gene.
    "All Cadence Breaks Out When Four Aviation Students Risk Lives to Halt Runaway
    Wagon." *College Training Detachment Newspaper,* Tennessee Polytechnic Institute.
    Undated article clipping, circa March 1943.

Tennessee Polytechnic Institute College Newspaper.
    "Greetings Cadets." Tennessee Polytechnic Institute. Undated article clipping, circa
    March 1943.

Thiery, Clément.
    "When the Free French Forces Trained in the U.S." *France-Amerique Magazine,*
    September 26, 2019. https://france-amerique.com/en/when-the-free-french-forces-
    trained-in-the-u-s/.

West, Jr., Thomas M.
    "Remembering Bechtel-McCone World War II in Birmingham." *JCHA Newsletter*
    (April 2012). http://www.jeffcohistory.com/newsletter_apr_12_pg4.html.

AIR FORCE HISTORICAL RESEARCH AGENCY (AFHRA)
MICROFILM RECORDS

Air Force Historical Research Agency (AFHRA).
    A History of the AAF PILOT SCHOOL (ADVANCED-SINGLE ENGINE),
    Marianna Army Air Field, Marianna, Florida. Official records on Reel B2385: AT-6
    Instructor's Manual, War Room description; Class 44-B graduates; Colonel John W.
    Persons; Majors Clifford Olson and Leslie Seppala.

    History of Bainbridge Army Air Field. Official records on Reel B2031: Class 44-B
    Report, January 1, 1943-February 1, 1944; Colonel Mills S. Savage records.

    History of Bainbridge Army Air Field. Official records on Reel B2032: Lieutenant
    Samuel H. Baron, Personnel list and transfer to the Infantry School at Fort Benning;
    Bivouac Exercise; Class 44-G Aviation Cadets; Colonel Mills S. Savage records;
    Second Lieutenant Robert Conary; Major James A. Gibson, Squadron II;
    Instrument Training; Weather Officers, February 1, 1944-July 1, 1944.

History of Tonopah Army Air Field. Official records on Reel B2617: *The Desert Bomber* issue dated December 8, 1944 for Colonel John A. Feagin biography; Chapter II Operations and Training April 1, 1945-April 30, 1945, Chapter IV, Life and Morale April 1, 1945-April 30, 1945 and May 1, 1945-May 31, 1945; Commendation for Safety Record letter dated 29 May 1945; *The Desert Bomber* issue dated 16 June 1945 for crew of the week runner-up; *The Desert Bomber* issue dated 11 August 1945 for air discipline.

Miami Beach Basic Training Center. Official records on Reel 2356: History of Basic Training Center #9, November 19, 1942-November 1, 1943.

U.S. Air Force Biography, Colonel Mills S. Savage. Official record, circa 1957.

GOVERNMENT WEBSITES

Biographical Directory of the United States Congress.
   "Brooks, Charles Wayland." Accessed October 16, 2022.
   https://bioguide.congress.gov/search/bio/B000874.

   "Church, Ralph Edwin." Accessed October 16, 2022.
   https://bioguide.congress.gov/search/bio/c000390.

   "McCormick, Ruth Hanna." Accessed October 16, 2022.
   https://bioguide.congress.gov/search/bio/M000372.

   "Nye, Gerald Prentice." Accessed October 16, 2022.
   https://bioguide.congress.gov/search/bio/N000176.

Library of Congress.
   "*Pm* (New York) 1940-1948." Accessed September 13, 2022.
   https://www.loc.gov/item/sn83030640.

National Archives.
   "Harry S. Truman Library and Museum," Accessed October 18, 2022.
   https://www.trumanlibrary.gov/.

National Hurricane Center and Central Pacific Hurricane Center, National Oceanic and Atmospheric Administration.
   "Hurricanes in History." Accessed October 17, 2022. https://www.nhc.noaa.gov/outreach/history/#great.

Naval History and Heritage Command, Histories, Naval Profiles.
   "Chester William Nimitz." Accessed July 28, 2021. https://www.history.navy.mil/research/histories/biographies-list/bios-n/nimitz-chester-w.html.

U.S. Air Force Biographies.
   "Brigadier General Arnold N. Krogstad." Accessed November 27, 2020. https://www.af.mil/AboutUs/Biographies/Display/Article/108098/brigadier-general-arnold-n-krogstad/.

   "Major General John W. Persons." Accessed October 6, 2019. https://www.af.mil/About-Us/Biographies/Display/Article/105948/major-general-john-w-persons/.

   "Major General Walter Reed Weaver." Accessed March 15, 2020. https://www.af.mil/About-Us/Biographies/Display/Article/2141849/major-general-walter-reed-weaver/.

ONLINE SOURCES

351st Bomb Group Association 1943-1945.
"Rader, Daniel Crew Member Search." Accessed January 12, 2023. http://www
.351st.org/loadlist/search.php.

"Stevens, Charles N. Crew Member Search." Accessed January 12, 2023. http://www
.351st.org/loadlist/search.php.

AFL-CIO America's Unions.
"Sidney Hillman." Accessed October 16, 2022. https://aflcio.org/about/history/
labor-history-people/sidney-hillman.

American Air Museum in Britain.
"Dorr Field." Accessed September 13, 2022. https://www.americanairmuseum.com/
place/159482.

American University Library Archives.
"Drew Pearson Biography." Accessed October 19, 2022. https://www.american.edu/
library/archives/pearson/drewpearson_bio.cfm.

ARCHIVEGRID.
"George E. Sokolsky Papers, 1916-1962." Accessed September 4, 2023.
https://researchworks.oclc.org/archivegrid/archiveComponent/754868998.

BIBLIO.
"Days of Our Years." Accessed October 16, 2022. https://www.biblio.com/book/
days-our-years-paassen-pierre-van/d/148900018?gclid=Cj0KCQjw166aBhDEARIs
AMEyZh5roUGuo5YHgiXDqHv_7QZ8ARBQF-OjoA-pRKE0qz4cGOf7ZY5
a9_saAoh6EALw_wcB.

"Moment in Peking, by Yutang, Lin." Accessed October 16, 2022.
https://www.biblio.com/moment-in-peking-by-yutang-lin/work/36145.

"Revelry by Adams, Samuel Hopkins." Accessed October 16, 2022.
https://www.biblio.com/book/revelry-adams-samuel-hopkins/d/1111111891.

"The Twenties (Our Times, Volume 6) by Mark Sullivan." Accessed October 16,
2022. https://www.biblio.com/book/twenties-our-times-volume-6-
mark/d/1398964437.

Britannica.
"Antoine de Saint-Exupery." Accessed September 13, 2022.
https://www.britannica.com/biography/Antoine-de-Saint-Exupery.

"James C. Petrillo American labor leader." Accessed October 16, 2022.
https://www.britannica.com/biography/James-C-Petrillo.

"John L. Lewis." Accessed March 28, 2022.
https://www.britannica.com/biography/John-L-Lewis.

"Joseph N. Pew, Jr. American Industrialist." Accessed October 17, 2022.
https://www.britannica.com/biography/Joseph-N-Pew-Jr.

"Lily Pons." Accessed March 20, 2022. https://www.britannica.com/biography/Lily-
Pons.

"Robert Frost." Accessed March 28, 2022.
https://www.britannica.com/biography/Robert-Frost.

"Theodore Dreiser." Accessed October 19, 2022.
https://www.britannica.com/biography/Theodore-Dreiser.

"Upton Sinclair." Accessed October 15, 2022.
https://www.britannica.com/biography/Upton-Sinclair.

"Walter Winchell." Accessed March 28, 2022.
https://www.britannica.com/biography/Walter-Winchell.

"Westbrook Pegler." Accessed October 19, 2022.
https://www.britannica.com/biography/Westbrook-Pegler.

Chicago Tribune Obituaries by Legacy.
"James R. 'Jim' Hoel." https://www.legacy.com/obituaries/chicagotribune/
obi*tuary.aspx?n=james-r-hoel-jim&pid=172006289.

Columbia University Libraries.
"Lincoln Steffens Papers, 1863-1936." Accessed September 13, 2022.
http://www.columbia.edu/cu/lweb/archival/collections/ldpd_4079365/.

The Comics Journal.
"Cecil Jensen, Elmo, and Colonel M'Cosmic: An Editoonist who also Drew a Comic
Strip." Accessed October 17, 2022. https://www.tcj.com/cecil-jensen-elmo-and-
colonel-mcosmic-the-first-editoonist-to-simultaneously-draw-a-comic-strip/.

The Daily Sentinel Obituaries by Legacy.
"Phillip H. Dodd." https://www.legacy.com/obituaries/gjsentinel/
obituary.aspx?n=philip-h-dodd&pid=160102935.

Detroit Free Press Obituaries.
"John V. Deaver." https://www.freep.com/obituaries/det086422.

Eggers Funeral Home.
"Lt. Col. Thomas Wilton Bonner" Accessed September 3, 2024.
https://www.eggersfuneralhome.com/obituary/lt-col-thomas-wilton-bonner.

Encyclopedia of Arkansas.
"Gerald Lyman Kenneth Smith 1898-1976." Accessed October 16, 2022.
https://encyclopediaofarkansas.net/entries/gerald-lyman-kenneth-smith-1767/.

Encyclopedia of Chicago.
"Fort Sheridan." Accessed September 1, 2019.
http://www.encyclopedia.chicagohistory.org/pages/478.html.

Encyclopedia of Trotskyism Online.
"John G. Wright, The Dean of Canterbury's *Soviet Power*, (February 1941)."
Accessed June 28, 2021.
https://www.marxists.org/history/etol/writers/wright/1941/02/dean.htm.

A Fan's Guide to Spy Series!
"Lanny Budd." Accessed October 15, 2022.
https://spyguysandgals.com/sgShowChar.aspx?id=1638.

Find A Grave.
"Mabel Dodd." Accessed August 30, 2023.
https://www.findagrave.com/memorial/233552717/mabel-dodd.

"William Ormond Butler." Accessed July 2, 2020.
https://www.findagrave.com/memorial/11274657/william-ormond-butler.

Franzo Senbusch Heritage Project.
"Grunow, William C." http://www.fhproject.org/Histories/ForestPark_Harlem/
William%20C%20Grunow.htm.

IMDB.
"Moon over Miami." Accessed May 15, 2021.
https://www.imdb.com/title/tt0033918/.

Jane Addams Hull-House Museum.
"About Jane Addams Hull-House Museum." Accessed September 13, 2021.
https://www.hullhousemuseum.org/about-jane-addams.

Merriam Webster Online Dictionary.
"Tonette." Accessed July 31, 2018. https://www.merriam-webster.com/dictionary/
tonette.

National Governors Association.
"Gov. Dwight Herbert Green." Accessed October 17, 2022.
https://www.nga.org/governor/dwight-herbert-green/.

"Gov. Thomas Edmund Dewey." Accessed September 13, 2022.
https://www.nga.org/governor/thomas-edmund-dewey/.

Nebraska State Historical Society.
"Walter Leonard Locke 1875-1957 [RG 1186.AM]." Accessed May 16, 2021.
https://history.nebraska.gov/collections/walter-leonard-locke-1875-1957-
rg1186am.

New World Encyclopedia.
"Robert R. McCormick." Accessed October 17, 2022.
https://www.newworldencyclopedia.org/entry/Robert_R._McCormick.

The Nobel Prize-1930 Literature Prize.
"Sinclair Lewis-Biographical." Accessed October 19, 2022.
https://www.nobelprize.org/prizes/literature/1930/lewis/biographical/.

Our State.
"Black Mountain College." Accessed August 10, 2019.
https://www.ourstate.com/mythic-mountain-college/.

Reference for Business.
"George S. May International Company - Company Profile, Information, Business
Description, History, Background Information on George S. May International
Company." Accessed March 20, 2022. https://www.referenceforbusiness.com/
history2/45/George-S-May-International-Company.html.

Spartacus Educational.
"John T. Flynn." Accessed October 17, 2022. https://spartacus-
educational.com/USAflynnJT.htm.

Tennessee Technological University Library, Special Collections.
"Sidney [Doc] McGee papersRG.0000.0008." Accessed August 5, 2021.
https://www.tntech.edu/library/pdf/RG8-SidneyMcGeePapers.pdf.

University of Iowa, The Biographical Dictionary of Iowa.
  "Smith, Ida B. Wise." Accessed September 5, 2024.
  https://uipress.lib.uiowa.edu/bdi/DetailsPage.aspx?id=348.

University of North Carolina Libraries.
  "A View to Hugh." Accessed July 28, 2018.
  https://blogs.lib.unc.edu/morton/index.php/2012/01/eleanor-roosevelt-visits-
  chapel-hill/.

Vorwerk & Wilson Families.
  "Christina Elizabeth Kammerer b. 2 June 1886, d. 14 January 1945."
  https://www.woodvorwerk.com/vorwerk/g1/p1632.htm.

World War II Flight Training Museum and the 63rd Army Air Forces Flying Training
  Detachment.
  "Army Air Forces Officers." Accessed November 13, 2020.
  https://wwiiflighttraining.org/?page_id=986.

  "Civilian Personnel—Flight Instructors." Accessed November 13, 2020.
  https://wwiiflighttraining.org/?page_id=949.

  "Class 1944-B." Accessed November 4, 2022.
  https://wwiiflighttraining.org/Cadets/Class-1944-B.php.

WorldCat.
  "The Big Bosses." Accessed August 4, 2021. https://www.worldcat.org/title/big-
  bosses/oclc/290649.

  "Co-operative Democracy: Attained Through Voluntary Association of the People as
  Consumers." Accessed August 4, 2021. https://www.worldcat.org/title/co-operative-
  democracy-attained-through-voluntary-association-of-the-people-as-consumers-a-
  discussion-of-the-co-operative-movement-its-philosophy-methods-
  accomplishments-and-possibilities-and-its-relation-to-the-state-to-science-art-and-
  commerce-and-to-other-systems-of-economic-organization/oclc/1442427.

  "World in Trance; From Versailles to Pearl Harbor." Accessed August 9, 2021.
  https://www.worldcat.org/title/world-in-trance-from-versailles-to-pearl-
  harbor/oclc/1493294.

INTERVIEWS, PERSONAL RECORDS AND UNPUBLISHED WRITINGS

Babcock, Robert.
  BMC File in Western Regional Archives, records held by the State of North
  Carolina, Department of Natural and Cultural Resources. Courtesy of Heather
  South, Lead Archivist, Western Regional Archives, State of North Carolina
  Department of Archives and History, received on August 16, 2019.

Grose, Peter.
  Telephone conversation with editor, September 25, 2017, Carlsbad, California.

Hanchett, Jane, Josephine, Frances, Alice Ann, William and Louise.
  "We Are Six" booklet. Evanston, Unpublished writings, 1931.

Hanchett, Leila A.
  American Red Cross Foreign Service Certificate

Hanchett, Lucie Alice Trowbridge.
"Personal Notes of Family Events 1910-1950," unpublished.

Hanchett, William.
"Biographical Sketch of Father and Grandfather," unpublished and undated.

Hanchett, William F. Jr.
Black Mountain College records 1941-1942, records held by the State of North Carolina, Department of Natural and Cultural Resources. This archive includes documentation concerning Evanston Township High School. Courtesy of Heather South, Lead Archivist, Western Regional Archives, State of North Carolina Department of Archives and History, received on August 16, 2019.

Hanchett, Jr., William F.
Military Service Record dated October 10, 1942-November 8, 1945.

Hanchett, Sr., William F.
Illinois Reserve Militia Discharge papers, personal record dated April 27, 1920.

Harris, Mary Emma.
Interview Transcript of former BMC student William Hanchett. February 15, 1998, Media AT1/VT2 Interview #211, conducted in San Diego, California. Courtesy of Black Mountain Project, Inc.

Hubbell, Delmer F. "Bill".
Military service information and photographs. Courtesy of the late Janet Fogg, author and historian of the 359th Fighter Group, received July 21, 2019.

Ramsey, Julia A.
"'Girls' In Name Only, A Study of American Red Cross Volunteers on the Frontlines of World War II." Master's thesis, Auburn University, 2011. https://etd.auburn.edu/bitstream/handle/10415/2616/ramsey_julia_ma_thesis_history_post_defense_and_AUETD_check_5.9.11.pdf?sequence=3.

Trowbridge, Lucius Atwater.
Personal Letters Collection, compiled in 1929. Reproduced by Clyde Louis Young, unpublished, dated July 2009.